SPORTS and ENTERTAINMENT MANAGEMENT

DECA PREP

Kaser and Brooks

THOMSON
SOUTH-WESTERN

Australia · Canada · Mexico · Singapore · Spain · United Kingdom · United States

Sports and Entertainment Management
Kenneth Kaser and John R. Brooks, Jr.

VP/Editorial Director
Jack W. Calhoun

VP/Editor-in-Chief
Dave Shaut

Senior Publisher
Karen Schmohe

Executive Editor
Eve Lewis

Project Manager
Enid Nagel

Production Manager
Patricia Matthews Boies

Production Editor
Colleen A. Farmer

VP/Director of Marketing
Carol Volz

Senior Marketing Manager
Nancy A. Long

Marketing Coordinator
Angela Russo

Manufacturing Coordinator
Kevin Kluck

Cover & Internal Design
Tippy McIntosh

Editorial Assistant
Linda Keith

Production Assistant
Nancy Stamper

Compositor
Navta

Printer
C&C Offset Printing Co., Ltd.

About the Authors

Ken Kaser has taught Marketing and Business in Texas and Nebraska for 25 years. He has been an innovative leader who has created new exciting courses that build strong programs. Ken has served as president of the Nebraska State Business Education Association and the Mountain-Plains Business Education Association. Teaching awards he has received include Nebraska Business Teacher of the Year, Texas Teacher of the Year, Mountain-Plain Business Teacher of the Year, and National Business Teacher of the Year.

Dr. John R. "Rusty" Brooks, Jr. (DBA) is Professor of Marketing and Area Coordinator for the Department of Marketing at Houston Baptist University. He holds the Prince-Chavanne Professorship in Christian Business Ethics. In Dr. Brooks' 30+ years as a professor, he has won four outstanding teaching awards. He is a professional consultant, member of several editorial review boards, and has served in numerous professional association capacities. Recently, Dr. Brooks has concentrated his writing efforts toward developing educational supplements that advance active learning and teaching pedagogy. He has over 50 publications in these areas. Dr. Brooks is an active spokesperson for the DECA program in the Houston area high schools.

Printed in China

6 7 8 9 10 08 07

ISBN-13: 978-0-538-43829-2

ISBN-10: 0-538-43829-0

For more information contact South-Western, 5191 Natorp Boulevard, Mason, Ohio, 45040.
Or you can visit our Internet site at http://www.swlearning.com

SPORTS and ENTERTAINMENT MANAGEMENT

CONTENTS

Chapter 1

What is Sports and Entertainment Management? 2

Lesson 1.1 Management Basics 4

Lesson 1.2 Sports Management 10

Lesson 1.3 Entertainment Management 15

Chapter Review 20

Chapter 2

College and Amateur Sports 26

Lesson 2.1 Managing College Athletics 28

Lesson 2.2 Managing Amateur Sports 34

Lesson 2.3 Economic Impact 39

Chapter Review 44

Chapter 3

Professional Sports 50

Lesson 3.1 Managing Big League Sports 52

Lesson 3.2 Organizing A Professional Team 59

Lesson 3.3 Agents, Managers, and Ethics 64

Chapter Review 72

Chapter 4

Sports and Entertainment Management 78

Lesson 4.1 Managing Local Events 80

Lesson 4.2 Managing College Events 86

Lesson 4.3 Managing Professional Sports 91

Lesson 4.4 Managing Other Events 95

Chapter Review 100

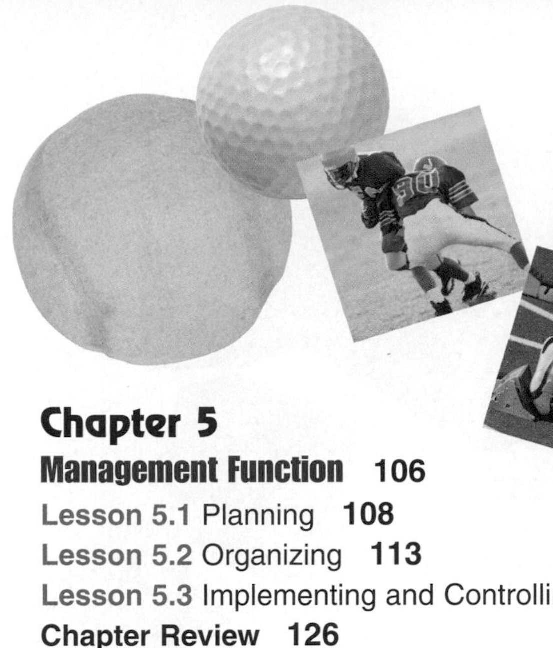

Chapter 5
Management Function 106

Lesson 5.1 Planning **108**
Lesson 5.2 Organizing **113**
Lesson 5.3 Implementing and Controlling **121**
Chapter Review 126

Chapter 6
Decision Making 132

Lesson 6.1 How Managers Make Decisions **134**
Lesson 6.2 Group Decision Making **141**
Lesson 6.3 Knowledge Management **147**
Chapter Review 152

Chapter 7
Management Strategies 158

Lesson 7.1 The Building Blocks of Strategy **160**
Lesson 7.2 The Process of Strategic Management **166**
Lesson 7.3 Strategic Planning Tools **174**
Chapter Review 182

Chapter 8
Organizing and Staffing 188

Lesson 8.1 Coordinating for Success **190**
Lesson 8.2 Networking and Delegation **196**
Lesson 8.3 Management Careers in Sports and Entertainment **201**
Chapter Review 206

Chapter 9
Leaders in a Changing Environment 212
Lesson 9.1 Characteristics of Leaders 214
Lesson 9.2 How Do Leaders Motivate? 221
Lesson 9.3 Agents of Change 227
Chapter Review 234

Chapter 10
Managing Groups and Teams 240
Lesson 10.1 Understanding Group Structures 242
Lesson 10.2 Building Successful Teams 249
Lesson 10.3 Designing a Team-Based Organization 255
Chapter Review 260

Chapter 11
Managing Operations 266
Lesson 11.1 Operations Management 268
Lesson 11.2 Control Through Evaluation 273
Chapter Review 280

Chapter 12
Managing With Information Technology 286
Lesson 12.1 Management Information Systems 288
Lesson 12.2 Implementing Strategies with an MIS 294
Chapter Review 300

Index 306

REVIEWERS

Michael Aleci
Smithtown, NY

Sandy Atkinson
Franklin, VA

Eddy Diaz
Hiahleah, FL

Thomas L. Farah
Green Bay, WI

Rich Gaard
Decorah, IA

Terri A. Heller
Manchester, MO

Bruce E. Herbert
Florence, OR

Perry A. Hughes
Stuart, VA

Paul Kluger
Manchester, MO

Kimberly C. Radford
Blacksburg, VA

Keri Schermerhorn
Lake Geneva, WI

Mark Steedly
Cincinnati, OH

Michael A Vialpando
Phoenix, AZ

Cynthia Yingling
Pittsburgh,PA

TO THE STUDENT

WELCOME TO SPORTS AND ENTERTAINMENT MANAGEMENT!

The field of sports and entertainment management is rapidly growing. Many universities, colleges, and high schools now offer specializations in sports and entertainment management or marketing. The general principles of management that are presented throughout this book are intended to be a guide in taking your first career step into the exciting world of sports and entertainment.

Managers create, oversee, and expand the operation of a business. The **basic principles of management** are visually identified by icons throughout the text.

BUSINESS INFORMATION MANAGEMENT
MANAGEMENT RESPONSIBILITIES
FINANCIAL MANAGEMENT
BUSINESS MANAGEMENT PRINCIPLES
PRODUCTION MANAGEMENT
MARKETING MANAGEMENT
HUMAN RESOURCES MANAGEMENT

Winning Strategies presents real world strategies used by successful sports and entertainment managers.

Opening Act begins each lesson and encourages you to explore the material in the upcoming lesson. Opening Act also gives you opportunities to work with other students in your class.

Cyber Management investigates how technology and the Internet help managers manage more effectively.

Ethics in Action examines legal and ethical issues that exist in sports and entertainment businesses.

The Global Manager presents global and international aspects of managing a sports or entertainment business.

Intermission provides you with an opportunity to assess your comprehension at key points in each lesson. Ongoing review and assessment helps you understand the material.

INTERMISSION

Time Out introduces you to interesting facts and statistics about sports and entertainment businesses.

sports.swlearning.com includes internet activities and crossword puzzles for every chapter.

POINT YOUR BROWSER
sports.swlearning.com

Managing Diversity focuses on the challenges of managing a diverse workforce.

Lead the Way acquaints you with people who have succeeded in sports and entertainment management.

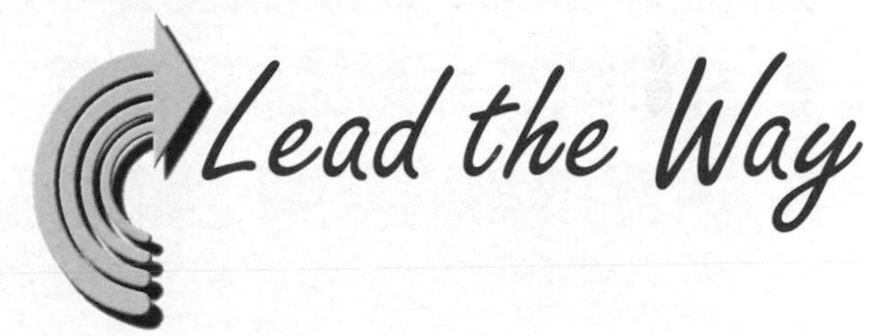

DECA Prep prepares you for competitive events with a Case Study and Event Prep in every Chapter.

CHAPTER 1

What is Sports and Entertainment Management?

©GETTY IMAGES/PHOTODISC

1.1 MANAGEMENT BASICS
1.2 SPORTS MANAGEMENT
1.3 ENTERTAINMENT MANAGEMENT

©GETTY IMAGES/PHOTODISC

©GETTY IMAGES/PHOTODISC

© GETTY IMAGES/PHOTODISC

WINNING Strategies

J.C. WINGO

Wingo has always been willing to take the risk necessary for success. J.C. joined the Denver Broncos as a free agent in 1972. When he was cut from the team in 1974, he looked for new opportunities in the sports field. Sports marketing, property development, and corporate sponsorship negotiations were three of Wingo's greatest strengths. Therefore, he organized United Sports Labs, Inc. to design and manufacture a line of sports protective products. That business eventually was sold to Riddell™, Inc. where J.C. became the president and chief operating officer. In 1995, J.C. organized Wingo Sports Group, which manufactures sports memorabilia such as foam fingers and football helmet-shaped air fresheners. Clients include Riddell, the Arena Football League, the Green Bay Packers™, and NFL on Fox.

The sports industry has been very good to J.C. Wingo, both on and off the field. Characteristics necessary to be a successful manager in this industry include

- Being a risk taker
- Believing in yourself
- Never accepting "no" as an answer
- Setting budgets and managing time
- Being specific about team goals
- Getting strong financial advice
- Recognizing your weaknesses and building a team of advisors to compensate for them

Success also depends on maintaining strong relationships with international factories, customers, and vendors.

THINK CRITICALLY

1. How did J.C. Wingo incorporate his athletic background into his current career?
2. List other characteristics necessary to operate a company like Wingo Sports Group.

LESSON 1.1

MANAGEMENT BASICS

Define management and its four functions.

Discuss the principles of business management.

List the steps in the decision-making process.

Major entertainment events like the Super Bowl, Final Four, concerts, and rodeos do not just happen. They require professional management to oversee the many details. Think of the last time you attended a major entertainment event. You purchased a ticket, paid for parking, bought food and souvenirs, appreciated the security, and enjoyed the entertainment. Sports and entertainment management involves planning, organizing, implementing, and controlling all parts of the event to make sure customers enjoy a great experience. The event must be organized and the entertainment must be scheduled to perform. Ticket sales must be managed to make sure that the maximum profit is earned. Ticket collectors, hosts, custodians, and security personnel must be in place. Someone must be in charge of publicity to advertise the event in the newspaper and on the Internet, television, and radio.

Work with a partner. Discuss the various aspects of planning, organizing, implementing, and controlling that were evident at a recent event you attended.

MANAGING SPORTS AND ENTERTAINMENT EVENTS

Profit is the goal for sports and entertainment events just as it is the catalyst for other business operations. Success depends upon having strong management strategies in place. **Management** is the process of accomplishing the goals of an organization through the effective use of people and other resources.

FUNCTIONS OF MANAGEMENT

The four functions of management are planning, organizing, implementing, and controlling.

Planning The **planning** function involves analyzing information and making decisions about what needs to be done. A good idea requires planning in order to maximize success and profits. Sports and entertainment event planners must determine if the event is feasible. Does the event have a large enough **target market**, or group that management is trying to reach, to make it financially worthwhile? How much money must be earned or raised to break even? Planners must analyze information to determine if an idea is an ambitious dream or a solid income producer. The planning of successful sports and entertainment events

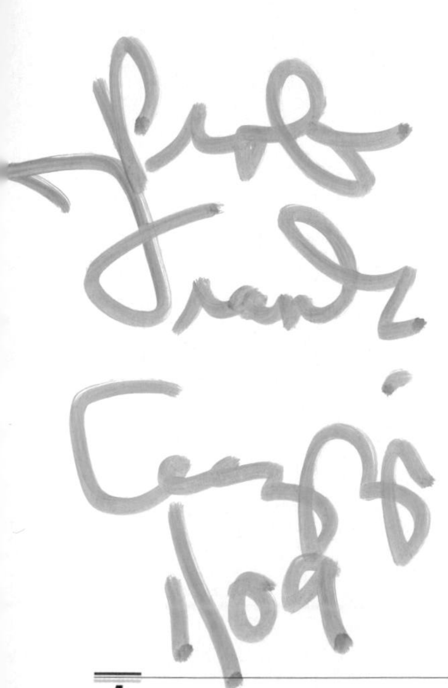

must take place far in advance. Once decision makers decide to go ahead with the event, they must determine all the steps that need to be completed. Factors to consider include the date, target markets, customer potential, competition, marketing strategies, sponsorships, security, facilities, and community or regional support.

Organizing The **organizing** function is concerned with accomplishing tasks most effectively and arranging resources to complete all necessary work. Many small communities have summer celebrations that include parades, fun runs, reunions, and carnivals. Organizing these events involves committees chaired by individuals who are event specialists. Event planning includes security, concessions, parking lot management, and maintenance. Events must be scheduled to attract the highest attendance at the two- or three-day celebration.

Implementing The **implementing** function involves carrying out plans and making sure that adequate personnel are available to accomplish all the necessary tasks. Successful implementing involves taking care of details, such as providing extra police officers to direct traffic, making sure that parking lots handle heavy traffic flow, and having enough restroom facilities.

Controlling The **controlling** function involves evaluating results to determine if objectives have been accomplished as planned. State fairs have a proud history of pulling people together from rural and urban areas to enjoy a wide variety of entertainment ranging from livestock shows to popular concerts. Stiff entertainment competition has made it difficult for state fair managers and boards of directors to plan events that will attract larger audiences. Managers must evaluate the event to determine how to improve the event in the future or if the event should not be pursued again.

College football generates big money for university athletic programs, and the cost for tickets may be pricing college students out of the entertainment venue. Games for national power programs top the list of schools where students pay the most for season tickets or even for tickets to see a single game. In 2003, the best seats at a Texas Tech game sold for $87 while Arizona charged $70, and tickets to an Oklahoma game sold for $60. Michigan and UCLA charged $58 with Ohio State, Nebraska, and USC close behind at $55.

THINK CRITICALLY

1. **Why are universities charging so much for football tickets to one game?**
2. **What could colleges and universities do to allow more students to purchase tickets to games while still earning big revenues?**

THE BEST LAID PLANS

Major events such as the Olympic Games are hosted by a city that has a diverse culture, an international airport with many flights, enough sporting venues, reliable public transportation, ample hotel rooms, strong hospitality, pleasant climate, and tight security. When a city is selected to host the Olympics, large sums of money are spent to improve the city. The best-laid plans include future uses for all of the new venues built specially for the Olympic Games. For example, the local university may use dorms built for housing Olympic athletes.

© GETTY IMAGES/PHOTODISC

Careful planning must take place. The Houston 2012 Committee was formed to promote Houston as the best city in the United States to host the 2012 Summer Olympics. The committee had to determine what features made Houston the best U.S. city. Houston's diverse culture was a definite plus, but its heavy traffic was a negative. The Olympic Selection Committee also considered many other features, including transportation, lodging facilities, and sports locales or venues. Being the fourth largest city in the U.S. did not guarantee that Houston would be one of the finalists.

The Olympic Selection Committee visited Houston during the summer of 2001 and was impressed with all four of the major sporting venues, including the new baseball field, basketball arena, professional football stadium, and state-of-the-art indoor running track planned for the old Astrodome. The committee liked that the four venues were in close proximity and that city leaders had agreed to build a light rail system that would connect all of the sporting venues.

Houston was on the list of the top four U.S. cities considered for the 2012 Summer Olympics. In the end, it didn't make the final cut.

TIME OUT

Eight U.S. cities—Tampa, Cincinnati, Dallas, Houston, Los Angeles, San Francisco, New York, and Washington, D.C.—vied for the honor of hosting the 2012 Summer Olympics. In November 2002, the International Olympic Committee selected New York City as the U.S. finalist to compete with other cities worldwide for the 2012 Summer Olympics.

INTERMISSION

Define briefly the four functions of management.

____

____

____

BUSINESS MANAGEMENT PRINCIPLES

Managers create, oversee, and expand the operation of a business organization by coordinating various resources, skills, and activities. Managers may be expected to play several roles by different individuals and groups. The ability to meet these multiple role demands makes the difference between a successful manager and an unsuccessful one.

Management Responsibilities Managers are responsible for accomplishing the goals of an organization through the effective use of people and other resources. Although their days may be interrupted by unanticipated events and problems, managers have regular duties to perform. They provide leadership for their part of the organization. Managers have formal and informal meetings and interactions with company personnel, other business people, and company visitors. They gather, review, and process information to make decisions and revise plans. They work with other managers and employees to determine ways to improve the performance of the organization.

Business Information Management All managers need information about target markets, the economy, competition, and business operations to make sound decisions. Information comes in many forms and from many sources. Information management uses technology, including the Internet, to effectively gather, organize, protect, and make information available to people in a form they can use.

Financial Management Good financial management is crucial for business success. Financial management involves obtaining funds to finance the business, managing the funds carefully, and keeping financial records accurately. All managers must understand finance and financial records to use them for both day-to-day planning and long-term planning.

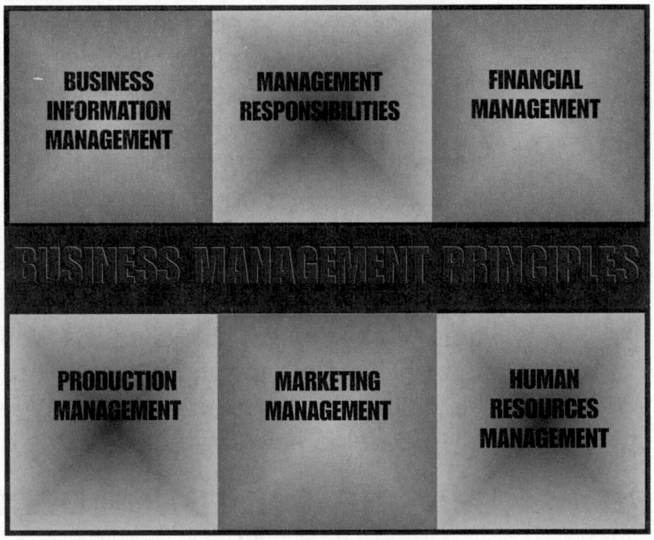

BUSINESS INFORMATION MANAGEMENT
MANAGEMENT RESPONSIBILITIES
FINANCIAL MANAGEMENT
BUSINESS MANAGEMENT PRINCIPLES
PRODUCTION MANAGEMENT
MARKETING MANAGEMENT
HUMAN RESOURCES MANAGEMENT

Production Management Production is all of the activities involved in creating products for sale. In sports and entertainment, the products are the events as well as the many related products such as posters, CDs, and apparel sold at the event or used in event promotion. Production management works with others to determine the products to be produced, obtains needed resources, organizes production facilities and personnel, and develops and maintains a production schedule and quality control.

Marketing Management Marketing involves all the activities used to plan, price, promote, and sell the event. These activities include customer and competitor research, event development, scheduling, advertising, pricing, and managing all of the marketing activities prior to, during, and after the event.

Human Resources Management Managing human resources involves determining the number and type of employees needed, recruiting and hiring the best people, offering needed training, and providing adequate compensation and benefits as well as a motivational work environment. Personnel is often the most important resource for the successful sports and entertainment organization.

INTERMISSION

Define two business management principles.

____

____

____

WHO IS RESPONSIBLE FOR WHAT?

Managers are responsible for making things happen in an organization. Higher-level managers usually complete planning and organizing activities. Lower-level managers perform implementing and controlling tasks. **Authority** is the right to make decisions about assigned work and to delegate assignments to others.

Supervisors are the first level of management and are responsible for directing the work of employees and conducting employee performance ratings or evaluations. For example, the supervisor of ticket sales for concerts or sporting events is responsible for coordinating employees to efficiently handle ticket receipts so that fans won't be waiting in long lines once the event starts.

Supervisors also serve as the communication link between management and employees. Well-managed organizations possess a sense of teamwork in which all individuals work together for the benefit of the entire team. These organizations may utilize **employee empowerment**, in which individuals have the authority to solve problems with available resources or to develop new strategies for the betterment of the organizations.

© GETTY IMAGES/PHOTODISC

MAKING THE TOUGH DECISIONS

Managers of entertainment events, ranging from rodeos and concerts to professional sporting events, need to be aware when performance is not meeting expectations. Computers are used to collect, store, and summarize information. When managers identify a problem, such as declining attendance, business research provides the information needed to correct the problem. Managers commonly follow the five steps of the decision-making process.

1. **Identify the Problem** Managers must determine what is causing declining attendance.
2. **List Possible Solutions** For example, what are the possible actions to turn around declining attendance at the event?
3. **Analyze Possible Solutions** Managers must analyze the solutions carefully and use research when necessary.
4. **Select the Plan** Managers must then determine the best way to implement the plan.
5. **Evaluate the Plan** The plan must be evaluated for effectiveness to make the best decisions in the future.

INTERMISSION

What is the management role of the supervisor?

____

____

UNDERSTAND MANAGEMENT CONCEPTS

Circle the best answer for each of the following questions.

1. Which of the following is not a function of management?
- **a.** controlling
- **b.** organizing
- **c.** financing
- **d.** planning

2. ___?___ are responsible for directing the work of employees.
- **a.** Supervisors
- **b.** CEOs
- **c.** Managers
- **d.** Presidents

THINK CRITICALLY

Answer the following questions as completely as possible. If necessary, use a separate sheet of paper.

3. Research Select a college bowl game. Where is the game played? Does the city meet the necessary criteria for success of a major event? Who would be a good corporate sponsor for this bowl game? Why?

____

____

____

4. Your city will host the Olympics. Explain the organizing, implementing, and controlling functions for this event.

____

____

____

5. Technology Explain the role of the computer in the decision-making process.

____

____

____

LESSON 1.2

SPORTS MANAGEMENT

Discuss the management of championship series for college sports.

Explain the financial and social impact that professional sports have on host cities.

OPENING ACT

Dear Event Staff Member:

Welcome to the Event Staff! We are very excited that you are joining us for this season at some of the best facilities in college athletics.

As a member of our event staff, you will be a major factor in orienting the guests to our facilities and making them comfortable in their surroundings. As a goodwill ambassador for this university, you are one of the people who will leave the greatest impression on our visitors.

Thank you for taking on this responsibility, and I look forward to seeing you throughout the season.

Sincerely,

Events Director

Work with a partner. Discuss ways that event staff members can assist guests at major sporting or entertainment events.

MANAGING SPORTS EVENTS EFFECTIVELY

Human resources management is the core of success for any organization. A professional management staff must be in place not only to maintain the facility but also to uphold the image of the organization.

Event staff members should take pride in the appearance of the facility. As the doors open on the first day of the season, everything must be clean and spotless. A good event management team will make sure that guests or fans are impressed with the facility and will want to come back for future events. A good service philosophy for the event staff includes knowledge, responsibility, courtesy, and professionalism. All staff members should know how to intelligently answer questions about the facilities, the operations, and the particular team or event.

Guests have high expectations for the entertainment dollars they spend. Therefore, event staff members should greet each guest in a friendly, sincere manner that will assure guests that they have selected the best entertainment venue. Experienced team members anticipate a guest's need for assistance and do not take rejection or disrespect personally.

© GETTY IMAGES/PHOTODISC

The safety and comfort of all guests should always come first. Even during a time when a small minority of sports fans may get out of control, most guests respect and enjoy the sport and the facilities. The challenge of the event management team members is to deal with that minority while maintaining a courteous, professional attitude toward the majority of the guests or fans.

Attitude makes the big difference when working at sports and entertainment events. The best event team members are enthusiastic, informed, and focused. These individuals are proud of their positions and are constantly looking for new and better ways to do their jobs. When a guest has a concern, informed event staff members listen carefully. They repeat the concern or problem clearly, apologize for any inconvenience that the situation has caused, acknowledge the guest's feelings, explain action that will be taken, and thank the guest for making the organization aware of the concern.

MANAGEMENT OF COLLEGE CHAMPIONSHIPS

The NCAA has championship series games for basketball, football, baseball, volleyball, and other sports. The Final Four starts in 16 host cities with 65 Division I-A basketball teams competing to be the national champion. The Final Four championship takes place in one location. Two weekends of these exciting games generate a lot of fan enthusiasm and revenue for cities hosting the event. Management is needed to select the teams, select the host cities, commit sponsors, negotiate television packages, and sell tickets. Hotels, restaurants, universities, shopping malls, and gas stations all receive financial benefits for being involved with the Final Four.

The Bowl Championship Series (BCS) determines the Division I-A National Champion in college football. The BCS consists of the Rose Bowl presented by AT&T™, Nokia™ Sugar Bowl, FedEx® Orange Bowl, and Tostitos™ Fiesta Bowl. In 2001, the four BCS Bowls combined to reach a record television audience of 127 million viewers. The average attendance for the games was 77,765, and overall attendance for all bowl games increased 7.6 percent to 1,291,557. BCS participants in the 2003 bowl games received between $11.78 million and $14.67 million depending on the conference affiliations of the participants.

INTERMISSION

Why is it important for event staff members to treat fans with respect even when the fans sometimes can be rude?

MANAGING PROFESSIONAL SPORTS

The theme for many professional sports teams today is "Build it or they will leave." Cities face the challenge of providing the best facilities to keep professional teams from moving to other locations. Satisfying the demands of professional teams requires strong financial management. Most cities trying to attract or keep professional sports teams must find ways to finance expensive sports arenas. Residents of these cities often vote on new taxes to pay for the necessary sports facilities. Cincinnati partially finances its new baseball field and football stadium with a half-cent sales tax passed by the voters. By the year 2016, the sales tax should generate $1.2 billion.

Financial management also involves finding corporations willing to make long-term financial commitments. Stadiums and other sports arenas are named after the corporate sponsors. Large stadiums with retractable roofs and state-of-the-art basketball arenas are now being built with multiple purposes in mind in order to maximize revenue. Reliant Stadium, home of the Houston Texans, has a retractable roof to let in the best weather and keep out the worst weather. This state-of-the-art stadium has real grass that can be removed like pieces of carpet to allow other events, including rodeos and concerts, to take place in the facility. However, each time the grass is removed from the stadium, it costs $30,000.

Bob McNair spent $700 million to get an NFL franchise in Houston, Texas. The open concourse and curved lines in Reliant Stadium make it more inviting to fans. All 168 luxury suites are located on the sidelines and licensed for 6, 8, or 10 years, costing $75,000–$250,000 per year. Major sponsors spend large sums of money to have their advertisements on each end zone of the stadium. Rotational signs can relay up to 25 messages during a game. Management is needed for sponsorships, ticket sales, concessions, field maintenance, transportation from satellite parking lots, and operation of the professional team.

the Global Manager

Mexico and the United States have much in common besides a shared border. Many residents in Texas are from Mexico, and an increasing percentage of the Texas population speaks Spanish as its first language. Houston, Texas has a population of more than four million people, and 37.9 percent of that population is Hispanic. The Houston Texans football team has KLAT La Tremenda as the flagship Spanish-language radio station broadcasting for the team. When the Texans entered their inaugural season, they realized the power of Hispanic Houston and recognized how many long-time fans they stood to gain. So get your team spirit pumping, strap on the pads, and ask yourself, "Are you ready for some fútbol Americano?"

THINK CRITICALLY

1. How would you describe the demographics of Houston, Texas?
2. Why was it a good move to have a Spanish radio station broadcast Texans games?

The 2003 Super Bowl in San Diego generated more than $300 million in revenues for the city. The Super Bowl is the nation's largest sports celebration, and enthusiastic fans eager to spend money on lodging, food and beverages, souvenirs, transportation, and other items spell a windfall for the host city.

The Super Bowl also has a major financial impact outside the host city. People throughout the world purchase food and beverages to host private Super Bowl parties. The gaming industry also experiences a windfall from the Super Bowl, which generates approximately $70 million annually for Nevada's legal sports books. College and high school bands invited to the Super Bowl event require management and special planning.

Safeco Field, home of the Seattle Mariners baseball team, is one of many stadiums with a retractable roof and real grass. Because it is challenging to keep the grass green when the roof is frequently closed, horticulturists grow two spare fields of grass to replace pieces of the field when necessary.

INTERMISSION

In the world of professional sports, what is meant by "Build it or they will leave"?

____

____

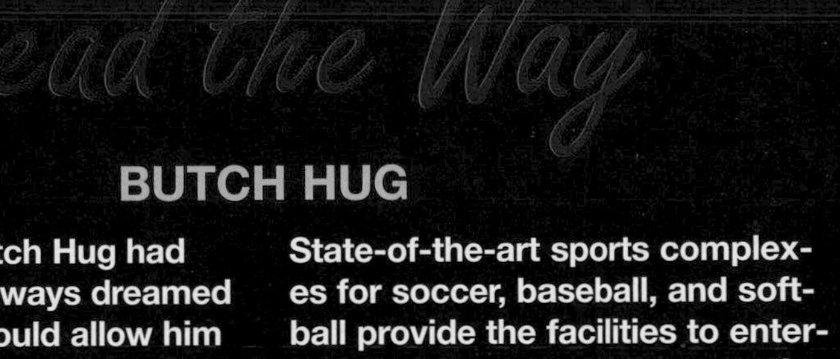

BUTCH HUG

Butch Hug had always dreamed of a career that would allow him to work in college athletics. He finally realized his dream when he landed the job of Events Director for the University of Nebraska Athletic Department. There is never a dull moment in this exciting position. Hug oversees 100 employees at six different athletic facilities. Memorial Stadium, home for Nebraska football, seats more than 76,000 fans and has sold out for 260 games. The Bob Devaney Sports Center can seat 14,302 spectators at Nebraska basketball games, state championships, and special state fair performances. State-of-the-art sports complexes for soccer, baseball, and softball provide the facilities to entertain fans throughout the rest of the year. The events director must make sure that individuals are in place to handle tickets, security, parking, concessions, and medical needs. For a major football game, this can involve 3,500 to 4,000 individuals working behind the scenes.

THINK CRITICALLY

1. **Why is the events director so important at a major university?**
2. **What departments are involved with a college sporting event?**

UNDERSTAND MANAGEMENT CONCEPTS

Circle the best answer for each of the following questions.

1. Which of the following characteristics is not necessary for the management team of sports and entertainment events?
   a. knowledge of the facilities
   b. positive, friendly attitude
   c. casual non-uniform dress code to make guests feel comfortable at the event
   d. sincerity

2. New professional sports complexes should serve multiple purposes
   a. because they are expensive to build
   b. since they usually require an additional city tax
   c. in order to maximize revenue from entertainment events
   d. all of the above

THINK CRITICALLY

Answer the following questions as completely as possible. If necessary, use a separate sheet of paper.

3. Communication You have been hired by a major university as the events director. This job requires you to write an employee handbook for the 100 employees you will manage. These employees are involved with guest relations. What are the five major ideas about customer relations that you want to stress to your employees?

____

____

____

4. Management Math Your city has decided to build a new professional football stadium. The voters have agreed to an 11% tax on hotels and rental cars to help pay for the facility. How much tax will someone pay for a weekly car rental that costs $360? How much tax will be charged on a hotel room that costs $150 per night?

____

____

5. Technology Visit the web site for the Super Bowl. What information is available at the web site?

____

____

ENTERTAINMENT MANAGEMENT

OPENING ACT

Many people choose summertime events, such as local festivals, county fairs, outdoor concerts, rodeos, and craft fairs, for relaxation and enjoyment. Entertainment events are much more comfortable for consumers when management has carefully planned all of the details, from ticket sales to parking and concessions. Management evaluates the success or failure of entertainment events based on attendance and repeat business potential. Management uses that information to improve future events.

Work with a partner. Select a summertime event, such as a state or county fair, which is held each year in your community. Make a list of changes and improvements that have occurred each year to increase your enjoyment of the event.

Explain the role of human resources management in community entertainment events.

Describe the challenges faced by state fairs.

LIMITED ONLY BY YOUR IMAGINATION

Entertainment possibilities are endless. The size of a community does not necessarily determine its ability to host an event. The New Orleans Mardi Gras is a major event held in February or March each year. Because New Orleans is a diverse city, it requires diverse entertainment, including country, jazz, rock, blues, and Zydeco music, to attract different target markets of customers to Mardi Gras.

HUMAN RESOURCES MANAGEMENT

Human resources management plays an important role in the success of entertainment events. Management for the Mardi Gras depends on dedicated individuals from the community who volunteer hundreds of hours to make sure that the event is a huge success. Planning involves determining the star-studded entertainment lineup. It also involves getting commitments from hotels and restaurants, contracting food and souvenir vendors, and organizing the various parades for which Mardi Gras is famous. Serving on one of the Mardi Gras committees is a great honor. Membership on the committees has its perks, such as receiving free parking on Grand Parade day and an invitation to the Thank You party after Mardi Gras.

©GETTY IMAGES/PHOTODISC

The Internet provides a fast, reasonably priced means of advertising sports and entertainment events. Concerts, rodeos, and celebrations for cities of all sizes successfully advertise on the Internet. Web sites contain numerous links allowing customers to view photos of the event, learn about the entertainers, and purchase tickets online. Sports and entertainment managers are increasingly relying on the Internet to successfully manage events.

THINK CRITICALLY

1. **Use the Internet to research an entertainment event. How many links are included on the web site? Describe four of the links.**
2. **What suggestions do you have to improve this web site?**

SMALL TOWN, BIG ENTERTAINMENT EVENT

Morristown, a small town located in the rolling hills of Eastern Ohio, hosts the Jamboree in the Hills Country Music Festival each summer. This event offers four days of outdoor country music concerts. It requires a covered stage and plenty of lodging and camping space for visitors. Individuals who purchase tickets to the event are required to bring their own lawn chairs. Known as the Super Bowl of Country Music, the festival is one of the nation's most highly regarded country music showcases. The event's managers know they have a successful idea that brings in large sums of money.

Jamboree in the Hills attracts current top country musicians for the four-day festival in July. Big-name entertainers like Martina McBride, Sara Evans, and Rascal Flatts perform. Jamboree In the Hills is one of the most respected country music events in the nation. Security personnel are on duty around the clock throughout the grounds for the entire festival. Strict enforcement of all laws and regulations is necessary to ensure that everyone there has an enjoyable experience.

Over the years, Jamboree in the Hills has become a traditional reunion spot for thousands of fans who choose the event as the site of family reunions, family vacations, and weddings. Between shows, organizers keep the crowd entertained with Bullmania, where 50 professional bull riders compete for cash prizes.

Country Stampede is a weekend country music and camping festival at the end of June in Manhattan, Kansas. The weekend is fun-filled and action-packed with great performers, fantastic food, colorful crafts, a swinging saloon, and much more. This major event is advertised in Kansas, Missouri, Kentucky, and surrounding states. The celebration is held at Tuttle Creek State Park, which is less than an hour from Topeka and Salina and approximately two hours from Wichita and Kansas City as well as Lincoln and Omaha, Nebraska. During the 2002 event, more than 140,000 people attended the weekend of country entertainment. A local radio station, 94 Country, sponsored the Country Giant Video Screen that allowed all guests to see performers larger than life, making them feel as if they were sitting in the front row.

COMEDY CLUBS

Today's serious world needs to take time out for a good laugh. Stand-up comedians perform at clubs, restaurants, and special venues to make people laugh. Some cities have comedy venues that have been around for years.

Comedy club managers must learn every aspect of the business, including hiring and supervising staff, booking comedians, overseeing maintenance of the club, and handling customer issues. Managers need outstanding communication skills, exceptional customer service skills, and attention to detail.

INTERMISSION

List four responsibilities of the Jamboree in the Hills management.

____

____

STRUGGLING STATE FAIRS

State fairs give rural and urban residents the opportunity to come together at the state's showcase entertainment event. State fairs can range in length from a 5-day event in Nevada and New Hampshire to a 24-day event in Texas.

Stiff entertainment competition has resulted in declining attendance at state fairs. Carnivals at state fairs are either permanently located on the fair grounds or are traveling shows. The carnivals face fierce competition from amusement parks like Universal Studios and Disney World.

Over three million people attend the Texas State Fair each year.

The population of the United States is becoming increasingly diverse. Sports and entertainment managers must recognize the changing demographics to successfully market their events. The 2000 Census indicated that San Francisco consisted of 43.8% Whites, 31.1% Asians, 14.1% Hispanics, 7.2% African-Americans, and 3.8% others. Wise marketing and management strategies take into consideration changing demographics. Successful managers understand that it is important to cater to all possible target markets.

THINK CRITICALLY

1. **How should professional sports teams in San Francisco promote to target markets considering the demographics of the city?**
2. **What kind of influence should these demographics have on individuals hired for management of entertainment events in San Francisco?**

The plight of state fairs depends upon the strength of management. During any given year, revenues for state fairs can range from record breaking to searching-for-new-life. Management for state fairs must focus on the bottom line—profit. Management must maintain facilities, contract with entertainment, determine promotional strategies, sell tickets, hire security, and attract sponsors.

Even with significant rain on the final weekend, the 2002 State Fair of Texas wrapped up a highly successful run characterized by enthusiastic crowds and quality attractions. State fair visitors spent slightly more than $21 million on food and amusement rides. This topped the 2000 total of $19.3 million but fell short of the 2001 record high of $21.4 million. New attractions proved to be crowd pleasers in 2002. From the 20-foot sand sculpture and the fascinating props and costumes in the Blockbuster movie memorabilia collection to the luxury showroom of premium-priced cars and the engaging "Little Hands on the Farm," visitors enjoyed the variety of exhibits offered. Country superstar Alan Jackson proved to be the top free concert attraction at the 2002 Chevrolet Main Stage. The biggest music event of 2002 came on the final Saturday. An all-star lineup drew a crowd of more than 40,000 to the Cotton Bowl for a seven-hour celebration of Texas music.

INTERMISSION

On what should management for state fairs focus?

____

____

UNDERSTANDING MANAGEMENT CONCEPTS

Circle the best answer for each of the following questions.

1. Fans of country, rock, and jazz music are examples of
- **a.** target markets
- **b.** demographics
- **c.** geographics
- **d.** general markets

2. Small towns
- **a.** cannot compete with big cities for major entertainment events
- **b.** are acquiring a greater share of the entertainment venues
- **c.** advertise entertainment events effectively through the Internet
- **d.** both b and c

THINK CRITICALLY

Answer the following questions as completely as possible. If necessary, use a separate sheet of paper.

3. Why are volunteers so important for events like Mardi Gras?

____

____

____

____

4. Describe a target market for an outdoor country music festival in Oklahoma.

____

____

____

____

5. You are the director of your state fair. Describe several new events that you could add to attract more people from the city to the fair.

____

____

____

____

REVIEW MANAGEMENT CONCEPTS

Write the letter of the term that matches each definition. Some terms will not be used.

a. authority	**e.** management
b. controlling	**f.** organizing
c. employee empowerment	**g.** planning
d. implementing	**h.** target market

____ **1.** Analyzing information and making decisions about what needs to be done

____ **2.** The process of accomplishing the goals of an organization through the effective use of people and other resources

____ **3.** Carrying out plans and making sure that adequate personnel are available to effectively accomplish all necessary tasks

____ **4.** Evaluating results to determine if objectives have been accomplished as planned

____ **5.** Giving authority to employees to solve problems with available resources

____ **6.** The group that management is trying to reach

____ **7.** The right to make decisions about assigned work and to delegate assignments to others

Circle the best answer.

8. Accomplishing tasks most effectively and arranging resources to complete all necessary work is
a. organizing
b. planning
c. controlling
d. implementing

9. Which of the following is not a step in the decision-making process?
a. obtain consensus before following through with a decision
b. analyze possible solutions
c. select a plan of action
d. identify the problem

10. Activities used to plan, price, promote, and sell an event are
a. production management
b. business information management
c. human resources management
d. marketing management

11. Planning and organizing activities are usually completed by
a. lower-level managers
b. supervisors
c. higher-level managers
d. employees

THINK CRITICALLY

12. Discuss with a classmate how you determine the amount of money that you are willing to spend on an entertainment event. Does your classmate have a similar viewpoint on money spent for entertainment?

13. You are the president of the Orange Bowl in Miami, Florida. FedEx® has just notified you that it no longer will sponsor the event. Which corporations will you approach as possible sponsors? Why? (Did you consider the product or service the sponsor offers? Did you consider the location of the sponsor?)

14. What are the four functions of management? Relate each function to a successful entertainment event.

15. Use the Internet to conduct research on the Jamboree in the Hills festival. Does the Jamboree in the Hills festival effectively use the Internet to advertise its entertainment events? Explain your answer.

16. Using the Internet or magazines in your library, find an article that deals with some phase of management for a sports or other entertainment event. List ten main points made in the article.

MAKE CONNECTIONS

17. Management Math You are the financial manager for a professional football team. The stadium holds 74,000 fans. Thirty percent of the seats in the stadium sell for $35 per game, forty percent of the seats sell for $50 per game, and thirty percent of the seats sell for $65 per game. What is the gross revenue for ticket sales for one game if there is a sell-out crowd?

18. Technology Use the Internet to find information about four professional sports stadiums or basketball arenas. What is the seating capacity? How much do tickets cost for sporting events? How old is the facility? What other events use the facility?

19. Communication You are the events director for a major university. Write a letter to welcome your events staff members. The letter should emphasize your expectations for top customer service.

20. Production Management Your class has decided to organize a 5K run/walk for the Heart Association. List all aspects of this event that must be covered. How will you deal with the liability of possible injuries suffered by participants in this event?

21. Management Responsibilities You are the community events coordinator for a professional team. You have decided to start a Kids Club to gain the interest of younger fans and their parents. During the year, you will schedule events for Kids Club members to meet some of the players, cheerleaders, and coaches. Also, you will give the kids promotional items in goody bags at the special events. What four events will you hold during the year for the Kids Club? Why? What will be the special attractions at these events? How will you measure the success of this promotional campaign? From what organizations will you pull volunteers to help you carry out the special events? What will be the perks for these volunteers?

22. Communication You are the manager of a state fair that has experienced declining attendance in the last two years. Write a one-page report detailing your suggestions for improving attendance at this year's state fair.

23. Technology Search the Internet for locations of small-town festivals. What kinds of events are being hosted by small communities? Prepare a chart comparing the attributes that make each event successful, including such things as location, promotions, advertising, and support from local businesses.

CASE STUDY

DECA PREP

An Association of Marketing Students

FROM WINDMILL FESTIVAL TO ROCK FESTIVAL

The 2nd Wind Ranch, located four miles north of the small town of Comstock, Nebraska, has become home to several successful entertainment events. And it all began with one man's fascination with windmills.

What began as a hobby for Henry Nuxoll has turned into the business of collecting and restoring windmills. He owns and operates 2nd Wind Ranch with his friend and partner Roland Shafer. The windmills range in diameter from 6 to 20 feet and are laid out in a 40-acre pasture on the ranch.

Windmills have intrigued Henry Nuxoll since boyhood. Roland Shafer, a welding helmet manufacturer, is helping make Nuxoll's dream come true. Nuxoll lost his 160-acre family ranch during the agricultural crisis of the 1980s.

The Dempster House

In 1998, he was able to buy the property again. That's when Nuxoll launched The Dempster House, a bed and breakfast, and the windmill collection. Dempster Manufacturing built many famed windmills in Beatrice, Nebraska. Since he was given a second chance to own the property, Nuxoll chose the name 2nd Wind Ranch. Since its opening, Nuxoll has added a restaurant and a mercantile, both located on the property. The bed and breakfast, the restaurant, and the mercantile employ 12 people, a number that is sure to increase.

2nd Wind Ranch is tucked in a green valley between untouched hills. It remains isolated from the hustle and bustle of city life and includes the peaceful background of beautiful countryside. What makes this place different is that it's a historic journey to the days of the pioneers who settled the West. Thirty windmills ranging from brand new to over 100 years old are laid out on a forty-acre pasture.

Comstock Windmill Festival

The 2nd Wind Ranch has put Comstock on the map with the Comstock Windmill Festival, a popular June country music festival. Comstock Rock is a second music celebration in September that attracts the attention of a different target market.

The Windmill World Trade Fair, held at the 2nd Wind Ranch during the summer of 2001, showcased 125 preserved windmills. This major event provided a gathering place for association members from the United States and Canada who have "a genuine love and respect for the preservation of windmills."

The 2nd Wind Ranch has become so much more than a quaint bed and breakfast. The small community of Comstock has become an entertainment attraction for fans of country and rock music. Each festival attracts crowds that dwarf the size of Comstock. Success comes from a great location, fun outdoor environment, excellent advertising through the Internet, and word of mouth from satisfied customers. The 2nd Wind Ranch is a classic example of how entrepreneurs even in the smallest setting can succeed with a large production.

Think Critically

1. How did the 2nd Wind Ranch become the location for major entertainment events?
2. List ways the four functions of management might be used to prepare 2nd Wind Ranch for the Comstock Windmill Festival.
3. What entertainment suggestions can you make for the 2nd Wind Ranch that will not commercialize the entertainment venue?
4. Visit the Windmill Festival on the Internet and describe the links that are included on the web site.

SPORTS AND ENTERTAINMENT MARKETING MANAGEMENT TEAM DECISION MAKING

You have been hired as a consultant by the athletic department of Rice University, a private school with only 40,000 alumni. The university's football stadium seats 70,000 people. Although the football team has experienced success the last three seasons, the alumni and current student population are not large enough to fill the stadium. The university is looking for creative ways to increase ticket sales at Rice's home football games.

Your task is to develop entertainment events throughout the year that will bring more people into the Rice University football stadium and ultimately will attract new target markets for football. Rice particularly wants to attract more families to the campus for events year-round in the hope that they will return in the fall and purchase football tickets.

Your strategy must include entertainment events for the stadium throughout the year, advertising campaigns, and special promotional strategies for the entertainment events and for Rice University football games.

Performance Indicators Evaluated

- Understand the challenges faced by Rice University Athletic Department.
- Devise strategies to attract new target markets to Rice University.
- Define events throughout the year to attract new customers to Rice University.
- Describe promotional strategies for the entertainment events and Rice football games.

Go to the DECA web site for more detailed information.

1. What entertainment events will attract large audiences ?
2. When will you schedule the special events? Why?
3. What target markets will you try to attract to Rice?
4. Outline your advertising and promotional strategies.

www.deca.org/publications/HS_Guide/guidetoc.html

CHAPTER 2

College and Amateur Sports

2.1 MANAGING COLLEGE ATHLETICS
2.2 MANAGING AMATEUR SPORTS
2.3 ECONOMIC IMPACT

© GETTY IMAGES/PHOTODISC

© GETTY IMAGES/PHOTODISC

© GETTY IMAGES/PHOTODISC

© GETTY IMAGES/PHOTODISC

WINNING Strategies

SUCCESS OF SPORTS CAMPS

Every summer, thousands of youngsters attend a wide array of sports camps throughout the United States. Camps range from one day to one week in length. College coaches, high school coaches, and professional athletes run some of the most popular sports camps. Many of these camp leaders rely on other individuals to manage all of the special events as well as the day-to-day activities of the sports camp.

Parents send their children to sports camps for a variety of reasons. Participants gain greater self-esteem, social skills, and athletic skills from the best camps. Camps run by popular college coaches tend to attract blue-chip athletes hoping to be recognized by the strongest athletic programs. Sports camps can serve as a channel for outstanding young athletes to get recognized by major universities.

Managers of sports camps must be involved with the planning, organizing, implementing, and controlling of the event. Camps at major universities are more likely than smaller, local camps to land nationally recognized sponsors. However, smaller camps sometimes can provide participants with equal or better experiences than larger, more heavily attended camps. Smaller camps often offer more individual attention. They frequently have the support and active participation of well-known athletes from the local community.

THINK CRITICALLY

1. What are some advantages of having popular athletes and successful business people involved in the organization of sports camps?
2. Why are more parents sending their children to sports camps?

MANAGING COLLEGE ATHLETICS

Discuss the functions of management for college sports.

Describe the levels of management, and explain the concept of Total Quality Management (TQM).

OPENING ACT

College sports programs require top management. Managers recruit players, promote events, sell tickets, and attract the best coaches. They follow the National Collegiate Athletic Association's rules and guidelines. Athletic directors are faced with making important management decisions. They must have successful, revenue generating sports teams to finance the numerous college athletic programs. Winning records and championships fill stadiums and coliseums. When a team is not winning, universities often search for new leadership to turn programs around.

Work with a partner. Discuss ways that new leadership can turn around a college athletic program.

MANAGING COLLEGIATE SPORTS

Successful collegiate sports programs hire the best coaches, recruit the most talented players, and keep the stands filled with paying fans. Universities count on the revenue from successful athletics to maintain diversified sports programs for both male and female students. Successful athletic programs result in greater attendance, more money donated by satisfied alumni, and attention from more corporate sponsors.

Management responsibilities are the obligations to carry out all necessary tasks for college sports events. In addition to the athletic directors, college presidents, and coaches, many dedicated people are needed for the management of ticket sales, sponsorships, and the event itself.

MANAGEMENT FUNCTIONS IN ACTION

Managers of college athletic programs must use the four functions of management in order for their programs to succeed.

Planning College athletic directors are faced with the challenge of scheduling non-conference games years in advance. Long-term successful programs try to negotiate schedules that require less-noted teams to play at the successful team's stadium or coliseum. This strategic planning is important for the home field advantage, a greater number of wins, and a better chance at the national championship. Sometimes less-noted teams will sign the contract to play at the dominant team's stadium in order to earn a percentage of the large amount of revenue from a sold-out stadium.

© GETTY IMAGES/PHOTODISC

Major universities understand the importance of national exposure on television and the resulting revenue from televised games. College teams in major conferences split the revenue from televised regular season games and bowl or championship games involving members of the conference. Football bowl games promise payouts to teams ranging from $500,000 to $13 million. Conferences have realigned to gain a better share of the television viewing audience. The Big Twelve Conference combined the Big Eight and four teams from Texas because the Houston/Dallas television audience is huge.

Athletic directors are in charge of financial management. Today's major universities are working with budgets ranging from $40 million to more than $100 million. The athletic director has the critical responsibility of accommodating all sports offered at the institution while attracting large numbers of fans and contributors. Large salaries for popular, successful coaches require a major percentage of the budget. There is a fine balancing act between charging acceptable ticket prices and offering the maximum number of top-quality sports for an athletic program. Athletic directors at some major universities have been forced to make budget cuts that eliminate certain sports.

Playing in championship tournaments and bowl games rewards successful college athletic teams. These games added to the regular season require careful planning and financing.

Organizing A college sporting event is much more than the game being played on the field or court. It literally is a recruiting tool for future students to attend the university. The event is also a public relations tool for taxpayers whose money is used to finance the university. Universities hire event management teams. Teams make sure that every aspect of the event, from ticket sales to the actual game, goes smoothly. Individuals involved with event management are, in a sense, hospitality agents hired to satisfy the needs of fans. Members of the event management team are responsible for customer satisfaction. They are also counted on to maintain security for sporting events. An increase in the number of unruly fans, requiring tighter security, has made it much more challenging to manage college athletic events. Guests from the opposing team should feel welcome and safe when attending an event at the hosting school.

Implementing Stadiums at universities have grown much taller. Luxury suites, previously common only for professional sports, are built atop the stadiums. They offer such amenities as comfortable seating and catered food in an enclosed, climate-controlled environment. Winning teams attract the attention of corporations and wealthy fans that pay big dollars to reserve the luxury suites.

Success on the field or on the court increases ticket sales and eventually can result in building new stadiums or coliseums. Winning at the college level also results in greater sales of merchandise bearing the college logo. Every sale of merchandise pays royalties (payments for the use of the logo) ranging from 8 to 14 percent to the universities.

© GETTY IMAGES/PHOTODISC

Controlling Management must evaluate results. Evaluation helps to determine if the university athletic department's objectives have been accomplished as planned. Controlling is a very important part of management because it determines what will take place in the future. The best management teams evaluate results to streamline the operation for the next season.

ROLE OF THE NCAA

The **National Collegiate Athletic Association (NCAA)** regulates collegiate athletics. The student-athlete is considered an integral part of the student body. In this regard, an amateur student-athlete is one who engages in a particular sport for the educational, physical, mental, and social benefits. Student athletes are ineligible for participation in an intercollegiate sport if they ever agree (orally or in writing) to be represented by an agent for marketing their athletic ability or reputation in the sport. Athletic directors and coaches are responsible for ensuring that the university's sports programs adhere to the NCAA's guidelines.

The NCAA is setting up a $17-million Student-Athlete Opportunity Fund that has no financial-need restrictions. It's to be used for "educational and developmental opportunities."

INTERMISSION

Give an example of each of the four management functions for a college sporting event.

NATURE OF MANAGEMENT

Managers are responsible for the success or failure of college athletic programs. They accumulate and determine the best ways to use the resources, and manage people effectively for success.

LEVELS OF MANAGEMENT

There is typically more than one level of management in most college athletic programs.

Executives are top-level managers who spend most of their time on management functions. Executives usually have other managers reporting to them.

Mid-managers spend most of their time on one management function, such as planning or controlling. A mid-manager might also be responsible for a specific part of a college sports program.

Supervisors work directly with employees and are called upon to translate the athletic department's plan into action. Usually supervisors are skilled, experienced workers promoted from areas where they work. Successful supervisors instill a team spirit in their employees by recognizing the value of human resources. Frequently, supervisors have little or no management training.

Major tasks for supervisors include implementing decisions of management, solving employee problems, and presenting employee concerns to management. The effectiveness of supervisors is measured by quality of work of the supervised employees, efficient use of resources, and satisfaction of the supervisors' employees. Supervisors must have good communication and human relation skills. They are responsible for their own work. They are also responsible for the work of their employees. The success or failure of the team is directly reflected on the supervisor.

Sometimes fan enthusiasm has turned ugly. A daylong summit on fan misbehavior emphasized the need to put the brakes on. The gathering of athletic, academic, event management, and law enforcement representatives led to new conference guidelines and the following recommendations.

1. **Shifting students' seating to remove them from the vicinity of the opposing team's bench**
2. **Inviting visiting schools' officials to pre-game planning sessions**
3. **Limiting or eliminating big-screen replays that may reveal officials' mistakes**
4. **Cracking down on even the smallest of criminal acts, including trespassing on playing fields and destruction of football goal posts**

Recommended practices were distributed to schools with major football and basketball programs at the start of the 2003 football season.

THINK CRITICALLY

1. **How are ethics involved with fan behavior?**
2. **Should the NCAA take more action regarding fan misbehavior?**

TOTAL QUALITY MANAGEMENT

Dr. W. Edwards Deming developed **Total Quality Management (TQM)** in the 1950s. He suggested that a long-term commitment to quality, customer satisfaction, and employee morale would lead to success. TQM emphasizes increasing quality and developing an effective organization. Customer satisfaction and employee motivation are top concerns of TQM. TQM relies on leadership and cooperation instead of the traditional management focus of closely supervising employee behavior. TQM managers constantly look for new and improved ways to complete their work in order to increase effectiveness and quality. Teamwork and employee involvement in decision making are emphasized by TQM. Total Quality Management views employees as valuable contributors to success and uses training and education to improve employee effectiveness and motivation. Universities count on event managers to be hospitality agents who effectively practice the TQM strategy.

INTERMISSION

Why is TQM so important for managing a successful college sports event?

___

___

© GETTY IMAGES/PHOTODISC

UNDERSTAND MANAGEMENT CONCEPTS

Circle the best answer for each of the following questions.

1. Management of college athletics
   a. focuses on reaching the goals of the university
   b. considers the financial impact on the university
   c. realizes the importance of fan satisfaction
   d. all of the above

2. Top-level managers who spend most of their time on management functions are
   a. supervisors
   b. executives
   c. employees
   d. mid-managers

THINK CRITICALLY

Answer the following questions as completely as possible. If necessary, use a separate sheet of paper.

3. What is TQM? Why is it so important for the management of collegiate sporting events?

____

____

____

4. Marketing Management How is a college sporting event considered a recruiting tool for future students to attend the university?

____

____

5. What is the role of the NCAA in college sports? Does the NCAA ever hinder the financial management function for college athletics? Explain.

____

____

____

6. Why are top athletic directors at major universities paid high salaries?

____

____

LESSON 2.2

MANAGING AMATEUR SPORTS

Describe the management functions necessary for amateur sports.

Explain the management of a successful sports camp.

OPENING ACT

The original purposes of amateur sports for youth were developing team skills, providing physical exercise, and offering participation in a social activity. However, amateur sports are attractive to individuals of all ages. A growing number of senior citizens now participate in amateur sports ranging from bowling to power walking. More than 40 percent of the U.S. population is overweight. Therefore, amateur sports are attractive as well for improving physical fitness. Sports camps and leagues focus not only on improving athletic skills but also on preparing young people for future professional careers. Amateur sports also have increased equipment sales. Amateur athletes want the best equipment and the latest styles, resulting in a multibillion-dollar industry. The marketing opportunities for amateur sports are endless.

Work with a partner. Make a list of potential marketing opportunities involving amateur sports.

GROWTH OF AMATEUR SPORTS

High school athletics are important social events for small and large cities. A small town often gains an image from its amateur sports. Communities rally behind their amateur high school athletic teams. In one small community that made it to the state basketball tournament, nearly everyone in town attended the tournament to support the local team. A sign along the highway read, "Will the last one out, please turn off the lights." Local amateur teams are a point of pride for many communities. Signs throughout small-town America brag about having a state champion sports team.

Cities and states are equally proud of their local amateur athletic heroes, especially young, emerging stars like Sarah Hughes. Sixteen-year-old Hughes surprised the world by winning the gold medal in women's figure skating at her first Olympic appearance. New York City and the State of New York are extremely proud of this famous amateur athlete.

Management of amateur sports has become increasingly important. Little league baseball, softball, soccer, hockey, and lacrosse require management to schedule games, maintain facilities, and hire the necessary employees for the amateur event. Amateur sports events require detailed planning. The participants, parents, and fans have great expectations for an enjoyable event.

MANAGEMENT FOR AMATEUR SPORTS

The functions of management are used to conduct amateur sports events.

MANAGEMENT RESPONSIBILITIES

Planning Managers in charge of tournaments for baseball, softball, soccer, lacrosse, football, and hockey must have the necessary organizational skills to work effectively with participants. Planners must consider fans, ticket sales, security, concessions, and rules of the sport. Planning an amateur sporting event takes into consideration all possible scenarios. A delicate balance must be maintained between healthy competition and good sportsmanship, and adults must set the example. There is an alarming trend of adults not maintaining their composure at amateur sporting events. This behavior has become so extreme that some parents are no longer allowed to attend their child's games.

Organizing High school football fields and basketball gymnasiums have been built and renovated for the best competition and fan comfort. Strategies must then be devised to attract people to the games. High school athletic directors are faced with tightening budgets that must pay for buses to the sporting events, referees, coaches' salaries, and the numerous other details associated with high school athletics.

Implementing Sporting events at high schools of all sizes require ticket sales, security, coaches, administrators, and concession operators. The main purpose of the event is to provide a satisfying experience for athletes and fans. Managers in charge of the sporting events are expected to help employees carry out the necessary tasks while financially breaking even or making a profit.

Controlling The best management teams streamline operations. Amateur sports managers are faced with improving tournaments, facilities, ticket efficiency, and other factors. High school athletic directors must consider ticket sales and create strategies to fill more seats. Sometimes the strategies include a recognition night for parents of players or hometown heroes from past championship teams. The athletic director and other managers are the strongest promoters of the events.

MAINSTREAM SPORTS ARE LOSING YOUNG PEOPLE

Mainstream sports are facing increased competition from video games, the Internet, wrestling, and alternative sports. Skateboarding has been the fastest-growing sport for the last five years. Few people realize the full extent of the decline in interest among kids and teens in the traditional sports of baseball, basketball, softball, and football. Television ratings are a good barometer of the success of sports with young people. Comparing 1997–98 to 2000–01, ratings were down across all four major pro sports for both kids (ages 2 to 11) and teens (ages 12 to 17) for the playoffs and down across every sport except baseball for the regular season.

School districts often face tough financial decisions in order to balance their budgets. Students at many public schools must now pay a fee ranging from $50 to more than $300, as well as purchase the necessary equipment, to participate in extracurricular activities and amateur sports.

© GETTY IMAGES/PHOTODISC

Like baseball and softball, wrestling survived a threat to its Olympic status. International Olympic Committee (IOC) officials postponed any decision on cutting either Greco-Roman or freestyle wrestling from the Summer Games program. The majority of proposed trims in other sports also were postponed at least through the 2008 Olympics. The IOC program commission recommended that the IOC cut three entire sports, including baseball and softball, as well as disciplines or events within nine other sports. After all the recommendations were reviewed, only three events were eliminated—one in sailing and two in shooting. The IOC is intent on maintaining the size of the Summer Olympics to ensure that a global range of cities is capable of hosting the event.

THINK CRITICALLY

1. What factors must be considered when cutting Olympic sports?
2. What can sports managers do to persuade the International Olympic Committee to retain their sport?

Pro sports leagues have poured millions of dollars into amateur sports programs aimed at getting kids to participate in their particular sports. Results have been disappointing since no league program has been able to counter the movement away from team sports. According to the National Sporting Goods Association, only soccer and golf have seen increases in youth participation (ages 7 to 17) among the traditional competitive sports, a group that includes baseball, basketball, football, hockey, softball, volleyball, and tennis. Nevertheless, professional sports leagues continue to invest in amateur sports. For example, the NBA has the Jr. NBA and Jr. WNBA recreational league programs. These programs involve more than 350,000 kids.

Marketing managers of amateur sports programs realize that if they want to win loyalty from kids and teens, they need to treat them like young adults. Whatever sports capture the fancy of people in their 20s will surely be a hit with youth. The NFL ranks Number 1 among all age groups in terms of team sports. "In order to reach kids, you have to speak to them in their language," says Timothy Garrell, vice president and publishing director at *Sports Illustrated for Kids.*

INTERMISSION

Give four reasons why amateur sports have become increasingly popular.

___

___

MANAGING SPORTS CAMPS

Buford Chambers is a retired business executive. Larry Micheaux is a former professional basketball player and current high school basketball coach. Together, they operate the Larry Micheaux June-Jam-Bo-Ree Basketball Camp in Stafford, Texas. The program provides basketball camps for youth between the ages of 6 and 18. Participants can develop their game at their own pace as well as attend more challenging camps. Guests from the ranks of professional players and coaches, as well as community leaders, make the camp exciting.

Running a successful sports camp requires planning, organizing, implementing, and controlling.

Planning involves scheduling camp dates, distributing information months before the camps take place, finding sponsorships, designing brochures and other forms of advertising, planning meals for the camps, ordering t-shirts and other memorabilia, and determining the necessary finances.

Organizing a camp requires managing finances, processing registrations, hiring coaches, and handling other details. When a camp advertises that a sports figure will make an appearance, it is essential that the appearance take place in order for the camp to maintain credibility.

Implementing a sports camp requires a smooth operation that covers all scheduled events. Meals, release of liability for injuries, parent consent forms, and end-of-camp tournaments are just a few of the responsibilities for camp organizers.

Controlling activities during the camp include collecting quotes to be used for future camp promotions, taking pictures of the event, and making sure that participants benefit from the experience. Each year, organizers of camps review the event to see what can be improved in the future.

Sports camps throughout the United States are reaching larger target markets by using the Internet for advertising. Major search engines make it easy to research all kinds of sports camps. Sports camp organizers must make sure that their web site is easy to use. Information about the sports camp must be clear. Links for sports camp web sites may include quotes from previous camp participants and their parents, pictures from previous camp sessions, the agenda for the camp, dates and costs for each camp session, and registration materials.

THINK CRITICALLY
Use the Internet to find three sports camps for the same sport. Compare the sites for information and ease of use. Report your findings.

INTERMISSION

What can camp managers do to attract more participants to their sports camps?

____

____

UNDERSTAND MANAGEMENT CONCEPTS

Circle the best answer for each of the following questions.

1. Amateur sports
  a. are only popular in large cities
  b. do not require a high level of management
  c. give a small community an identity
  d. are only for young people

2. The planners of amateur sporting events must consider
  a. security
  b. fans
  c. ticket sales
  d. all of the above

THINK CRITICALLY

Answer the following questions as completely as possible. If necessary, use a separate sheet of paper.

3. Technology You are in charge of designing a web site for a baseball sports camp. Describe five links you will include for this web site.

____

____

____

4. Marketing Management Describe a promotional strategy to increase youth attendance at a high school baseball game.

____

____

____

5. How has the image of amateur sports been tarnished by fan behavior?

____

____

6. In what ways are mainstream sports attempting to increase loyalty among young people?

____

____

____

ECONOMIC IMPACT

OPENING ACT

Athletic programs at major universities throughout the country fund as many as 24 sports. Athletic directors at major universities are faced with balancing budgets ranging from $40 million to $60 million each year. During a time when state and federal governments are facing massive shortfalls in revenues, universities also feel the pinch. Athletic directors must make tough decisions that range from cutting funds to actually cutting sports from the total program. Athletic directors must also consider which sports are generating the most revenue for the athletic program and the equity issue of distributing funds to other sports within the program.

Work with a partner. Make a list of the pros and cons of allocating athletic funds based on the amount of revenue that each program generates.

Explain the financial impact of college athletics.

Describe the influence of amateur sports on family spending.

FINANCIAL IMPACT OF COLLEGE ATHLETICS

Athletic programs at major universities are huge financial operations that cultivate the talents of amateur athletes. Tight economic times mean less money is available to universities while costs of operating successful sports programs continue to rise. Universities have annual athletic budgets as high as $60 million for more than 20 sports. For example, the University of Nebraska football team generated $36 million in 2002 for the athletic program, which had a $47-million budget to finance 23 sports.

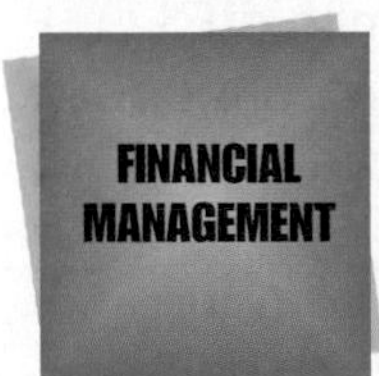

© GETTY IMAGES/PHOTODISC

A report issued in 2002 by the Commission on Opportunity in Athletics indicates that reform is needed to make Title IX fairer to male athletes. The report gives the Education Secretary wide latitude in deciding how to change underlying regulations of the law that bans sex discrimination at schools that receive federal funds. It is clear Title IX enforcement requires reform in order to make the law clearer, fairer, more enforceable, and truly open to all, according to the executive summary of the report. Title IX proponents believe that the recommendations could result in lost opportunities for female athletes.

THINK CRITICALLY

1. **Who will benefit the most from this report?**
2. **Is it fair to set guidelines for supporting women's sports but not men's? Defend your answer.**

TOUGH DECISIONS

Athletic departments at major universities want to offer the greatest number of winning sports programs possible. This goal is becoming increasingly difficult to accomplish with state funding cuts and increased costs for multiple sports programs. Universities that support more than 20 sports realize that money spent does not necessarily indicate success or failure for a program.

Athletic directors are faced with balancing large budgets for competitive programs. When there is a shortfall of revenue, tough decisions must be made. Tiering or regionalizing some sports are two options to save money. **Tiering** involves funding five or six sports at a high level, five or six at a medium level, and five or six at a low level. This decision does not eliminate any sports from the program but becomes controversial when deciding which sports receive the higher amount of support. **Regionalizing** is a second option for athletic departments with tight budget constraints. To save money, the school sets geographic limits on recruiting and travel. A third, unpopular option is to cut sports from the athletic program.

Title IX laws must be considered before cutting programs from the athletic department. **Title IX** bans sex discrimination at schools that receive federal funding and sets parameters for female sports that must be met by athletic programs.

WHAT ABOUT PAYING ATHLETES?

The NCAA regulates athletes. It is a voluntary organization that prohibits payment to college players. Athletes receive scholarships that pay for food and housing, and they can apply for Pell Grants based on need. The NCAA allows student-athletes to take a job, buy special insurance for their skill, and investigate their chances of being drafted by professional teams. An increasing number of amateur athletes are choosing to skip their junior and senior years in college to join professional teams. Professional baseball and basketball teams are even drafting athletes directly from high school and offering multimillion-dollar contracts. Graduation rates for athletes at successful programs are not encouraging, with some universities only graduating 25 to 40 percent of their athletes.

State legislatures have looked into the possibility of paying college athletes. However, they realize that such action would be an NCAA violation. Paying college and university amateur athletes would require large sums of money. State legislatures dealing with tightening budgets would be hard-pressed to find enough money to pay college athletes even a small amount. Ultimately the National Football League, National Basketball Association, Major League Baseball, National Hockey League, and U.S. Olympics benefit from athletes who are trained at colleges. Some individuals suggest that these organizations should help pay for the training of their future stars.

Perhaps the NCAA could help pay the bill with the money earned from television networks for broadcasting championship games. CBS agreed to pay $6 billion to carry the Final Four, which determines the national college basketball champion, in 2003. ABC paid the NCAA $535 million for the Bowl Championship Series (BCS) to determine the 2003 national college football champion.

INTERMISSION

Why is tiering of sports at a university controversial?

____

____

THE BIG BUSINESS OF AMATEUR SPORTS

Individuals participating in sports spend large sums of money on equipment, lessons, physical therapy for injuries, travel, hotel rooms, and meals associated with amateur sporting events. Even state governments realize the financial value of amateur sports. The Minnesota Amateur Sports Commission was created to generate interest in and support for amateur sports throughout the state. The economic impact of amateur sports in Minnesota was $51.8 million in 2000 and $55 million in 2001. Many states have state Olympics to recognize amateur athletes and enthusiasts. Participating sports range from traditional basketball and baseball to the less common chess game.

Athletics have always involved a sense of healthy competition. Communities compete to host amateur sports events because they realize the potential revenue for hotels, restaurants, and other retailers. Amateur sports also give businesses in the community an opportunity for sponsorship. The sponsorship can range from paying for the printed programs at the event and having an advertisement in the program to paying for uniforms bearing the company name and providing team transportation to sporting events. Tight economic conditions will open more opportunities for sponsorship of amateur sports.

© GETTY IMAGES/PHOTODISC

WHAT FAMILIES SPEND

Amateur sports definitely make up a percentage of the family budget, whether it is the cost of attending the event, buying the equipment, or actually participating in the sport. Spectators pay from $5 to more than $50 to watch amateur sports. Retailers that sell athletic shoes, jerseys, protective gear, and numerous other amateur athletic devices are reaping huge financial benefits. People selling concessions, programs, and souvenirs can earn big money.

Every weekend soccer fields, swimming pools, baseball fields, football fields, basketball arenas, and running tracks are filled with amateur athletes and spectators. The great increase in sales of sports utility vehicles can be attributed in huge part to families participating in amateur sports.

INTERMISSION

Explain the impact that amateur sports have had on family budgets.

____

____

Lead the Way

STEVE PEDERSON

In 2002, Steve Pederson was named the Athletic Director at his alma mater, the University of Nebraska, after managing programs at the University of Tennessee and the University of Pittsburgh.

When Pederson arrived, he immediately proclaimed the Year of the Fans to show appreciation for Nebraska's dedicated fans. He also made plans to bring back the Herbie Husker mascot and the old football uniform. Because he believed that fan suggestions were more useful than survey results, Pederson encouraged fans to e-mail him with ideas for improving the university's athletic programs.

With Pederson's arrival, individual ticket prices for the 2003 home football games were decreased by $1.75. This bold move cost the university more than $1 million in lost revenue from ticket sales for one football season. However, Pederson is counting on this goodwill gesture to increase the amount of money given by donors to the university athletic department.

THINK CRITICALLY

1. **Describe the career path for a university athletic director.**
2. **What strategies are being used to increase fan satisfaction at the University of Nebraska?**

UNDERSTAND MANAGEMENT CONCEPTS

Circle the best answer for each of the following questions.

1. Some athletic directors use __?__ to save money in the athletic budget.
a. tiering
b. regionalizing
c. program expansion
d. both a and b

2. Laws that set parameters for female sports are established by
a. the NCAA
b. Title IX
c. the Commission on Opportunity in Athletics
d. none of the above

THINK CRITICALLY

Answer the following questions as completely as possible. If necessary, use a separate sheet of paper.

3. How are the sales of sports utility vehicles related to amateur sports?

____

____

4. Management Math What percentage of the University of Nebraska's $47-million annual athletics budget does its football team generate by earning $36 million in revenue?

____

____

5. Technology Use the Internet to research the College World Series. Design a brochure to highlight Omaha, Nebraska, site of the College World Series.

____

____

6. Communication Compose a letter to the NCAA giving at least three reasons why college athletes should be paid for playing sports.

____

____

____

____

REVIEW

REVIEW MANAGEMENT CONCEPTS

Write the letter of the term that matches each definition. Some terms will not be used.

____ **1.** Top-level managers who spend most of their time on management functions
____ **2.** Managers who work directly with employees to translate the athletic department's plan into action
____ **3.** Long-term commitment to quality, customer satisfaction, and employee morale
____ **4.** Regulates collegiate athletics
____ **5.** Funding five or six sports at a high level, five or six at a medium level, and five or six at a low level
____ **6.** Law that sets parameters for female sports that must be met by athletic programs at universities
____ **7.** Setting geographic limits on recruiting and travel for athletic departments at universities

a. executives
b. mid-managers
c. NCAA
d. regionalizing
e. supervisors
f. tiering
g. Title IX
h. TQM

Circle the best answer.

8. Amateur athletes
a. participate in sports for pay
b. are growing in number
c. spend small sums of money on sports gear
d. only participate in high school sports

9. Management of college athletics
a. considers the financial impact to the universities
b. is not concerned with fan satisfaction
c. has become an increasingly easy task
d. none of the above

10. Amateur sports
a. are dominated by young people
b. are for all age groups
c. can be a stepping stone for professional sports careers
d. both b and c

11. The NCAA
a. regulates collegiate sports
b. hires university athletic directors
c. provides agents for amateur athletes
d. none of the above

THINK CRITICALLY

12. Use the Internet to compare the prices of three sports camps for the same sport. Design a comparison table to show potential customers what each camp offers.

13. Design a brochure for BASEBALL USA that advertises the instruction, camps, tournaments, and other services.

14. You are the athletic director at a major university that is experiencing a financial crunch. Explain the options of regionalizing and tiering sports. What would you do?

15. Use the Internet to research the NCAA. What is the mission (purpose) of the NCAA? List five rules (regulations) for amateur athletes. What other information is included on this web site?

16. Fans at your university have become increasingly unruly with a winning season in football. The campus police are unable to control 76,000 unruly fans who storm the field and tear down goal posts. Twenty fans suffered injuries at the last sporting event. You are the athletic director and must devise a plan to get better control at football games. Compose a letter to be published in the local newspaper.

MAKE CONNECTIONS

17. Management Math Rosenblatt Stadium, home of the College World Series, seats 23,145 fans. Box seats make up 60% of the stadium and cost $29 for the championship game. Reserved seats make up 30% of the stadium and cost $23 per seat. General admission seats make up 10% of the stadium and cost $7 each. How many seats make up each category of seating? How much revenue will be generated from each type of seat? How much ticket revenue will be generated from a sold-out stadium?

18. History Use the Internet to find information about the history of amateur sports at your favorite university. Write a one-page paper about the growth of the amateur sports program.

19. Communication Write a letter to parents to welcome their child to your sports camp. The letter should provide parents with an agenda and all necessary details to make them feel comfortable leaving their child in your care.

20. Marketing Management Your restaurant has decided to sponsor the local basketball team in your community (population 15,000). What promotional items will you produce to show your support while advertising your business? Draw samples of the promotional items and explain why they will be successful.

21. Marketing Management Your car dealership sells sports utility vehicles (SUVs). You realize that a large percentage of your target market is composed of families who are active in amateur sports. Design a newspaper advertisement for your SUVs that targets amateur sports families.

22. Management Math Plan a budget for a family of four to attend a three-day softball tournament in your capital city. Make sure you budget for transportation, gas, food, hotel, and other miscellaneous expenses.

23. Research Amateur sports have increased the sales of sporting gear. Select an amateur sport and research the price of three related pieces of sports equipment or gear purchased for the sport. Compare the prices at three competing retailers.

24. Marketing Management Professional sports are losing the interest of youth. Choose a professional sport. Describe in detail a special promotional strategy to attract more youth to that sport.

NASCAR'S IMAGE AND TEENAGERS

NASCAR™ is the fastest growing stock car circuit. It has attracted younger fans. They watch races on television with their parents. However, NASCAR's aggressive courting of corporate America is a turn-off for teens more interested in extreme sports.

EA Sports makes stock car video games. EA Sports believes NASCAR is blatantly commercial. It will always be avoided by a youthful demographic that seeks entertainment categorized as underground or sub-cultural.

NASCAR wants to find a way to blend into the teenage marketplace. Then an array of potential sponsors and advertisers could include jeans, fashion-conscious shoes, apparel, and game software.

Most experts agree that NASCAR relates powerfully with pre-teens. Recent ad campaigns have emphasized the generational fan connection between parents and children.

Hit or Miss

So far the marketing strategy is hit or miss. A FOX™ Family cartoon series, "NASCAR Racers," is unlikely to return to the airways. The series, developed with NASCAR's input, was intent on building young fans' interest and selling tie-in merchandise. The strategy failed on both counts. A stock car comic book series developed in 2000 also was not successful.

Youth appeal is more likely with traditional licensed products. NASCAR's $1.2-billion collectibles industry includes 50 licensees for youth-oriented products such as school supplies, posters, stickers, puzzles, and miniature race cars from Hot Wheels™ and other toy makers.

NASCAR's vice president of strategic marketing and licensing believes the sport must project shared values with the teenage market. NASCAR is unique because athletes stay in the sport for a long time. Support for popular NASCAR drivers can be passed down through generations of fans.

Jeff Gordon, three-time Winston Cup champion, is popular with younger fans. Gordon teamed with collectibles manufacturer Action Performance Company™ and Warner Brothers to manufacture collectible model cars that feature familiar icons like Bugs Bunny™, Road Runner™, and Daffy Duck™. Gordon realizes the importance of younger fans. Action Performance projected $20 million in sales of the collectible cars.

Teen Market

NASCAR realizes the teen market is crucial to its survival. FOX attracts younger viewers. Second-half partner NBC™ advertised coverage of the Pepsi™ 400 with promotional spots starring Gordon and pop star Britney Spears. The Spears–Gordon pairing opened the door for more teen appeal. NASCAR fans will start enjoying younger grand marshals and pop singers for the national anthem.

Domino's Pizza™ has signed a five-year, $30-million sponsorship to be the official pizza of NASCAR. The pizza chain, with 4,800 U.S. locations, will support its first major sports sponsorship. At least $30 million in media, promotions, and rights fees will occur over the life of the deal. Additional marketing support is anticipated from local Domino's franchisees. Domino's realized that the NASCAR fan indexed well against Domino's consumers. NASCAR's ratings are only second to the NFL nationally among sports, and the brand loyalty of its consumer is a big plus. Domino's also has an all-family target. Creative opportunities exist with NASCAR's emphasis on speed and Domino's emphasis on delivery. Eighty percent of Domino's franchisees support NASCAR promotionally.

Think Critically

1. Why has NASCAR sponsorship changed?

2. What should be done to attract a younger fan base?

3. In what way is NASCAR's fan base unique?

4. Who would be a good NASCAR sponsor to attract a younger audience?

SPORTS AND ENTERTAINMENT MARKETING MANAGEMENT TEAM DECISION MAKING

NASCAR realizes the importance of the teenage target market. This market will determine the future success of NASCAR. You have been hired by NASCAR to design a new promotional strategy to attract a greater share of teenage fans. You have a $5-million budget to design new advertisements, hire new spokespersons, attract new sponsors, design special promotions at the races, and develop relationships with products for NASCAR tie-ins. Outline your annual promotional strategy for NASCAR with projected expenditures.

Performance indicators Evaluated

- Understand NASCAR's mission to broaden its target market.
- Discuss the importance of the teenage target market to NASCAR.
- Budget promotional money through various outlets.
- Define the relationship between the target market and promotional strategies.

Go to the DECA web site for more detailed information.

1. Who will be the new sponsors for NASCAR?
2. Why will these sponsors be attractive to teenagers?
3. What individuals will be good spokespersons for NASCAR?
4. Why will these spokespersons attract the attention of teenagers?
5. What special promotions will attract greater attendance of teenagers and more television viewers?

www.deca.org/publications/HS_Guide/guidetoc.html

CHAPTER 3

Professional Sports

© GETTY IMAGES/PHOTODISC

3.1 MANAGING BIG LEAGUE SPORTS
3.2 ORGANIZING A PROFESSIONAL TEAM
3.3 AGENTS, MANAGERS, AND ETHICS

© GETTY IMAGES/PHOTODISC

© GETTY IMAGES/PHOTODISC

© GETTY IMAGES/PHOTODISC

WINNING Strategies

YOUR FOOT IN THE DOOR

Growing up in Kingwood, Texas, Adam Wright set a goal of working for a professional sports team after graduating from college. Adam attended Kingwood Junior College for two years. He then completed his degree at the University of Indiana, which had a strong Sports Management program.

When Adam graduated from Indiana University, he contacted the Houston Texans about an internship. The Texans were impressed with Adam's determination and his willingness to do anything—including accepting an unpaid internship—to get his foot in the door. Two weeks after the initial meeting, the Texans offered Adam a paid internship.

In less than a year, his hard work, outstanding attitude, and team effort earned Adam a full-time position as client services coordinator. His responsibilities include managing more than 30 corporate sponsors' accounts. Adam fulfills promises of the clients' contracts by staying in touch with all clients at least once a month. Communication and execution of sponsorships are important elements necessary for long-term success.

Adam Wright earned his position with the Houston Texans. Getting his foot in the door was the first step to career success. Working for a professional sports team requires individuals to handle intense, stressful work environments. Employees often work 80-hour workweeks during the season. The sports management industry is intensely competitive, making it hard to get your foot in the door. However, future career possibilities are outstanding for dedicated individuals.

THINK CRITICALLY

1. How did Adam get his foot in the door with the Houston Texans?
2. What characteristics are necessary to survive in the competitive field of sports and entertainment management?

MANAGING BIG LEAGUE SPORTS

Explain the importance of management for success in big league sports.

Describe ways professional sports teams generate money.

Discuss how opportunities have expanded for women in professional sports.

OPENING ACT

Big league sports offer great potential to earn large sums of money with a first-class team. However, the number of sports management positions is limited. Individuals who work for professional sports teams must have a college education, a strong work ethic, and a total commitment to the success of the team. The number of people necessary to run a successful professional athletic program goes far beyond the coaching staff and players. Professional sports teams have specialized coaches, trainers, team doctors, equipment managers, and travel coordinators. A typical sales and marketing department for a professional team can have 30 to 40 employees. These individuals ensure that all phases of the operation run smoothly. Networking, dedication, hard work, and willingness to prove yourself by working as an intern are some of the keys to success in sports management.

Work with a partner. Outline a strategy for becoming an employee for a professional sports team. Discuss the sacrifices involved with a career in professional sports management.

MANAGING BIG MONEY

It takes large sums of money to successfully operate professional sports teams. Sound financial management is necessary to build the latest state-of-the-art stadiums and arenas and to pay player salaries that are well into the millions. Designing the latest equipment and gear for the multitude of sports and planning hospitality venues to accommodate big league sports also require reliable financial management. Effective financial control is also equally important for negotiating television contracts, sponsorships, and endorsements. The four functions of management are key to managing a professional sports team.

PLANNING BIG LEAGUE SPORTS EVENTS

Planning involves analyzing information and making decisions about what needs to be done to host a Super Bowl or to determine the best television schedule for a professional team. More than ever before, planning is based upon the financial return. Showing multiple professional games at the same time on different networks and paying millions or billions of dollars to televise a championship event require detailed planning.

Strategic planning looks at the long-term big picture for the entire business. Cities throughout the United States have strategic plans for attracting professional teams and building the facilities necessary to entice the teams to stay. The first step of strategic planning, external analysis, occurs when managers study factors outside the organization that can affect operations. Managers focus attention on customers, competitors, the economy, and government. *Internal analysis* is the second step of strategic planning. Managers look at internal factors such as operations, finances, personnel, and other resources that can affect the success of the business. Managers must agree on the **mission**, or the most important purposes or directions, for the organization based upon all information collected.

Operational planning includes short-term activities for each part of the business. Finding a new sponsor for a major professional sport such as NASCAR is an example of operational planning.

ORGANIZING RESOURCES

Big league sporting events earn large sums of money. Financial and human resources must be in place to run a first-class operation. Managers must be willing to *delegate* duties, or transfer the responsibility of tasks, to other individuals who will most likely accomplish the goals. Delegation carries the risk of others not fulfilling the expectations of their manager. Team relationships must be strong for an organization to be successful.

IMPLEMENTING THE GAME PLAN

Implementing is the process of carrying out the plans of the organization without losing sight of short-term and long-term goals. **Short-term goals** are usually accomplished in less than a year. **Long-term goals** take more than one year to complete. One example of a short-term goal is to devise a solution to the traffic jams created during the first game of the season. More police officers directing traffic and satellite shuttle buses from park-and-ride locations are two short-term solutions to the traffic problems. Long-term goals may include adding seats and luxury suites to a stadium, building a new basketball arena, or increasing the size of parking lots.

© GETTY IMAGES/PHOTODISC

The mission of the Chicago Bulls states that the "organization is a sports entertainment company dedicated to winning NBA Championships, growing new basketball fans, and providing superior entertainment, value, and service."

The Internet provides easy access to information about stadiums and other sporting venues. Most sites show pictures of the sports venue. The more sophisticated sites also can provide a virtual view from each seat in the stadium. Technology has made it possible for people to learn in advance what their view of a game will be from different seats.

THINK CRITICALLY

1. **Use the Internet to locate the web site of your favorite professional sports team. Does the web site give a good picture of the complete sporting venue? Does the site offer a virtual view to give you an idea of how you would see the game from different seats?**
2. **What does this web site do well? How could the site be improved?**

To implement a successful professional sports program, managers must initiate effective communications. These communications should motivate employees, develop competent work teams, and guide operations management.

Communication is necessary to implement the work of any organization. Effective managers must be able to communicate plans and directions. They must gather information from employees to improve the organization. They also must work to identify and resolve communication problems. Managers must have both personal and organizational communication skills. One of the most important communication skills involves listening to employees. Employees provide management with valuable input to decide the best way for completing organizational tasks. Encouraging involvement during the decision-making process gains employees' commitment to achieving company goals.

CONTROLLING PROFESSIONAL SPORTS

The first step of the controlling function involves establishing standards for each of the organization's goals. A standard for a big sporting event may include selling all tickets for a game two weeks before the event. Another standard may be making sporting venues safe for fans by taking all necessary security precautions. Measuring performance and comparing it to the established standards help determine if goals have been met. It is easy to prove if standards for ticket and concession sales have met the goals set by the organization. Measuring security at the sporting event is more difficult. Quantity standards, quality standards, time standards, and cost standards must be measured to determine the effectiveness of any organization.

Quantity standards measure the amount of sales and sponsorship goals. Leaders in sales and promotions for professional sports teams spend much time and energy maintaining profitable relationships with sponsors. Quantity standards also involve ticket sales and the number of games televised to generate big revenue.

Quality standards measure how well a task has been completed, with perfection being the ultimate goal. Haste can result in waste. There must be a delicate balance between speed of completion and quality.

Time standards are directly related to quantity and quality standards. Every organization wants to be as efficient as possible with a minimum amount of error.

Cost standards are an important measure of financial success for an organization. Profit is the bottom line for big league sports. Management can increase profits by either increasing sales revenue or decreasing costs. Employees and managers who monitor performance to control cost can save large sums of money for their organization.

Big league sports must calculate results of their efforts in order to determine what strategies to use in the future. Controlling is important for maximizing revenue. Controlling involves not only financial management but also factors such as crowd control, traffic maintenance, and security, among many other details. Managers who discover that performance is not meeting standards can take steps to improve performance, change policies and procedures, or revise the standards. Managers must make sure that work is well organized. Employees must be empowered to effectively complete their jobs. Effective management provides all necessary resources for employees to complete their tasks. Management sets the tone for successful teams to meet standards.

STAYING IN THE GAME FINANCIALLY

Big league sports go well beyond game day, athletes, and fans. Manufacturers of sports equipment have a significant financial stake in the industry. With sports comes the risk of injury. Manufacturers of sporting goods such as bats and football helmets must have *liability insurance* to cover possible damages from a lawsuit due to player injuries.

© GETTY IMAGES/PHOTODISC

Major League Baseball's new regulations require manufacturers to purchase $10 million of liability insurance coverage. Manufacturers must also pay a $10,000 annual administrative fee for the insurance coverage.

INTERMISSION

What standards must be measured to determine the effectiveness of any organization?

Sports today have crossed international borders. Fans in Europe travel freely to other countries in order to support their favorite soccer teams. The Winter and Summer Olympics bring together athletes and fans from around the world. Management of international sporting events has become more challenging than ever before. The threat of terrorism must be seriously considered when many countries are assembled for a major sporting event such as the World Cup Soccer Championship or the Olympics. Tightened security since 9/11/01 presents a greater challenge of maintaining control of fans whose behavior at athletic events is declining.

THINK CRITICALLY

1. What might hinder sports fans from attending international events?
2. What special security measures should be enforced to maintain safety for fans of international sporting events?

MULTISPORT MECCAS

A popular strategy used by professional sports teams to pressure cities and counties to build new sports venues is "Build it or they will leave." These venues frequently are funded by taxpayer dollars. Many cities have hotel and car rental taxes that pay for new stadiums and arenas, which can cost more than $750 million. A corporate sponsor that wants its name attached to a professional sports venue will pay as much as $350 million for a multi-year contract.

Professional sports venues have become entertainment centers. Fans can enjoy a nice meal in a restaurant, shop for souvenirs in the upscale stores, and entertain children with a merry-go-round or swimming pool, as well as actually watch the sporting event.

TOUCHING THE TIP OF THE ICEBERG

Large sums of money are required for more than paying professional players, building state-of-the-art sports complexes, or obtaining the rights to become the official sponsor for a sports venue. Fans in the United States and throughout the world are willing to pay huge prices to attend the Super Bowl or NBA Championships. Additionally, big league sports keep money flowing into sporting goods stores, memorabilia shops, hotels, restaurants, retail stores, airports, and many other outlets. Adding the name of a professional team to a $3 t-shirt increases the value of the shirt to nearly $30.

INTERMISSION

Why is it important for sports complexes to have multiple uses?

____

____

WOMEN'S PROFESSIONAL SPORTS

Women's opportunities in sports have expanded rapidly since the 1972 Title IX law was passed. Title IX requires that high schools and colleges provide equal funding for men's and women's athletics. Twenty years ago, the assumption was that women were not interested in playing male sports. In reality, few programs were available for women to try these sports.

More people now appreciate female versions of popular sports due to increased media coverage. The WNBA does not sell out arenas like the NBA, and its players do not earn millions each year. However, it represents a powerful image to girls across America who now have role models who compete in professional sports. The U.S. Women's Soccer Team's World Cup victory in the summer of 1999 was a turning point that helped women achieve equal recognition for their athletic abilities.

Football has not gained much momentum for women since Title IX. The females who currently play professionally are mostly older women who have little training in football. Many professional women football players come from strong soccer or rugby backgrounds. These women may not be prepared to enter the "professional" level of another sport. Nonetheless, a crowd of 2,200 watched the first game of the newly formed Women's Professional Football League (WPFL) at the Orange Bowl in Miami on October 14, 2000.

A five-year, $40-million endorsement deal between Reebok™ and tennis star Venus Williams set a new benchmark for female athletes. Williams played the 2000 season without any endorsement contracts. She gained corporate popularity when she won the Wimbledon singles and doubles titles, the U.S. Open, and the Olympic singles and doubles titles. Venus and her sister Serena are aiming to become the new endorsement champions. They currently have deals with Wilsons Leather™, Avon™, Nortel Networks™, Puma™, Wrigley™, and McDonald's. Awareness of the two sisters among the public is at an all-time high.

THINK CRITICALLY

1. **Why was Reebok willing to pay Venus Williams so much to endorse its products?**
2. **Why do you think Venus and Serena Williams are such popular endorsers?**

INTERMISSION

Why do you think football has not become as popular as other sports with female athletes?

____

____

UNDERSTAND MANAGEMENT CONCEPTS
Circle the best answer for each of the following questions.

1. Goals that take more than one year to complete are
a. short-term goals
b. long-term goals
c. external goals
d. none of the above

2. Looking at the long-term big picture for the entire business is
a. internal analysis
b. external analysis
c. strategic planning
d. operational planning

THINK CRITICALLY
Answer the following questions as completely as possible. If necessary, use a separate sheet of paper.

3. Production Management Research the history of AstroTurf and predict what type of playing surface will take its place. Explain why your product will be superior to AstroTurf.

4. Marketing Management You are in charge of special promotional events during a minor league baseball game. Describe in detail three promotional activities to get fans involved during the game.

5. Technology Your city will host a new professional team with a new sporting venue. Design an electronic presentation to convince a local corporation that a luxury suite is crucial for entertaining business guests at professional sporting events. The stadium is being built and will be ready three weeks before the first game. Thus, you are selling a product/service that currently does not exist.

ORGANIZING A PROFESSIONAL TEAM

OPENING ACT

Paul Tagliabue is the commissioner for the National Football League (NFL). From September to February, Tagliabue controls the passion of America—32 teams of the NFL. Fans treat Tagliabue like a celebrity, frequently requesting his autograph. Tagliabue is in a position where everything is falling into place financially. The NFL recently signed a $2-billion satellite television deal. Twenty new football-only stadiums were built or remodeled between 1993 and 2003. Sponsors somehow keep pumping out big dollars to get a piece of the NFL brand. Revenues have doubled since 1997 ($4.8 billion in 2002) and are estimated to grow by $1 billion between 2003 and 2005. Commissioner Paul Tagliabue believes that he inherited an entertainment business. Tagliabue is a visionary who cut deals with new media and created an acceptable player salary cap. He negotiated growing television revenues to ensure that new stadiums could be financed.

Work with a partner to discuss why commissioners of professional sports have so much power. How can these individuals use their power to make a positive impact in a community?

Describe the purpose and structure of an organizational chart.

Explain how organizations measure the success of the business plan.

THE ORGANIZING FUNCTION

Organizing determines how plans can be accomplished most effectively. Organizing is all about arranging resources and developing relationships between employees and departments. Each employee must have a clear understanding of his or her responsibility to the department and the entire organization. Employees for a professional sport realize that every person is important for the success of the organization.

ORGANIZATIONAL CHARTS

Organizational charts are illustrations that show the structure of an organization, the major job classifications, and the chain of command. Organizational charts clearly show each employee's department and supervisor and identify lines of authority and formal communication.

Most new employees receive a handbook that explains the organization of the business. The organizational chart lets employees know where they fit into the company. The organizational chart also identifies career opportunities that may exist within the organization.

RESPONSIBILITIES FOR INDIVIDUALS

The Sales & Marketing Department organizational chart for a professional team can have as many as 35 management positions. The chart may also include numerous additional employees who are supervised by the individuals involved in management. Management positions include Vice President of Corporate Sales, Director of Ticket Operations, Director of Marketing, and Director of Customer Service. Management positions even exist for the Mascot Coordinator and Cheerleader Coordinator.

Each manager listed on the organizational chart has specific duties. The Vice President of Corporate Sales for a professional sports team is in charge of sponsor sales and client services. The Director of Ticket Operations is responsible for ticket sales, ticket service, and luxury suite sales. The Director of Marketing handles special events, advertising and promotions, game-day entertainment, and specialty merchandise. The Director of Customer Service oversees club services, luxury suite services, and training of employees. The Senior Vice President, Chief Sales and Marketing Officer serves as the leader who ensures that all four departments work together smoothly to accomplish the organization's goals.

Job descriptions define the requirements for each position in an organization. Job descriptions include skills required for the position and the basic function—the job description narrowed down to one paragraph. Detailed job descriptions can list as many as 20 duties and responsibilities. Duties include travel requirements, physical demands, audiovisual demands, specific actions, work environment, repetitive motions, and job requirements. Good job descriptions include *measurements of success* that describe how the employee will be evaluated.

One professional football team uses extensive job descriptions that identify not only the department and who the individual reports to in the organization but also the required minimum education and work experience.

INTERMISSION

What is the purpose of an organizational chart?

____

____

MEASURING THE SUCCESS OF THE BUSINESS PLAN

A **business plan** outlines the mission, objectives, goals, strategies, and measures of an organization.

- **Mission** is the general statement of the organization's purpose.
- **Objectives** are specific company priorities.
- **Goals** are tangible, measurable outcomes for company objectives.
- **Strategies** are specific initiatives to deliver company goals and objectives.
- **Measures** are standards to evaluate the success of each strategy in delivering goals and objectives.

The mission, objectives, goals, strategies, and measures flow through the organization and are interconnected. For example, an organizational objective will likely be the mission of one or more of the departments.

An organization tests its business plan by using the 4 S's (selective, sufficient, synchronized, and sustainable).

Selective An organization's business plan must be selective. Important choices define the type of business and customer. They also define by omission who is not a customer, who is not served, and who is not employed.

Sufficient A successful organization must determine if its business plan is sufficient. If the plan is sufficient, the organization will achieve its goals by executing its strategies. Also it must determine if goals that are reached will result in the organization achieving its objectives. Will the achieved objectives adequately fulfill the organization's mission?

The 4 S's of a Business Plan

- Selective
- Sufficient
- Synchronized
- Sustainable

Synchronized A successful business plan is synchronized. All pieces of the organization work collectively in a smooth, effective, and efficient manner. Total productivity and impact should be greater than the sum of individual efforts. The collective results of the organization's employees are called **synergy**.

Sustainable A sustainable business plan looks at the "competitive advantage" that can be used for leverage. Leverage is the organization's advantage over its competitors. Successful organizations have a unique approach, and customers are willing to pay for the advantages over the competition.

INTERMISSION

How can an organization measure the success of its business plan?

____

____

FELICIA HALL

Felicia Hall began her career in sports as an intern with the National Collegiate Athletic Association (NCAA). She was Manager of Women's Basketball for NIKE's™ Sports Marketing Department before becoming the Director of Business Operations for the WNBA's Charlotte Sting. Hall describes her average day as anything but typical. She is responsible for all aspects of the management functions. That means staff meetings every other week with all department heads, including marketing, broadcasting, game operations, advertising and public relations, ticket sales, corporate sales, and accounting. There are also luncheons, speaking engagements, and other various public appearances to heighten brand awareness of the Charlotte Sting. Hall is in constant contact with season ticket holders, sponsors, and civic organizations. She works hand-in-hand with college coaches, sports agents, and members of the WNBA office in New York City. Hall says that effective communication is at the core of her central responsibilities.

THINK CRITICALLY

1. Why is effective communication so important to a sports management position?
2. What career advice would you give to women who are interested in a position similar to Felicia Hall's?

UNDERSTANDING MANAGEMENT CONCEPTS

Circle the best answer for each of the following questions.

1. Organizational charts
   a. show the structure of organizations
   b. indicate the chain of command in an organization
   c. show major job classifications
   d. all of the above

2. The ___?___ is the general statement of the organization's purpose.
   a. mission **c.** strategy
   b. goal **d.** objective

THINK CRITICALLY

Answer the following questions as completely as possible. If necessary, use a separate sheet of paper.

3. Marketing Management List five products that famous female athletes might endorse. Match the five products to five popular female athletes and explain your pairings.

____

____

____

4. Technology Using the Internet, locate and print the organizational chart for a sports or entertainment organization. How many levels of management does the chart include? How many people are included in the organizational chart?

____

____

____

5. Communication You are the president of a professional sports organization. Identify the organization and write its mission statement.

____

____

____

____

____

LESSON 3.3

AGENTS, MANAGERS, AND ETHICS

Identify the characteristics of successful sports agents.

Explain the standard fee structures of sports agents and describe how agents recruit clients.

Discuss the roles of team owners and general managers.

OPENING ACT

Sports agents who represent top professional athletes make large sums of money from the deals they negotiate for their clients' salaries and endorsement packages. Sports agents make as much as four percent of the amounts they negotiate for the athletes they represent. Popular athletes like Tiger Woods, Shaquille O'Neal, Mia Hamm, and Venus Williams are likely candidates for lucrative endorsement deals. Venus Williams has a five-year endorsement contract with Reebok worth almost $40 million. Mia Hamm makes up to $15 million per year from endorsements. Tiger Woods has a five-year contract with NIKE worth $100 million. Woods makes an estimated $54 million per year from endorsements with 11 companies. Most reputable sports agents have a solid legal background. Many are attorneys who know all the details involved with contracts. Professional athletes must know how to manage their personal finances while counting on agents to land new contract terms and endorsement deals.

Work with a partner to discuss the role of sports agents. How are ethics involved with the sports agent career? Why must professional athletes conduct careful research before choosing an agent?

TALK TO MY AGENT

Professional athletes have the potential to earn large sums of money from contracts and endorsements. It is important for athletes to be in charge of their finances and to have solid knowledge about their investments. Often, they do not have the time or expertise to work out the legal terms of contracts and endorsements.

Athletes hire **agents** as legal representatives who negotiate new contracts and endorsement agreements. A large percentage of the agents are attorneys who are well-versed in contract law. Good agents can represent up to 12 athletes at one time. The biggest incentive for being an agent is the possibility of high income. Income for an agent is based upon a percentage of the amount negotiated for the athlete. Professional athletes must hire trustworthy agents. Untrustworthy agents take some athletes on a financial roller coaster ride.

AGENTS AND LEADERSHIP

Agents are managers for the professional athletes they represent. They have the responsibility to effectively represent their clients. Leadership is one of the most important qualities that an agent must possess. **Leadership** is the ability to influence individuals and organizations to cooperatively achieve goals that benefit both parties. Agents bring together players and sports franchises to negotiate the best financial agreements. Agents who earn the respect and business of professional athletes accomplish successful negotiations because they are leaders. Leaders keep up to date on the latest trends in the professional sports industry.

Agents must have strong human relations skills to work well with people. Good agents gain respect by being knowledgeable, fair, and accurate. The individual athlete and sports franchise must trust the honesty of the sports agent. A spirit of trust will make it easier to avoid negative feelings, misunderstandings, and a mutual lack of respect.

Octagon is the sports, entertainment, and event marketing arm of the Interpublic Group. Octagon was recently slapped with a third lawsuit alleging tampering with players under contract to other agents. In a $41-million suit, Andrew Joel claimed that Octagon agent Andre Colona stole the NFL's 2001 No. 1 draft pick, Michael Vick. Joel alleges that Colona and other Octagon representatives met secretly with Vick when Vick was still under contract to Joel. Veteran agent Frank Bauer, who lost the NFL's 2002 No. 1 pick, David Carr, to Octagon also filed a lawsuit. James Sims, another veteran football agent, has alleged that his former employee, Doug Hendrickson, now an Octagon agent, violated the Players Union's rules against soliciting players when he took at least six of Sims' clients with him to Octagon.

THINK CRITICALLY

1. **What is the ethical issue involving Octagon?**
2. **What do you think has led to the actions of Octagon in this case?**

LEADERSHIP CHARACTERISTICS

Leaders have the responsibility of creating an atmosphere that encourages employees to do their best work to make the business successful. Frequently, sports franchises and successful athletes have conflicting goals and needs. Successful agents have the ability to create a productive atmosphere. The best agents have the talent to create a win–win situation for both parties.

Leaders influence people to take steps for the success of the organization and the individuals who make up the organization. Agents influence the athletes they represent, sports franchises, and corporations that want endorsements in order to work out the best agreements.

Position power comes from the position the agent holds in the organization. Agents who have earned respect will be more likely to gain the attention of athletes, sports franchises, and corporations. A track record of successful negotiations for top athletes will increase the position power of an agent.

Reward power is based upon the ability to control rewards and punishments. Top agents who have the ability to negotiate the best agreements for their clients and sports franchises gain respect. Agents will withdraw from agreements when they think their client can do better with another organization.

CHARACTERISTICS OF SUCCESSFUL AGENTS

Agents who are leaders in the field exhibit some common characteristics. Leaders must be able to carefully review all facts and apply this knowledge. Agents must consider previous experiences and new information and use good judgment to make the best decisions. Agents must be *objective* or able to look at all sides of a problem and not make biased judgments or statements. Leaders gather information and do not rush into actions before considering possible results.

© DIGITAL VISION

Agents who are leaders in the field show initiative. They have ambition and persistence in reaching goals. Success depends on being a self-starter. Good agents have drive and are highly motivated to win the trust of the best professional athletes. Successful agents are dependable and consistent in their actions. Others rely on the commitments they make. Some of the best agents view the relationship between the agent and athlete as a business that ends in friendship.

Agents understand the importance of negotiation and cooperation. This quality requires good communication and listening skills while keeping in mind the client's objectives. Successful leaders must have the courage to pursue unlikely agreements and the confidence to meet high personal expectations. While agents can become highly emotional when negotiating deals, they must recognize that the feelings and ideas of others are important. Agents must try to understand how others function in the negotiation process.

Leaders are honest and have high standards of personal integrity. Agents unfortunately have gained a bad reputation because of a small number of individuals in the profession who have demonstrated less-than-honest behavior. **Ethics** involves doing the right thing even when it is more tempting or profitable to do otherwise. The potential for large sums of money sometimes causes individuals to overlook ethics while chasing financial gain. Sports agents know college talent who will be highly sought after by professional franchises. Sports agents also know that the National College Athletic Association (NCAA) has specific rules prohibiting them from communicating with college athletes or offering them financial incentives. Although the rules are clear, some agents are willing to overlook ethics in order to reap the greatest financial gain even if it jeopardizes the individual athletes or the universities they attend.

Many athletes choose attorneys to represent them as agents due to their perceived competence, education, and training. However, suspicion about agents still exists among professional players. One former professional basketball player expressed a popular view regarding lawyers who represent athletes when he said, “Lawyers do the same things agents do: they lie, connive, cheat, and hurt athlete–clients.”

INTERMISSION

What are the characteristics that define successful sports agents?

____

____

FEES AND COMPETITION

Successful, experienced sports agents receive lucrative fees. The level of competition to provide service and to obtain the first client is extraordinary. Sports agents are faced with a large number of competitors for a limited number of clients. As the number of sports agents has increased, so have the harsh methods of competition.

WHAT DO AGENTS CHARGE?

The standard fee for agents representing NBA players is two to four percent of the negotiated contracts. Some agents choose instead to charge $400 or more per hour for their legal services. Sports agent Lon Babby charged professional athlete Grant Hill $100,000 to negotiate Hill's first contract—a six-year, $45-million deal with the Detroit Pistons. Hill would have been charged $1.8 million if he had paid the standard four-percent agent fee.

THE COMPETITION HEATS UP

Competition among sports agents is fierce and can lead to unethical behavior. A prospective agent is not difficult to find. The first question that most athletes ask agents is, “Who else do you represent?” The answer to that question signals the success of the agent. Success for sports agents is also measured by the amounts attached to contracts. Breaking into the sports agent business is a difficult process. Until you negotiate a contract for your first client, you are frozen out while other agents with clients continue to score.

Sports agents realize that sending letters to athletes does not work. Student athletes receive numerous pieces of mail (featuring models, yachts, and sunny beaches in Miami) with an invitation to the athlete to

Charles C. “Cash and Carry” Pyle was considered by most to be the first sports agent. He negotiated a $3,000-per-game contract for Red Grange to play professional football for the Chicago Bears in 1933.

Today, salaries ranging in the tens of millions of dollars are common.

come for a visit. When Mike Rozier won the Heisman Trophy, he received 1,200 letters from prospective agents whom he did not know. Face-to-face meetings between agents and prospective players are much more successful than flooding the mail with numerous letters.

© GETTY IMAGES/PHOTODISC

The NCAA does not allow agents to give money to college student athletes. Unethical agents have worked around this rule by lending money to athletes and requiring the athlete to repay the loan when they are drafted by a professional team. The athletes are tied to the agent who gave them a loan. Loans to college athletes present a barrier to honest agents.

Most athletes are interested in what the agent can do for them immediately. Some of the more well-known incidents include an agent taking Florida State football players on a $6,000 shopping spree at Foot Locker in 1994 and an agent paying $3,900 to University of Southern California football player Shawn Walters. Other examples include the payment of a $2,500 promissory note to University of Alabama basketball star Derrick McKey and the offer of $65,000 to former Louisiana State linebacker Michael Brooks.

© GETTY IMAGES/PHOTODISC

TAKING IT TO THE STREETS

One popular recruitment technique used by sports agents is to hire *street agents* or *runners* to secure clients. The street agent pays a fee to the athlete's coach or someone with influence over the athlete. The runner funnels money and gifts from the agent to the athlete to establish an indirect relationship between the athlete and the agent. Money may be funneled to high school coaches, friends, roommates, family members, or anyone who can win over players with flattery, cash, and other gifts. Later, the agent makes it clear to the player that he or she should show gratitude for the gifts from the agent, or the athlete may even face threats. Incentives of cash and shoes close the deal for many younger, inexperienced players.

The NCAA does not prohibit an agent from having contact with an athlete. Some universities prohibit agents from visiting their campuses while athletes are still participating on the collegiate level. State legislatures have passed regulations for agents wishing to contact athletes whose collegiate eligibility has not yet expired. The agents first must register, pay a fee, and contact the administration of the student athlete's college.

Myron Piggie coached a youth basketball team in Kansas City, Missouri. He was a classic street agent who held control over young collegiate stars and professionals. Piggie influenced which schools athletes attended and which agents they chose. However, Piggie's criminal activity finally caught up with him. He was charged with defrauding the NCAA and four universities for risking the status of amateurs by providing them with money and other gifts. Piggie was jailed for fraudulent activities and sentenced to 37 months for conspiracy to commit mail and wire fraud.

GOOD VERSUS EVIL

Some agents have given the profession a bad reputation with mismanagement of finances and excessive fees. Conflicts of interest when negotiating with more than one athlete and undisclosed lists of players that the agent represents cause further problems. The negative reputation of sports agents usually comes from the unethical individuals who mismanage athletes' finances. David Ware is an agent who stated at an NFL Players' Agents meeting that he resented accusations that agents ". . .are a little higher than snakes and a little lower than scorpions." He preferred that agents be described as having the ". . .obligation to be a zealous [enthusiastic] advocate of the client."

© GETTY IMAGES/PHOTODISC

Sometimes the agent who puts forth the most effort for the athlete is paid the lowest fee. Rookie free agents (undrafted players who are free to sign with any team) often ask an agent to contact teams interested in giving the athlete a tryout. Frequently the agent contacts more than two dozen teams. Even when an athlete impresses a team enough to earn a contract, the agent is not guaranteed a fee because of the possibility of the player being cut from the roster.

Baseball agents are often more patient than other sports agents because they serve time in the minor leagues, making little or no fees while waiting for their client to be called up to the major league team. During the time that athletes are in the minor leagues, their agents provide them with sports equipment and financial support in expectation that the athlete will eventually make it big.

The bottom line in the highly competitive world of sports agents is that only a few agents gain major benefits.

What are some of the unethical behaviors that have given sports agents a bad reputation?

____

____

____

OWNERS AND GENERAL MANAGERS

Owners of professional teams pull together large sums of money to attract and keep a sports franchise in a city. These individuals are highly visible in the community and have a lot of political influence. Owners do everything possible to win a championship. They demonstrate their commitment to winning by acquiring the game's finest talent. This goal comes with a big price tag. Owners obviously must have plenty of money and a love of the sport.

Some owners like Jerry Jones cannot get enough of the limelight and have their own radio talk shows. Jones also is very visible on the playing field and appears to be highly involved with the coaching aspect of the Dallas Cowboys. Owners like Leslie Alexander of the Houston Rockets make a team commitment to the community. Building a better quality of life for Houston is the driving force of Alexander and the Rockets franchise. Five years of intense community involvement have produced more than $15 million in donations to local charities. Fundraising and city youth programs are some of the special projects that professional teams embrace.

General managers work hard to attract the best professional players to a team. These individuals know how to put together a coaching staff and players that have a chemistry for championship teams. General managers are required to manage large budgets. They must demonstrate negotiation skills with players, coaches, cities, and the general public. General managers must display a respect for fans who fill the seats and generate a large portion of the revenue for the team.

INTERMISSION

What are some ways that a professional sports team and its owner can demonstrate commitment to their local community?

____

____

UNDERSTANDING MANAGEMENT CONCEPTS

Circle the best answer for each of the following questions.

1. ___?___ comes from the respect the agent has earned.

a. Reward power
b. Position power
c. Negotiation
d. Ethics

2. Agents must

a. have good negotiating skills
b. be honest
c. keep up to date on all the latest issues surrounding the sports they represent
d. all of the above

THINK CRITICALLY

Answer the following questions as completely as possible. If necessary, use a separate sheet of paper.

3. Technology Use the Internet to find three articles about sports agents. What are the main points covered in each article?

____

____

____

____

4. Management Math You are an agent for five professional athletes who have the following annual salaries: \$2 million, \$7 million, \$550,000, \$1.5 million, and \$4 million. Your commission is four percent. How much annual commission will you make from representing these five athletes?

____

____

____

5. Research Use the Internet to research the National College Athletic Association (NCAA). List five of its specific rules concerning agents.

____

____

____

CHAPTER 3 REVIEW

REVIEW MANAGEMENT CONCEPTS

Write the letter of the term that matches each definition. Some terms will not be used.

____ **1.** Plans that take more than one year to complete	**a.** agents
____ **2.** The collective results of an organization's employees	**b.** business plan
____ **3.** Illustrations that show the structure of an organization, the major job classifications, and the chain of command for personnel	**c.** ethics
____ **4.** The most important purposes or directions for the organization based upon all information collected	**d.** job descriptions
____ **5.** Power that comes from the position held in the organization	**e.** leadership
____ **6.** Doing the right thing even when it is more tempting or profitable to do otherwise	**f.** long-term goals
____ **7.** Outlines the mission, objectives, goals, strategies, and measures of an organization	**g.** mission
____ **8.** Power that is based upon the ability to control rewards and punishments	**h.** operational planning
____ **9.** Legal representatives who negotiate new contracts and endorsement agreements for athletes	**i.** organizational charts
____ **10.** Plans accomplished in less than a year	**j.** position power
____ **11.** Looks at the long-term big picture for entire business	**k.** reward power
	l. short-term goals
	m. strategic planning
	n. synergy

Circle the best answer.

12. Which of the following is not looked at for external analysis?
- **a.** company personnel
- **b.** economy
- **c.** customers
- **d.** competitors

13. New professional stadiums are being built
- **a.** against the will of voters
- **b.** with special tax dollars
- **c.** due to the demands by professional teams and fans
- **d.** both b and c

14. ___?___ are specific initiatives to deliver company goals and objectives.
- **a.** Strategies
- **b.** Missions
- **c.** Measures
- **d.** Standards

THINK CRITICALLY

15. Describe the 4 S's used by a professional sports team to measure the success of its business plan. Explain these 4 S's for an organization in your school, such as DECA.

16. Most professional business people have a code of ethics to use as a guideline for ethical issues. Write ten rules for sports agents to follow as an "Agents' Code of Ethics."

17. What is the purpose of an organizational chart? Locate an organizational chart on the Internet or request a chart from a businessperson. Attach the chart to this assignment. How many levels are represented in this chart? What position is at the top of the chart?

18. Search newspapers, magazines, or the Internet to find articles about the salaries of three professional basketball players. How much will the agent for each player earn based on a four-percent commission?

19. Design a collage or poster with pictures of stadiums and other sporting venues. Include the means of funding these venues on your poster. You may find pictures of stadiums on the Internet.

MAKE CONNECTIONS

20. Management Math You are in charge of selling season tickets for a new stadium. Your goal is to sell 20,000 season tickets at $5,000 each before the stadium is built. You have been given a one-percent commission incentive. How much money will you make if you sell all 20,000 season tickets?

21. Technology Use the Internet to find the mission statement for three professional sports teams. Compare the three mission statements and point out the similarities and differences.

22. Communication You are the athletic director for a major university that has a very successful football program. You have noticed that professional agents are trying to contact the athletes. Write a letter to the agents reminding them of the NCAA rules and the rules for your university concerning agents.

23. Marketing Management You are in charge of corporate sponsorships for a professional team. How will you keep your top sponsors happy? List six events that you will host during the year to show your appreciation and maintain your corporate sponsors.

24. Marketing Management You are the ticket manager for a professional team that does not have sell-out crowds. Devise a special promotional strategy to sell out one game. Write a one-page paper that describes your marketing strategy. Will this strategy be a one-time offer or will it be used more frequently? Why?

25. History Visit the web site for the Women's Professional Football League. Write a one-page paper detailing the history of women's professional football.

26. Marketing Management You are the marketing manager for a professional football team. Your team already generates revenue from the sale of t-shirts, sweatshirts, and jerseys that carry the team logo. Make a list of other team merchandise that could be designed and sold to generate additional income.

27. Communication As a new professional sports agent, you are competing with many seasoned agents for new athlete–clients. You know that writing letters to prospective clients does not work well and that landing face-to-face meetings is crucial to your success. Work with a partner and develop a list of creative ways that you will contact prospective athlete–clients to schedule face-to-face meetings.

FROM "KNOW 'EM" TO "SEE 'EM"

In November 2001, the fate of the Minnesota Twins baseball team looked shaky at best. Baseball owners voted 28-2 to eliminate two Major League teams before the start of the 2002 season. Though the two teams were not identified, all evidence pointed to the Minnesota Twins and the Montreal Expos. These teams held a long record of failing to generate enough revenue to operate a profitable major-league franchise. The Twins had also failed to generate government support for a new ballpark.

Injunction Issued

The Minnesota Twins' saving grace came in the form of an injunction issued by the Hennepin County District Court. The court's ruling forced the team to honor its 2002 lease of the Metrodome stadium. The attempt to eliminate the team actually played to the Twins' advantage. In May 2002, government funding was approved for a new stadium.

In an effort to boost attendance, the Minnesota Twins ran two years of advertisements in 2001 and 2002 asking fans to "Get To Know 'Em." After nearly making it to the World Series in 2002, the Minnesota Twins now have a new message they are pitching to fans.

New Message

The team's new message is "Gotta See 'Em." This ad campaign was launched in February 2003 with the goal of driving more people to the stands earlier in the season. The advertisement theme intends to capitalize on the club's success in 2002 that resulted in an American League Central Division championship.

New Attendance Goals

Nancy O'Brien, Director of Advertising for the Minnesota Twins, hopes to drive people from their seats at home into the seats at the ballpark. The late-season surge in 2002 allowed the Twins to meet a rather modest 2002 attendance goal of 1.8 million to 2 million.

The stands had less than 50 percent capacity during the regular 2002 season while nearly 250,000 people attended playoff games in the league divisional and championship series. With the new campaign, the Twins hope to attract 2.2 million people for the 2003 season, an overall attendance increase of 16 percent.

If the Twins reach that goal, they'll have their highest attendance since 1992, when they hit 2.5 million for a 90-victory season. It would be their first 2-million season since 1993.

At the end of January 2003, 90 percent of 2002's season-ticket holders had renewed. This pace was the best renewal rate at this point of the year in about a decade. After selling 6,000 season tickets in 2002, the team was at 7,500 by February 2003, with the goal of 9,500 in sight.

Introduces New Players

The new advertisement campaign is an extension of the 2001 "Get To Know 'Em" campaign created by Hunt Adkins Advertising, the marketing communications firm for the Minnesota Twins. This campaign introduced fans to a number of new players, such as shortstop Cristian Guzman and left fielder Jacque Jones, by using newspapers, radio, and television. The campaign highlighted the players' hobbies and skills.

The cost to create and deliver the new round of promotions is in the low six-figure range. The "Get To Know 'Em" campaign cost $1.75 million.

The success of the 2001 campaign excites officials about the "Gotta See 'Em" campaign. Minnesota Twins officials are capitalizing on what the players are known for while encouraging people to come out to the games and enjoy the live experience.

The new campaign featured pitcher Eddie Guardado and catcher A. J. Pierzynski. Future ads plan to feature additional players as well as team manager Ron Gardenhire.

Think Critically

1. **What is the main purpose of the Minnesota Twins' new promotional campaign?**
2. **What two things have served as incentives for increased fan interest since 2002?**
3. **Why is it important for professional athletes to be visible in the community?**
4. **Go to the Minnesota Twins web site and list five sources of information about the team and ticket sales.**

SPORTS AND ENTERTAINMENT MARKETING MANAGEMENT TEAM DECISION MAKING

You have been hired as the community relations person for a professional sports team. The team has been criticized for not being visible enough in the community and not being a positive role model for youth.

Your position requires you to develop four community service projects and a career day for youth in which the team and management will be visibly involved in the community.

Performance Indicators Evaluated

- Explain the rationale for community service.
- Describe community service projects to be performed.
- Define the activities for a career day.
- Explain the strategy for completing the community service projects.

Go to the DECA web site for more detailed information.

1. What community service projects will you select for the team? Why?
2. Outline the agenda for a three-hour career day for 400 high school students from your city and surrounding communities. The career day event will end with students attending a professional game and observing key marketing employees from the sports franchise.
3. Describe the types of media you will use to announce the team's commitment to the community.

www.deca.org/publications/HS_Guide/guidetoc.html

CHAPTER 4

Sports and Entertainment Management

4.1 MANAGING LOCAL EVENTS
4.2 MANAGING COLLEGE EVENTS
4.3 MANAGING PROFESSIONAL SPORTS
4.4 MANAGING OTHER EVENTS

© ROYALTY FREE/CORBIS

EVERYTHING'S COMING UP ROSES!

For more than 100 years, millions of people around the world have tuned in on January 1 to watch the Tournament of Roses Parade. Thousands more camp out along the Pasadena parade route to view the magnificent floats made of millions of flowers.

The Tournament of Roses Parade and the Rose Bowl game are huge events that require intense planning. More than 100,000 fans attend the Rose Bowl game each year. Hotels, restaurants, and other hospitality venues must prepare for the influx of visitors. Parade organizers must handle management issues ranging from crowd control and security to smooth operation of the parade. Pasadena presents its best hospitality each year to keep visitors coming back.

The Tournament of Roses Parade has a proud history of special events each year. These events are often influenced by the mood of the country at the time. The terrorist attacks of September 11, 2001 influenced the special patriotic opening of the Rose Parade in 2002. The parade included flyovers by the Marine Corps and the U.S. Air Force.

Shirley Temple Black holds the honor of being the only Grand Marshal to host the parade as a child and as an adult. She led the 50th Tournament of Roses Parade in 1939 and the centennial celebration of the Tournament of Roses Parade in 1989.

In 1994, the 105th Tournament of Roses Parade aired for the first time in its entirety in the People's Republic of China. Approximately 2.4 million Chinese-Americans viewed the parade. The Rose Parade continues to draw spectators of all ages and nationalities.

THINK CRITICALLY

1. How has the Tournament of Roses Parade benefited the city of Pasadena?
2. How has the parade adjusted to international interest in the event?

LESSON 4.1

MANAGING LOCAL EVENTS

Describe three types of plans necessary for organizing entertainment events.

Explain the importance of budgets as related to entertainment management.

Describe the management necessary for major events.

OPENING ACT

The Boston Marathon is the world's oldest annual marathon. This American classic is distinguished as a premiere running event due to its tradition and qualifying requirements for runners. The Boston Marathon uses the ChampionChip computer timing system. Digital clocks display elapsed time at every mile and five-kilometer marker. The Boston Marathon course is lined with 24 fluid-replacement stations and 26 first-aid stations. All marathon entrants receive admission to the pre- and post-race parties. Entrants also receive a race program and results booklet, a T-shirt, and transportation to the start of the course. Finishers receive a commemorative medallion.

Work with a partner to discuss possible sponsors for the Boston Marathon. How could the sponsors receive visibility during the race?

THE IMPORTANCE OF PLANNING

Communities of all sizes organize entertainment events each year. A successful event depends upon a business plan. A *business plan* is a written description of the event, its goals and objectives, and how they will be achieved. Legal factors such as licenses, leases, and contracts are included in the business plan. Job descriptions describing employee skills needed to successfully complete tasks are also included.

An entertainment event requires cash for start-up and continuous cash flow to carry out the event. The **financial plan** must include projected income, expenses, and profit for the entertainment event. An entertainment event also requires a marketing plan to determine the target market, demand for the event, prices to charge, and competition. The **marketing plan** is a detailed written description of all marketing activities that must be accomplished in order to make an event successful. The plan identifies ways in which the event's success will be evaluated. This evaluation determines if the marketing activities were successful and the goals were accomplished.

Goals and objectives play an important role in the business plan. Goals involve the expected short-term and long-term results. Results are usually expressed in terms of sales volume or profits. Success of an event depends heavily on location, size of the event, risks, and demand for the type of entertainment. Event planners realize that there are many competitors in the sports and entertainment market.

STRATEGIC PLANNING

Strategic planning is the long-term preparation for an entertainment event. Managers should look at the organization's strengths and weaknesses when planning an event. Strengths for the organization might include the experience of the planners, past successes with similar events, and new features to attract future crowds. Weaknesses may include the size of the budget and target market as well as the lack of experience managing events.

Successful attendance rates for entertainment events vary according to the size of the community and the expectations of the planners. Event planners must look at opportunities and threats, and then take the risk of planning new events with expectations of success. Communities of all sizes have opportunities to host profitable entertainment events. Threats to an event's success include competitors, poor weather, and weak economic conditions. It is crucial that event planners are aware of the competition. Consumers have numerous entertainment options but limited financial resources.

Planners depend on the mission of the event for directions to successfully accomplish entertainment goals. Each person responsible for an entertainment event must know his or her responsibilities. Goals must be specific and provide a definite roadmap for success.

TIME OUT

The formula for a nightclub disaster includes too many people, too few exits, and too little time to escape. In 2003, two nightclub calamities in the same week left 118 people dead. Neither of these nightclubs had an emergency plan in place for crowd management and evacuation.

INTERMISSION

What are the differences among a business plan, a financial plan, and a marketing plan?

____

____

PRODUCING THE EVENT

The production of an entertainment event requires thorough and careful planning. A budget must be set, and work must be divided efficiently among the team members.

SETTING THE BUDGET

Businesses make plans based upon a budget. The **budget** is a specific financial plan that assists managers in determining the best way to use available financial resources to reach goals. The budget estimates sales, expenses, the number of people who can be hired, and the amount of work each individual must accomplish in order to carry out the entertainment event successfully. Whether an event is large or small, the event manager must check the estimates against actual conditions. The comparison determines whether the business plan is on, under, or over budget. Factors to consider when developing the event budget include

- Previous attendance
- Changes in competition
- Population shifts
- Capacity
- Season of the year
- Economic trends
- Factors such as weather
- Amount of promotion
- Spending habits of attendees

To develop a budget successfully, the event manager must conduct research on these factors. Notes should be taken when planning entertainment events to conduct business more efficiently in the future. Past budgets are looked at to determine how much will be spent on upcoming events.

DIVIDING THE WORK

The most successful organizations determine the strengths of their team members and rely on those individual strengths. Entertainment event planners must determine the total work to be done and divide it into units, such as divisions. The first consideration for grouping employees is based upon broad categories such as marketing promotions, logistics, and financial management. Major divisions may need to be divided further into departments or work units of reasonable size. Each department should be composed of related tasks. Work should flow smoothly within and among departments. All tasks should have team members assigned to complete them.

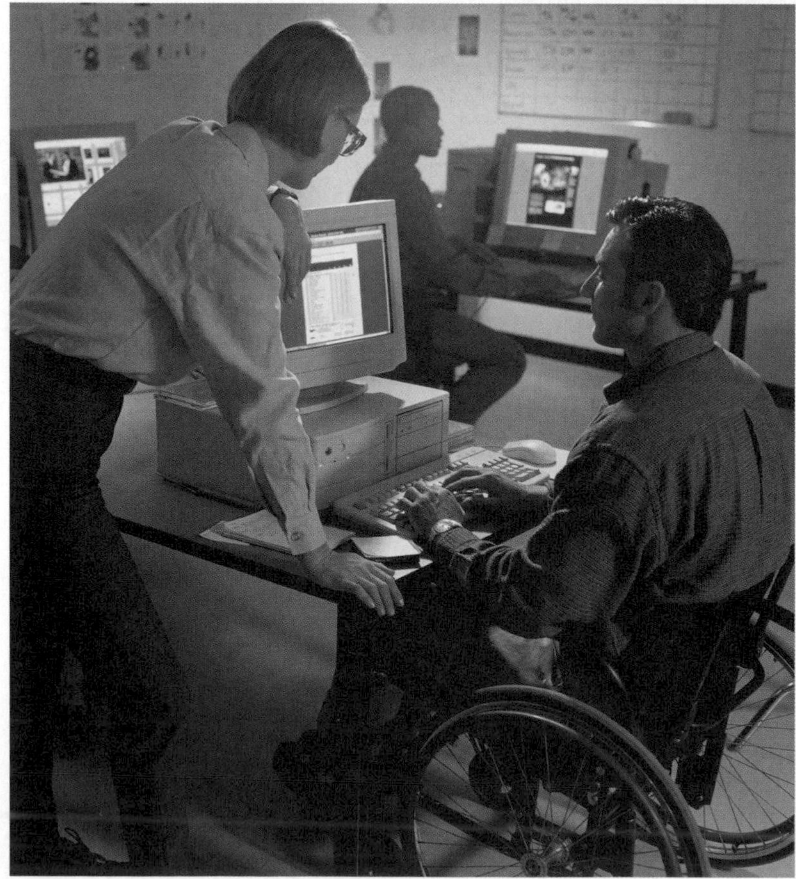
© GETTY IMAGES/PHOTODISC

Determining how to divide work into efficient units is based on the type of work to be done and the amount of work to be done. Successful organizations are looking for workers who function effectively as a team. The team takes responsibility for completion of the entire task. The agent for a band must make sure that all concert contracts are legally acceptable. Agents ensure that clients' special requests—such as requests for special foods on the day of the performance—are met. The stage crew ensures that all equipment is properly set up for the best-sounding concert. Ushers and ticket takers must be in place on time to properly run the concert. Security is responsible for maintaining the safety of the fans. Each team member must fulfill his or her role effectively for the event to be successful.

Location and facilities play an important role in the success of an entertainment event. A small community may have an annual summer event that requires blocking off a main street to set up a carnival, food stands, and other entertainment venues. Key team players must make sure that all tasks are carried out in order to have the celebration up and running on time. The Fleming County Covered Bridge Festival is held in late August at the site of the Goddard Bridge, a well-known covered bridge in Kentucky. Organizers of this rural festival must consider traffic control and the safety of thousands of people who will attend. Booths must be set up for the hundreds of food and crafts vendors who participate in the event.

INTERMISSION

Why should organizations pay special attention to the strengths of their team members?

____

____

MAJOR EVENTS

World-known annual events require huge budgets and specific policies and procedures. Committed team members who work together make the events successful.

NEW YEAR'S EVE IN TIMES SQUARE

Times Square is the center of worldwide attention on New Year's Eve. In 1904, the owners of One Times Square began a rooftop celebration to usher in the New Year. The tradition of lowering the ball in Times Square has become a universal symbol of welcoming the New Year. Times Square 2003 was a spectacular event full of sights, sounds, and special effects. Revelers began lining up as early as 5:00 A.M. to grab a prime spot at the festivities. Hundreds of thousands of people rang out the old year by personally observing the dropping of the New Year's Eve Ball designed by Waterford Crystal.

MACY'S THANKSGIVING DAY PARADE

Since 1924, Macy's® department store has provided a tradition that ushers in the Christmas season—its annual Thanksgiving Day Parade. Large balloons first appeared in the parade in 1927. The parade grew throughout the 1930s. Even during the Great Depression, more than a million people lined the parade route. New balloons such as Disney characters were among the favorites. Radio audiences could hear the ceremonies and Santa's arrival at 34th Street. The parade was not held from 1940 to 1944 during World War II when rubber and helium could not be wasted. It resumed in 1945 and was televised in New York City.

Macy's Thanksgiving Day Parade assumed its hold on the nation in the 1950s with nationwide television exposure. The most bittersweet parade took place in 1963, less than a week after President Kennedy's assassination. The country was in mourning, but the parade went on to not disappoint millions of children.

Some of the most popular balloons during the '60s, '70s, and '80s included Snoopy, Kermit the Frog, and Superman. The winds were so bad during the 1971 parade that balloons had to be cancelled.

The Macy's Thanksgiving Day Parade is a true New York experience that is special for adults and children. Individuals who plan to attend the Macy's Thanksgiving Day Parade should prepare for big crowds. Spectators can attend pre-Thanksgiving Day Parade preparations on Wednesday evening to get a sneak peak at the giant helium balloons.

the Global Manager

The holiday of Cinco de Mayo on May 5 honors the victory of the Mexicans over the French army at The Battle of Puebla in 1862. Cinco de Mayo is primarily a regional holiday celebrated throughout the state of Puebla. Cinco de Mayo celebrations are increasingly popular along the U.S.–Mexico border and in parts of the United States that have a high Mexican-American population. Festivities feature foods, beverages, music, and customs unique to Mexico. Entertainment businesses in the United States and Mexico successfully promote the holiday by offering Mexican foods, beverages, and festive items. Cinco de Mayo is being adopted into the holiday calendar of more people every year.

THINK CRITICALLY

1. Why has Cinco de Mayo become more popular in the United States?
2. What types of businesses might benefit from this holiday?

INTERMISSION

Why is management necessary for major events like the Macy's Thanksgiving Day Parade?

____

____

UNDERSTAND MANAGEMENT CONCEPTS

Circle the best answer for each of the following questions.

1. A specific financial plan that assists managers in determining the best way to use available financial resources is a
   a. budget
   b. business plan
   c. strategic plan
   d. marketing plan
2. A written description of an event, its goals and objectives, and how they will be achieved is a
   a. financial plan
   b. marketing plan
   c. business plan
   d. none of the above

THINK CRITICALLY

Answer the following questions as completely as possible. If necessary, use a separate sheet of paper.

3. **Technology** Visit the web site for one of the major events discussed in this lesson. Print the first page for the event. Then list ten types of management skills necessary to successfully produce the event.

   ____

   ____

   ____

   ____

4. **Financial Management** You are in charge of the financial planning for an after-prom party at your school. Develop a detailed budget for this event using spreadsheet software.

   ____

   ____

   ____

5. Explain the importance of a marketing plan. What elements might be included in the marketing plan?

   ____

   ____

   ____

   ____

MANAGING COLLEGE EVENTS

Define the four types of economic utility as they relate to collegiate entertainment events.

Describe the factors of production in a market economy.

Explain how universities increase revenues through entertainment events.

OPENING ACT

In 1909, a group of Texas A&M cadets staged a pep rally, complete with a bonfire, to boost the spirits of their athletic teams. Other bonfires followed and became the most visible symbol of the school's "Aggie spirit." The bonfire became the world's largest annual bonfire. The project brought together Aggies of all ages and backgrounds in a unified effort. Construction became as important as the burning. On November 18, 1999, an early morning collapse during the construction of the bonfire stack took the lives of 11 students and one alumnus and injured an additional 27 people. The accident forever changed the Texas A&M community. That tragic event ended the 90-year tradition as Texas A&M realized the huge liability associated with the bonfire. Current students and alumni want to revive the tradition. Some groups are organizing their own bonfires off campus.

Work with a partner to determine events for Texas A&M students and alumni to substitute for the annual bonfire.

ECONOMIC ENVIRONMENT

The science of **economics** relates to producing and using goods and services that people want. College students are a ripe target market for entertainment events such as homecoming, concerts, and other campus activities. Colleges schedule entertainment events to meet the demands of students and alumni. The price charged for these events is based on consumer supply and demand. **Supply** is the amount that will be offered for sale at a particular time and at a certain price. **Demand** is the amount that will be bought at a given time at a given price. When a football program has a stadium that holds 80,000 people and it sells out for each home game, consumer demand raises the price for tickets.

© GETTY IMAGES/PHOTODISC

Most colleges and universities have tight budgets due to decreased state funding. Colleges schedule entertainment events for stadiums and basketball arenas to earn additional revenue. Concerts held at major universities bring more people to campus. Additional events scheduled at major universities serve as a public relations tool. Public relations create a greater awareness of what the university has to offer.

UTILITY

Utility is the ability of a service or good to satisfy a want. Most consumers are not very excited about a plain white T-shirt. When a T-shirt has the name of a popular university printed on it, the shirt has added value. Fans are willing to pay even higher prices for T-shirts displaying the university logo or other related images. Universities earn up to 14 percent in royalties from merchandise bearing their logos or names.

Form utility involves changing the form or shape of a product to make it useful for prospective customers. While a plain white T-shirt may not be exciting to many consumers, that same shirt screen-printed with the name or logo of a popular university gains value due to form utility.

Possession utility is created when ownership of a good or service is transferred from one person to another. It also can occur through renting and borrowing. The excitement generated by a successful football or basketball team increases the prices for merchandise bearing the college's logo or name. The enthusiasm for a winning team results in fans' increased willingness to purchase higher-priced merchandise. Possession utility becomes more valuable, causing prices to go up.

Time utility involves having the entertainment event available when the largest target market can be involved.

Place utility involves offering an entertainment event at a location where the target market demand is greatest. Country music is popular in the central portion of the United States. A country music concert at a major university in Texas, Oklahoma, Kansas, or Nebraska has place utility. These locations will attract country music fans from surrounding states.

CBS hosts a well-known sports information web site, CBS SportsLine .com. It has agreed to produce and host the official NCAA sports championship site. The new site will replace the old championship sites. Many advertisers for the 2002 NCAA Basketball Tournament purchased advertisements that appeared on both CBS Television and CBS SportsLine.com. Coca-Cola™, General Motors™, and Monster.com are a few of the companies that took advantage of the multiple advertising.

THINK CRITICALLY

1. **Why would a major television network want to produce and host a web site?**
2. **What advantages exist for the sponsors of CBS SportsLine.com?**

INTERMISSION

What are the four types of economic utility? How are they related to an entertainment event?

____

____

FACTORS OF PRODUCTION

Four basic resources are used to create useful goods and services. These **factors of production** include natural resources, labor, capital goods, and entrepreneurship.

Natural resources are anything provided by nature that influences the productive ability of a venue. Examples of natural resources include mild climate and water for a collegiate rowing event.

Labor is the physical or mental human effort that goes into the production of goods and services. Technology increases the importance of mental effort when organizing entertainment events.

Capital goods are buildings, tools, machines, and other equipment used to produce goods or services to satisfy needs of consumers. Entertainment venues at universities are classified as capital goods.

Entrepreneurship involves taking the risk of planning, managing, and producing an entertainment event. Entrepreneurship brings together natural resources, labor, and capital goods. Event planners must take the risk of pulling together productive resources for a successful entertainment event.

Cities in Florida and Texas embrace (or brace for) the large crowds of students during spring break each year. Young people crowd the beaches to play volleyball, work on tans, and pick up t-shirts and other freebies from promotional stands. Some of the most visible companies at spring break promote controversial products.

THINK CRITICALLY

1. **What companies should be visible at spring break hot spots? Why?**
2. **Why is spring break a controversial event each year?**

ECONOMIC SYSTEMS

Because productive resources are scarce, difficult decisions must be made about how to use these limited resources. An **economic system** is an organized way to decide how to use productive resources.

Market economy is an economic system in which consumer buying decisions determine what, how, and for whom goods and services will be produced. Entertainment consumers tend to be unpredictable, making it challenging for managers to organize successful collegiate events.

Scarcity involves limited financial resources for unlimited wants. College students in a market economy have limited resources to spend on entertainment events. Entertainment planners are aware of scarcity and try to plan events that students will choose over competitors.

Capitalism allows individuals to freely produce and distribute legal entertainment events. Capitalism, or the *free enterprise system*, is practiced in the United States. Three basic characteristics of capitalism include the right to own private property, the right to make a profit, and the right to set prices and to compete. Collegiate event planners must pay attention to the competition, which is a vital component of the free enterprise system.

Competition is the rivalry among sellers for consumers' dollars. Competition benefits both consumers and producers. Managers of collegiate events must improve the quality of products and services offered to maintain a fair market share. Competition helps to ensure that consumers receive quality products and services at fair prices.

Socialism is a political system in which the government controls the use of the country's factors of production. The government partially decides how scarce resources are used to satisfy the many wants of people. Socialism does allow individuals to own property, with varying amounts of control by government. A socialist government influences the entertainment events that take place at that country's universities. Socialism of different forms exists in many countries, especially in Western European countries such as Sweden and Italy.

Communism is an extreme form of socialism in which most national factors of production are owned by the government. Managers do not determine which entertainment events are available to consumers. A communist country's government makes such decisions. Cuba and North Korea are examples of communist countries.

TIME OUT

In a market economy, individual citizens, rather than the government, own most of the factors of production.

INTERMISSION

How is entertainment management different for capitalism than for communism?

____

____

COLLEGIATE EVENTS

The NCAA Tournament is an annual event that takes place during March. The college basketball tournament starts out with 65 teams competing to get to the Final Four. Major universities compete to host the first games of the NCAA Tournament at 16 sites. Hosting games for the NCAA Tournament earns schools additional revenue.

Large sports stadiums and arenas have the potential to host entertainment events such as concerts and rodeos. These non-sporting events bring in additional revenue to universities.

Homecoming is an entertaining event for college students and alumni. Homecoming events include the football game, alumni parties, and special festivities on campus. Homecoming also provides a promotional strategy to gather contributions from alumni.

INTERMISSION

Why do universities want to host events like the NCAA tournament?

____

____

UNDERSTAND MANAGEMENT CONCEPTS

Circle the best answer for each of the following questions.

1. Which of the following is not a form of utility?
a. time utility
b. place utility
c. space utility
d. possession utility

2. The factors of production include
a. capital goods
b. labor
c. natural resources
d. all of the above

THINK CRITICALLY

Answer the following questions as completely as possible. If necessary, use a separate sheet of paper.

3. Research Find out the seating capacity for the football stadium or basketball arena of your favorite university. Outline six events other than sports that could take place at the stadium or the arena. Explain the rationale and the potential income for each event.

____

____

4. Technology Use the Internet to search for information about corporate sponsors for a major collegiate event. You have the responsibility to persuade these corporations to continue their sponsorship of the event. List the reasons for continued sponsorship and the types of advertising that the sponsors will receive.

____

____

5. Management Math You are the activities director for a major university. A popular country music group will perform a concert at your football stadium, which seats 76,000 people. Forty percent of the seats will sell for $40. Thirty percent of the seats will sell for $25. The remaining thirty percent of the seats will sell for $15. The concert is expected to sell out in less than six hours. The country music group will be paid $20,000 for its two-hour performance. What is the gross profit from the concert after you pay the group?

____

____

____

MANAGING PROFESSIONAL SPORTS

OPENING ACT

World-class sports stadiums provide opportunities for additional revenue-earning events. Cities attract professional sports teams with new facilities that are paid for by taxes and corporate sponsorships. Many of the new football stadiums have retractable roofs that open to let in the good weather and close to keep out the bad weather. Taxpayers are more likely to pay for new arenas that have multiple uses. Reliant Stadium, home of the Houston Texans, is filled with tons of dirt every March for the Houston Rodeo and Livestock Show. The football stadium becomes a showcase for barrel racing, bull riding, and concerts. Taxpayers like the idea of a sports facility being used for more than five months during the year.

Work with a partner to determine activities that can take place in a new professional baseball facility with a retractable roof during the baseball off-season. Outline the events and the revenue possibilities.

Describe the job positions and responsibilities involved in sports management.

Explain the importance of community involvement for professional sports teams.

SPORTS MANAGEMENT JOBS

Professional sports management involves all the responsibilities necessary to successfully implement and carry out a professional sporting event. Sports management positions carry a variety of job titles, such as

- Marketing and promotions director
- Corporate sales director
- Director of ticketing and finance
- Sporting goods sales manager
- Facilities coordinator
- Athletic business manager
- Fitness manager

Typical sports management jobs require knowledge of business aspects related to sports. Management positions normally require 50- to 60-hour workweeks, including night and weekend hours. Job duties often involve working with corporations in special event promotions and sponsorships. Responsibilities may include accounting, ticketing, or financial operations of a sporting event. Event management, media relations, or the sales of licensed sports products are possible duties. Additional responsibilities include developing risk management plans for current legal issues in sports.

The field of professional sports management is extremely competitive. Most jobs require an internship for hands-on experience. Graduate internships usually do not pay, but academic credit hours are earned toward graduation. The opportunity to network and learn from professionals is one of the greatest benefits of unpaid internships. Sports management careers offer the opportunity to work with people who share a love for the sport. Individuals in sports management usually receive excellent health and wellness benefits.

The popularity of professional sports has increased significantly in major U.S. cities and promises continued growth. Jobs in marketing and promotions, sports information, and community relations continue to expand. Employment opportunities for sports agents and arena managers continue to grow.

INTERMISSION

List five possible sports management jobs.

____

____

COMMUNITY INVOLVEMENT

Professional sports franchises must demonstrate a commitment to the community that supports the team and sports facility. Most sports organizations have a paid position for a community relations coordinator. Involvement with a charity event such as a 5K run increases the organization's visibility in the community. The involvement also demonstrates the goodwill of contributing to a worthwhile cause.

A 5K run is a major event that requires extensive planning. Corporate sponsors must be committed. The route for runners must be planned. Registration packets must be designed and distributed. T-shirts must be designed and manufactured. Entry fees must be collected. On the day of the race, water stations must be set up and information booths must be patrolled. Radio and television stations are frequently contacted for favorable publicity. Complimentary food and beverages are usually provided at the post-race party, along with music and prize giveaways.

Some of the most successful charity runs are scheduled on the same day as another major event, such as the NFL Draft. Run participants can mingle with professional teams' players, cheerleaders, and mascots at the post-race party.

TIME OUT

The New York Jets and Kraft/Nabisco™ are teaming up to develop Jets-themed promotional projects. The first joint venture in April 2003 was called the Taste of New York. This special event featured current and former Jets players and gave attendees a chance to sample food from 20 top New York-area restaurants.

CATERING TO YOUNG FANS

The community relations coordinator for a professional sports franchise frequently starts a Kids' Club to gain the enthusiasm of young fans and their families. Young fans can join the club for a $20 to $30 annual membership. Kids' Club members are invited to attend special events throughout the year where players, cheerleaders, and mascots make appearances.

INTERMISSION

Why is it important for professional sports teams to be visible in the community?

____

____

Lead the Way

AMY TRASK

Amy Trask began attending Raiders football games in Oakland while she was working on a bachelor's degree at the University of California in the late 1970s. After graduation, she attended law school at the University of Southern California in Los Angeles. Coincidentally, the Raiders moved from Oakland to Los Angeles the same year, 1982.

The team played its games in the Los Angeles Memorial Coliseum adjacent to the USC campus. Trask took advantage of the close location and joined the Raiders for an internship in the early 1980s. She went to work for an L.A. law firm after earning her law degree. Trask then accepted a job in the Raiders' legal department in 1987.

Since then Trask has steadily moved up and branched out. Her legal duties have expanded into dealings with media outlets, public officials, business partners, and travel agents. As chief executive, Trask's most visible role is in representing the Raiders at the NFL Owners' Meetings, a traditionally male-dominated gathering. In a recent special report, the *Sports Business Journal* ranked Trask fifth among the most influential women in sports.

Trask is proud of the revolutionary steps taken by the Raiders. Owner Al Davis was the first modern NFL owner to hire an African-American head coach (Art Shell in 1989). Davis was among the only owners ever to hire a Latino head coach (Tom Flores in 1979). In addition to Trask, the Raiders currently employ high-ranking women in legal affairs (Roxanne Kosarzycki) and business affairs (Dawn Roberts).

THINK CRITICALLY

1. What has led to Amy Trask's success?
2. Do you think that a woman can perform as well as a man in a high-ranking professional sports management job? Why or why not?

UNDERSTANDING MANAGEMENT CONCEPTS

Circle the best answer for each of the following questions.

1. Typical sports management jobs
   - **a.** include 20- to 40-hour workweeks
   - **b.** require knowledge of business aspects related to sports
   - **c.** are easy to find
   - **d.** provide no health benefits to employees
2. Professional sports teams get involved in the community to
   - **a.** demonstrate goodwill
   - **b.** gain the enthusiasm of young fans
   - **c.** gain visibility
   - **d.** all of the above

THINK CRITICALLY

Answer the following questions as completely as possible. If necessary, use a separate sheet of paper.

3. Select three major charities for a professional sports franchise to adopt as community service projects during the year. Outline an event to raise money for each of the charities.

   ____

   ____

4. **Technology** Use the Internet to find information about three available sports management jobs. Print each job description. Highlight the job title, city where the job is located, and job requirements.

   ____

   ____

   ____

5. You are the community project director for a professional basketball franchise. The franchise wants to increase the interest of youth in the community. Give examples of three events to accomplish this goal.

   ____

   ____

   ____

   ____

   ____

MANAGING OTHER EVENTS

OPENING ACT

Universal Studios Orlando Resort is a 500-acre theme resort with world-class hotels surrounded by entertainment events throughout the park. Universal Orlando has made a great impact in the world of theme parks due to the latest rides and wise use of technology. The resort offers a wide array of entertainment for individuals of all ages, excellent hotels and convention facilities, and strong corporate partners. Major corporate partners for Universal Orlando include Toyota™, MasterCard™, Gatorade™, Minute Maid™, U.S. Airways™, Sherwin Williams™, and Kodak™.

Work with a partner to schedule events for Universal Orlando during the slow months of January and February. Who is your target market for these events? What types of promotion will you use for the best results?

Explain the various types of organizational structures.

Describe the value of special events and their importance during shoulder periods.

ORGANIZATIONAL STRUCTURE

The organizational structure of a sports and entertainment management organization indicates relationships among departments and personnel. These relationships influence lines of communication and decision making. Two popular types of organizational structure include line organizations and line-and-staff organizations. Matrix organizations and team organizations are additional types of organizational structure.

Line organizations trace all authority and responsibility in a direct line from the top executive down to the lowest employee level. Lines that join the boxes in an organizational chart indicate the *lines of authority*. The president or CEO has direct control over all work units of a line organization. Responsibility, authority, and accountability are passed from one person to another throughout all levels of the organization. Each person is responsible to only one manager, making it an efficient operation. Too many layers of management can lead to poor communication between departments within the organization.

Unity of command means that employees report to only one supervisor at a time. Employees need clear assignments of responsibility and authority for their tasks. Workers must know who is in charge of each activity. **Span of control** is the number of employees that a manager supervises directly. Managers cannot effectively supervise too many people. However, valuable time is wasted when managers are not

© GETTY IMAGES/PHOTODISC

assigned enough people to supervise. The span of control is larger at the lower levels of an organization than at the higher levels. Well-trained and motivated employees do not require as much direct supervision as individuals who rely heavily on managers for direction.

Line-and-staff organizations give managers direct control over the units and employees they supervise. *Staff specialists* are available to assist managers of line-and-staff organizations. Staff specialists give advice and assistance to line personnel. Specialists in the areas of law, information management, strategic planning, and human resources provide valuable advice to the line-and-staff organization.

Matrix organizations are newer, more flexible structures also referred to as *project organizations*. The matrix organization forms temporary work teams to complete specific projects. A project manager directs the temporary work team. The matrix organization changes regularly, making it difficult to develop an organizational chart. The matrix organizational structure works well for advertising and special promotions. This structure brings together people with the necessary skills for each project. The matrix organization uses the specific skills of managers and employees as effectively as possible. Managers must define authority and responsibility when assigning new projects to employees.

Team organizations are the newest type of organizational structure. This structure divides employees into permanent work teams. The teams have responsibility and authority for important business activities. Management control over daily work is limited. Team leaders replace the traditional position of supervisor and act as facilitators. Team leaders help identify problems and work with the team to solve the problems as a group.

Self-directed work teams are organized without a permanent team leader. Team members are collectively responsible for work assigned to the team. Self-directed work teams have a manager for team members to consult when solving difficult problems. Team members work together to establish goals and to plan and organize their work.

BUSINESS ORGANIZATION

As competition increases and customers expect increased quality and service, the organization of a business becomes important.

Centralized organizations have a few top managers who do all major planning and decision making. Larger organizations often have communication problems when using a centralized organizational structure. An overabundance of rules and policies sometimes makes employees of a centralized organization feel unimportant to the business.

Decentralized organizations divide large businesses into smaller operating units. Managers have greater responsibility and authority for the operation of their units. An entertainment organization could be decentralized into work units by categories of target markets or business functions.

Flattened organizations have fewer levels of management than traditional structures. The flattened organization achieves improved communication because information flows through fewer levels of the business. More coordination and cooperation are necessary because there is less specialization within the organization.

INTERMISSION

Define two types of organizational structure.

MORE THAN A THEME PARK

Managers of Florida's Universal Studios Orlando Resort realize the value of expanding the uses for its venue. Orlando has a 2.1-million-square-foot convention center. Meetings attended by 3.7 million people each year bring $3.2 billion into the Orlando economy. Orlando has experienced 24 percent growth in convention hotel lodging during the past five years. The city will have 115,000 hotel rooms by 2005.

Managers of Universal Orlando realize the opportunities that exist to attract meeting business in Orlando. The theme park earns more than $100 million in revenue each year. The Resort Sales Team and the Park and Events Sales Team set ambitious goals to increase revenue. Strategies to increase revenue include attracting more meeting and after-park-hours business.

MAKING THE BAD TIMES GOOD

Peak times for theme parks occur during the summer. Non-peak times at theme parks like Universal Orlando are referred to as *shoulder periods.* Special events drive attendance during shoulder periods. Guest satisfaction and repeat business are top goals for special events managers during shoulder periods at the theme park.

Mardi Gras at Universal Orlando is a celebration that takes place for ten weeks during March and April. Ten "super concerts" attract customers through the turnstiles.

Rock the Universe at Universal Orlando is a two-day Christian event that occurs the first weekend in September. This celebration includes music, ministry, fellowship, and fun.

Florida is the number one destination in the United States for tourists from the United Kingdom (UK). Orlando is the most popular city for tourists from the UK to visit. Universal Orlando has an office in the UK and two offices in Brazil. Sales promotions drive 55 percent of the attendance at Universal Orlando from the UK and Brazil.

THINK CRITICALLY

1. **Why is it important for entertainment businesses like Universal Orlando to have offices in other countries?**
2. **Why do you think Orlando is the most popular city to visit for tourists from the UK?**

Businesses form partnerships to attract additional opportunities. Dunkin' Donuts™ in New York offers a special promotion during the winter that gives customers a chance to win a trip to Universal Orlando to escape the cold weather.

Halloween Horror Nights take place every October. Universal Orlando dares people to take part in the biggest, most horrific annual Halloween party. Participants should be prepared to scream as hundreds of mutants, maniacs, and monsters emerge from the darkness.

CREATING A SPECIAL EVENT

Planning a special event for the shoulder season at Universal Orlando begins by developing a **proforma**. This financial document projects attendance and revenue necessary to successfully undertake the event.

The second phase of planning involves writing a business plan that serves as a strategic road map. The business plan also will be used after the event concludes to make improvements for the future. A new event is usually given a three-year window to become profitable.

MARKETING AND SALES

Brand marketing is the hub of Universal Orlando's marketing program. **Brand marketing** is the process of creating a perception that separates an organization from its competitors. Marketing managers realize that recognition of the Universal name, or brand, is an important influence in increasing sales.

Selling additional products to customers beyond the initial purchase is known as **upselling**. Universal Orlando's success depends on upselling. Additional revenue is generated from food, games, and merchandise. Successful upselling efforts result in consumers purchasing more than their original intentions. Universal Orlando and other theme parks rely on upselling to increase revenue.

© GETTY IMAGES/PHOTODISC

Universal Orlando's management understands the importance of *synergy*, the strength gained from partnerships and teams working together. Partnerships with key sponsors such as Gatorade, Toyota, and Sherwin Williams provide avenues to attract more people to Universal Orlando.

INTERMISSION

What challenges do shoulder periods present for entertainment venues?

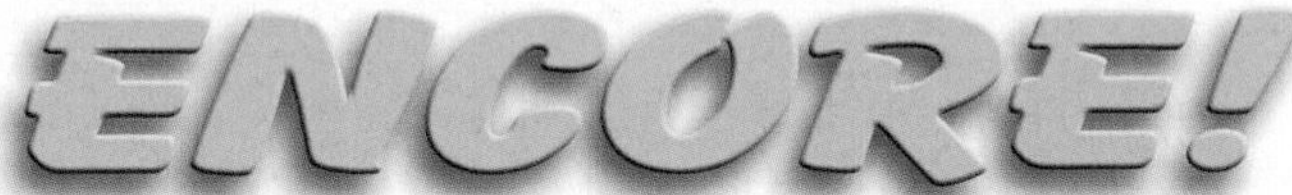

UNDERSTANDING MANAGEMENT CONCEPTS

Circle the best answer for each of the following questions.

1. An organizational structure that divides employees into permanent teams with the authority and responsibility for implementing business activities is a

a. team organization
b. centralized organization
c. decentralized organization
d. flattened organization

2. The first step in planning a special event for the shoulder season of a theme park is

a. writing a business plan
b. upselling
c. brand marketing
d. developing a proforma

THINK CRITICALLY

Answer the following questions as completely as possible. If necessary, use a separate sheet of paper.

3. Draw the organizational chart for a business or other organization in your community.

____

____

____

4. Communication The Hard Rock Café at Universal Orlando offers a restaurant, meeting place, and catering service. Write three paragraphs to brand market each of these functions for the Hard Rock Café.

____

____

____

____

5. Choose three types of entertainment events, and give several examples of upselling for each type.

____

____

____

____

CHAPTER 4 REVIEW

REVIEW MANAGEMENT CONCEPTS

Write the letter of the term that matches each definition. Some terms will not be used.

____ **1.** Includes project income, expenses, and profit for an entertainment event
____ **2.** A specific financial plan to determine the best way to use available financial resources
____ **3.** The amount that will be bought at a given time at a given price
____ **4.** A detailed description of all marketing activities that must be accomplished in order to make an event successful
____ **5.** Limited financial resources for unlimited wants
____ **6.** The ability of a service or good to satisfy a want
____ **7.** The amount that will be offered for sale at a particular time and at a certain price
____ **8.** The number of employees that a manager supervises directly
____ **9.** The process of creating a perception that separates an organization from its competitors
____ **10.** Selling additional products to customers beyond the initial purchase

a. brand marketing
b. budget
c. demand
d. economic system
e. economics
f. factors of production
g. financial plan
h. marketing plan
i. proforma
j. scarcity
k. span of control
l. supply
m. unity of command
n. upselling
o. utility

Circle the best answer.

11. Careers in sports management
- **a.** are very competitive
- **b.** frequently require individuals to participate in internships
- **c.** frequently have 50- to 60-hour workweeks
- **d.** all of the above

12. Shoulder periods
- **a.** are busy periods for a business
- **b.** require creative marketing strategies to bring in more business
- **c.** are slow periods for a business
- **d.** both b and c

13. More coordination and cooperation are necessary because there is less specialization within the
- **a.** decentralized organization
- **b.** flattened organization
- **c.** centralized organization
- **d.** matrix organization

THINK CRITICALLY

14. Work with a partner to discuss strategies and events to fill major hotels located at theme parks in warm climates during shoulder periods.

15. Sports and entertainment management is a competitive career field. Outline a strategy for a graduating high school senior to ultimately land a sports and entertainment management career. (Your strategy should include a college offering this major and internships for experience.)

16. What are the four utilities for a good or service associated with sports and entertainment management? Give an example of each type of utility.

17. What are the major differences between centralized and decentralized organizations? List the advantages and disadvantages of each.

18. List the steps that are involved in the creation of a special event for a shoulder period. Begin with the development of the financial pro-forma. What is the importance of each step? Explain why a new event might need three years to become profitable.

MAKE CONNECTIONS

19. Management Math You plan to work for a professional football team in the corporate sponsorship department. You are aware of the long hours that you must work each week to be successful in this career. One of your coworkers has told you to be prepared to work 60 hours per week. Your organization gives you two weeks of vacation during the year. How many hours will you work during the year?

20. Technology Use the Internet to visit the web site of your favorite U.S. theme park. List three different price packages that are available at the theme park. Devise additional price packages with special incentives to attract more customers during the shoulder periods.

21. Communication Compose a letter to student organizations such as DECA, FBLA, and Student Council to let these groups know about the Halloween festivities at Universal Orlando. Offer these student organizations special group rates to attend the Halloween activities at the theme park.

22. Human Resources Management You are in charge of seasonal employees for a major theme park. Compose a job description outlining the theme park's expectations for seasonal employees. The job description should include dress code, customer service requirements, and team requirements to make your theme park the leader among other parks.

23. Management Responsibilities You are in charge of security at a favorite local entertainment venue. You have booked a popular musical group that will draw a sell-out crowd. What steps will you take to provide security throughout the event? What measures will you have in place to ensure the safety of the crowd? In case of an emergency, such as a fire, what emergency plan will you have for the safe evacuation of all patrons?

24. Communication You are the marketing director for a major university planning its annual homecoming weekend. Your school relies heavily on alumni donations throughout the year. Write a letter to alumni detailing the planned events. Invite them to attend the upcoming homecoming weekend and solicit their financial support for the school.

25. History The number of Mexican-Americans in your local community has steadily increased over the past few years. Your community is seriously considering a Cinco de Mayo celebration. You have been asked to research the historical background of Cinco de Mayo. You will present a report along with your recommendations for the celebration at the next meeting of the city council. Using the Internet, conduct research about Cinco de Mayo, its historical background, and the types of events that are typically held during its annual celebration. Prepare a one-page written report that you will present to the city council.

26. Marketing Management Your city, a popular warm-weather recreational area, would like to increase revenues by attracting more visitors during spring break. What kinds of local events will you plan to attract more visitors to your city? What major corporations will you approach as potential sponsors for these events? What kind of visibility will you offer these sponsors before, during, and after the spring break events?

THE UPSELLING STRATEGY

Most businesses will tell you that the key to their success is upselling. Profits come when you get the customer to buy a larger, more expensive, or more comprehensive product or service.

Every day, consumers encounter upselling. Fast-food restaurants ask customers if they want to increase their drink size or add fries to their hamburger order for an additional price.

Hair styling salons offer basic hair cuts plus a variety of additional services. These additions are designed to raise the price of the service purchased. Once customers have their hair cut or styled, stylists ask if they want to purchase shampoo, conditioner, brushes, or other hair care products. National chain hair salons produce their own product lines to upsell to customers.

Full-service car washes offer the basic service for a base price. Add-on services such as wax and wheel cleaning are offered to upsell the basic product.

Hotels offer deluxe rooms with additional services or features for higher prices. Some hotels offer brunch for an additional cost to the hotel room. Customers receive a good meal while the hotel receives additional revenue.

Airlines are also involved in the business of upselling. When customers reserve a plane ticket, they can purchase a basic coach ticket, or they can upgrade to first class or business class for a higher price. Many airlines have reward cards that allow frequent fliers to collect miles toward free flights or upgrades.

Even credit cards are involved in upselling. Customers are offered a credit card that accumulates advantage points or better repayment plans. The only catch to a better credit card is that the consumer usually pays a higher interest rate or annual fee.

Car dealerships practice upselling. The sticker price on new cars shows the base price without all the bells and whistles. It also shows a much higher price for cars that have extra features. Consumers are encouraged to add features for a higher price.

Car dealerships and other businesses that sell high-priced items, such as computers and major appliances, encourage customers to purchase extended warranties. These warranties cover the purchased item beyond the manufacturer's warranty.

Think Critically

1. **Why is upselling so popular?**
2. **Do you think consumers appreciate or resent upselling strategies? Explain.**
3. **Give an example of a recent personal upselling experience.**
4. **What is the best way for sales associates to upsell a product?**
5. **Give an example of a base price for a new car. Also give an example of upselling this product (tell what additional features have increased the price of the car).**

SPORTS AND ENTERTAINMENT MARKETING MANAGEMENT TEAM DECISION MAKING

An important part of the overall success of theme parks is selling additional products to customers. Theme parks like Universal Orlando depend on generating more revenue than just the initial admission sale. Additional revenue is derived from foods, games, and merchandise. Universal Orlando wants to sell customers more products and services than they originally intended to purchase.

You are on the sales team of a popular theme park and resort. You are in charge of devising strategies to upsell the following items.

Annual passes If local customers buy a one-day ticket to a park, you want them to consider upgrading to an annual pass. This increases revenue and attendance to the park.

Multi-day tickets If guests purchase a one-day ticket, you would like them to consider upgrading to a multi-day ticket (two-day, three-day, or flexible ticket).

Resorts You want to ensure that all guests are aware of the resort's first-class, on-site hotels. Resort guests are likely to spend the majority of their vacation on the resort property.

Merchandise It is critical to the resort's success that it maximizes the revenue from merchandise.

Food and beverage It is just as important that the resort maximizes the revenue from food.

Entertainment At the end of the day in the theme park, you want guests to know that the fun continues at restaurants, retail outlets, and movie theaters associated with your resort. The resort has a large number of businesses on the property that rely on park guests for part of their daily business.

Performance Indicators Evaluated

- Define the importance of upselling.
- Explain strategies for upselling tickets and merchandise at a theme park and resort.
- Describe promotions to increase sales.
- Explain the value of related merchandise sales.

Go to the DECA web site for more detailed information.

1. What features should you highlight to attract more business to the theme park and resort?
2. What is your strategy for upselling annual passes to the theme park? Why do you think this strategy will be successful?
3. Outline a complete strategy to upsell your resort.

www.deca.org/publications/HS_Guide/guidetoc.html

CHAPTER 5

Management Functions

5.1 PLANNING

5.2 ORGANIZING

5.3 IMPLEMENTING AND CONTROLLING

© GETTY IMAGES/PHOTODISC

© GETTY IMAGES/PHOTODISC

© GETTY IMAGES/PHOTODISC

WINNING Strategies

DREAM FOOTBALL

Catherine Masters is founder and CEO of the National Women's Football Association (NWFA). Masters' ideal football game is 25 to 30 women cracking helmets and catching passes in front of a crowd of screaming fans. She pulled off the organizational feat in August of 2000. The Nashville Dream met the Alabama Renegades for the NWFA's first women's full-contact professional football game. One year later, the NWFA had expanded to ten teams. Since then, it hasn't looked back. By 2003, the NWFA had 30 active teams representing cities across the nation.

Masters pulled off this challenge by using sound planning and organizational principles. Masters has been around sports for many years. Her experience includes stints as a tennis scout, a promoter of minor league baseball, and an outdoor event planner. As a past Executive Director for the National Women's Business Association, Masters also knows the value of networking.

Masters' NWFA dream began with an understanding of the female spirit and its competitive nature. Women participate in almost all major sports, so why not football? Masters and her group of owners insist that a professional women's football league can succeed. The keys to success are good management structures, solid financing, and the right target audience.

THINK CRITICALLY

1. How did Catherine Masters make her dream come true?
2. List the characteristics necessary to make women's professional football successful.

LESSON 5.1

PLANNING

Discuss the purpose and benefits of planning.

Describe the planning process.

OPENING ACT

Memo to the Planning Committee:

As a member of our planning staff, you are responsible for planning the activities that guide and direct our charitable event. Without your hard work, this concert benefiting the March of Dimes would not occur. As you know, our goal is to raise $300,000 for this worthy cause. Bruce Hornsby and the Range, Clint Black, and Amy Grant have graciously donated their time and music to this event. We believe that the diversity of these musical performers will draw a great crowd.

The March of Dimes™ and the children it serves wish to thank you in advance for your time and energy.

Sincerely,

Events Director

Work with a partner. Discuss the activities that the planning committee would need to arrange in order to ensure that this concert is a success.

THE PURPOSE OF THE PLANNING PROCESS

Planning is the process of deciding what objectives to follow in the future and what to do to achieve those objectives. Good managers must have a plan to succeed. When managers plan, they effectively take charge of the future. Managers in successful organizations do not just sit back and let things happen. They make things happen.

Planning means that every employee becomes actively involved in the actions of the organization. This involvement produces many benefits. First, if everyone in the organization is involved in the planning process, then the plans are naturally better. Second, knowing the big picture helps employees understand the direction of the organization. Third, by knowing and contributing to the planning process, employees become empowered and feel a sense of self-worth. Finally, by participating in the planning process, all members of the organization become more future-oriented. They are better prepared to meet the challenges that the future brings.

Consider the problem facing many sports managers today as kids continue to lose interest in sports. To the planner, this means that future fan interest and revenues are in danger. Statistics indicate that television viewership, fan interest, and participation in sports by kids ages 2-11 and 12-17 are down. To counter this trend, planners are actively trying to add the fun back into their sports. The NBA is sponsoring nationwide Fan-Jams where kids can learn about basketball from the pros. The WNBA encourages its athletes to get close to kids through mentor programs. NASCAR is trying new licensing approaches to stimulate teen interest. The NFL is testing the carnival atmosphere of the NFL Experience to encourage young fans to dream about football and its stars. Whether these techniques will stimulate youth interest in sports cannot be determined for a few years. In the meantime, planners will continue to focus on youth and their interests.

©DIGITAL VISION

TIME OUT

Do teens care much for golf? For many years, the answer was no. However, Golden Tee, the most popular video game ever, may be changing teens' minds. The game is teaching Gen-Y youth about the sport and is getting them onto golf courses around the country.

TYPES OF PLANS

There are many types of plans. Plans can be informal or formal. An **informal plan** is a loose collection of thoughts about how to do something. Informal plans frequently change. For example, if you were planning to get together with friends on Friday evening, the time and place to meet may change. A **formal plan**, on the other hand, is usually written and well thought out. The formal plan in a sports and entertainment management organization addresses many factors. These factors may include the environment and the size and type of business concerned. Other factors might include who will carry out the plan and the end result expected.

Plans often are linked to business functions. Plans may be short range or long range in nature. For example, many cities conduct annual Yellow Duck Races in the spring. These races raise thousands of dollars and draw people outdoors and into local parks. Thousands of numbered yellow ducks are dumped into a local waterway. The ducks then make their way to a finish point. The first duck across the finish line—and the lucky person with that duck's number—is declared the winner. A short-range plan for this event indicates how to monitor the race and declare a winner. A long-range plan specifies how funds are collected, audited, and distributed to the needy.

INTERMISSION

How does an informal plan differ from a formal plan?

____

____

THE PLANNING PROCESS

Managers often struggle with the planning process. Although simple in description and concept, planning is often difficult because it is hard to communicate your thoughts and actions to others.

The steps of the planning process are

1. **Establish Objectives** What do you want to accomplish?
2. **Analyze the Situation** What does the plan relate to and what is its background?
3. **Determine Alternative Courses of Action** What are several ways to solve your problem?
4. **Evaluate Alternatives** What are the pros and cons of each solution?
5. **Choose an Alternative and Implement Your Plan** What is the best course of action to take? How will you put your plan into action?

Consider how you might apply the planning process to the decision of choosing a path to an education beyond high school. Following are the basic planning steps that you might choose.

1. Set an objective of attending a college, university, or other educational institution.
2. Analyze your current situation based on your skills, test scores, interests, financial condition, and preferences.
3. Determine which colleges, universities, or other educational institutions match your situation. In other words, identify the paths that are open to you.
4. Evaluate each of your alternatives in light of your situation.
5. Choose your educational option and write it down. Develop a budget for reaching your goal. Complete an application, visit the campus, and pay your deposit.

© DIGITAL VISION

If you are able to accomplish these five steps, you have just designed a **descriptive plan**. A descriptive plan states what is to be achieved and how. If you match your career goals with your descriptive plan, you have constructed a longer-term strategic plan. The steps to realizing your strategic plan, such as career counseling, graduating from college, and interviewing, would include shorter-term operational plans.

Managers who learn the art of planning lead their organizations to successful business ventures. These managers are able to capitalize on opportunities as they arise.

INTERMISSION

Why is it important to follow the steps of the planning process to reach a goal or objective?

Lead the Way

OAKLAND RAIDERS

In reviewing what works in sports management, a positive image is not always necessary. More important are a sound financial plan and a creative marketing plan. These strategies and talented football players brought the Oakland Raiders once again to the Super Bowl in 2003.

By almost every standard except image, the Oakland Raiders is considered to be one of the best-run teams in the NFL. Some believe it is the organization's winning tradition. Others say it is the outspoken owner, Al Davis. Still others believe it is the coaches and players themselves. What makes this team special is that it makes money and it wins!

Few teams bring in the licensing dollars that flow to the Raiders. The silver and black colors and the patch-eyed Raider can be seen on almost every street corner. However, because of its often unfair association with gangs, many schools have outlawed Raiders-wear. This ban still has not slowed the Raiders' popularity with teen and adult fans.

The Raiders organization believes that good management is at the core of a dynasty. This organization intends to use sound planning to stay on top of the highly competitive game of professional football.

THINK CRITICALLY

1. **Why are good plans so important to winning in sports?**
2. **What makes the Oakland Raiders a leading organization in spite of its sometimes negative image?**

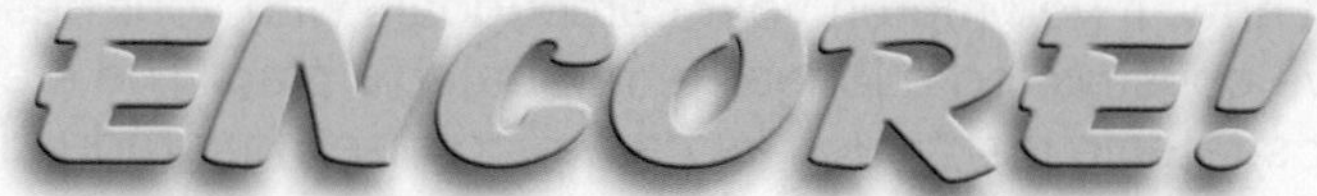

UNDERSTANDING MANAGEMENT CONCEPTS

Circle the best answer for each of the following questions.

1. When planning, a specific result you want to achieve is
a. an alternative
b. a situation
c. a function
d. an objective

2. A plan that states what is to be achieved and how is
a. a descriptive plan
b. an operational plan
c. a strategic plan
d. an informal plan

THINK CRITICALLY

Answer the following questions as completely as possible. If necessary, use a separate sheet of paper.

3. Communication You have been hired by a local ice skating rink as the events director. You must plan at least one event at the rink in each of the next three months. What events would be appropriate for the ice rink? Write a brief plan for one of the proposed events.

____

____

____

4. Management Math If sales receipts for a concert totaled $300,000 and expenses for the concert were $250,000, what amount of profit would be shared by the organizers of the event? What factors might determine the plan for distributing this money?

____

____

____

____

5. Technology Search the Internet to locate the web site for the USA Volleyball Organization. What information is available at the web site? Write a long-range plan for keeping the web site current.

____

____

____

____

ORGANIZING

OPENING ACT

Organizing is the process of arranging activities in such a way that goals are accomplished. Consider a softball game at a Sunday picnic. For the game to be played (the goal), the players must bring the equipment, choose sides, choose someone to officiate and keep score, and start and stop the game (activities). The organizing function accomplishes these tasks.

To succeed in today's competitive environment, sports and entertainment businesses must be well-organized. A first step in organizing effectively is to draw up an organizational chart. This chart shows the structure of the business by listing each manager's position by job title. Lines show who accomplishes what tasks and who is accountable to whom.

Work with a partner. Discuss the various aspects of organizing an event at your school. Draw an organizational chart that shows who is responsible for the activities necessary to make the event a success.

Describe the reasons for and benefits of organizing.

Explain factors that affect the structure of an organization.

Describe how authority is delegated in organizations.

ORGANIZING SPORTS AND ENTERTAINMENT EVENTS

Organizing is concerned with accomplishing tasks most effectively and arranging resources to complete all necessary work. An **organization** consists of people whose specialized tasks are coordinated to contribute to the company's goals.

REASONS FOR ORGANIZING

Sports and entertainment event managers must be skilled in organizing in order to establish lines of authority. Clear lines of authority help to create order within a group. This order allows the group to function effectively.

© GETTY IMAGES/PHOTODISC

Organizing improves the efficiency and quality of work through synergy. When individuals or groups work together to produce a whole greater than the sum of the parts, synergy occurs. In football, each player is assigned a particular position and role to play in the game. However, offensive and defensive formations are much more than just individuals playing a game. Organization of these formations produces synergy. Managers attempt to create this same effect.

Organizing improves and enhances communication. Businesses must carefully define channels of communication within the organization. *Upward communication* occurs when an employee tells a supervisor about a problem. *Downward communication* happens when a supervisor tells an employee how to meet a goal or objective. Both types of communication are essential for an organization to be successful.

the Global Manager

Lana Corbi is an up-and-coming global entertainment manager. As the CEO of the Hallmark Channel, Corbi has a difficult organizing task in front of her. Her responsibility is making the Hallmark Channel a credible media and entertainment force. However, she does not have to start from scratch. The Hallmark Channel has already received high marks for programming and entertainment events. Corbi wants to increase the number of Hallmark Channel viewers to 50 million. She also wants to encourage international broadcast deals. Corbi plans to use original programming, specials, and outstanding dramas to accomplish her goals. She also plans to add programming with an international message.

THINK CRITICALLY

1. What are some things Lana Corbi should consider in order to accomplish her goals?
2. What should be the Hallmark Channel's focus if it desires to create an international presence?

BENEFITS OF ORGANIZING

Throughout history, people have shown a desire to organize. This desire led to the development of organizations. The use of an organization allows people to

- become specialized in their work tasks
- implement new advances in technology more rapidly
- understand and react to external forces more efficiently
- use power and authority more productively

Specialization occurs when work is given to those people who can best accomplish the tasks. A field manager for the Boston Red Sox may be good at creating team lineups, picking pitchers for a game, and deciding when to bunt or steal. However, this manager does not negotiate contracts, sell tickets, create advertising, or clean the stadium after a game.

New technology has dramatically impacted all forms of businesses, including sports and entertainment organizations. When popular Latin recording star Jennifer Lopez gives a concert, her entertainment organization combines the live event with modern technology. Satellite broadcasting, the Internet, and high-tech special effects bring the fans an uplifting experience. Without organizing, coordination and success would be difficult to achieve.

External forces lie outside an organization's control. For example, an organization cannot control the economy, culture, laws and regulations, competition, or target market. The organization is affected by these external forces and must be aware of their impact on decision making. For example, raising ticket prices is usually a poor strategy when the country is going through an economic downturn. Many sports and entertainment organizations have learned this lesson the hard way.

Organizing can aid managers in exercising power and control. Power is the ability to influence, command, or apply force. Power is associated with authority. Authority comes with a position and represents the legitimate exercise of power. Consider the power and authority held by a manager of a large organization. If power and authority are used poorly or harshly, no one will be willing to work in the organization. If power and authority are used wisely and responsibly, the organization will likely meet its goals. Commissioner of Major League Baseball "Bud" Selig has a difficult task. He must represent owners, players, fans, and even the game itself. Each of these groups often has ideas and positions that are in conflict with the other groups. If Selig favors one group over another, he loses credibility. Selig uses his power and authority to keep the organization of Major League Baseball operating smoothly and profitably.

ETHICS in Action

Professional athletes and entertainers have special responsibilities because of the influence they have over youth markets. Children trade player cards. They buy music and merchandise developed by or endorsed by sports and entertainment stars. Many of these celebrities also endorse tobacco, alcohol, or other adult products. Legislators are concerned that celebrities' endorsement of these products adversely affects underage consumers. "Don't Do It!" campaigns sponsored by nonprofit groups are offset by "Try It, You'll Like It!" messages from celebrities.

THINK CRITICALLY

1. **Should sports and entertainment celebrities endorse controversial products? Why or why not?**
2. **Without attempting to control free speech, what would be an ethical solution to this problem?**

INTERMISSION

List the benefits of organizing.

____

____

ORGANIZATIONAL STRUCTURE AND DEPARTMENTS

Organizational structure defines how far the organization reaches and indicates the framework within which it operates. The structure of an organization reflects how groups compete for resources and where responsibilities lie. Structure also guides how information is transmitted and how managers make decisions. Many people believe that a manager or employee should be able to work effectively no matter what type of organizational structure exists. However, efficient organizational structure helps foster efficient performance and vice versa.

© GETTY IMAGES/PHOTODISC

The Montreal Expos are a good example. Major League Baseball (MLB) recently took over the team from previous management. The team was averaging only 3,000 season ticket sales and had few premier seats in its stadium. It had no local television partners and was losing players and fans at an alarming rate. The team's organizational structure was an example of chaos and poor management. Now that MLB has taken over the team, a new home is being sought. New management is being hired, and new management strategies are being tested. Only time will tell whether the attempts will be successful or not.

FACTORS OF STRUCTURE

There are several factors that affect which structure is best for an organization. Failure to account for these factors can result in difficulties such as those experienced by the Montreal Expos. The four key factors in determining the proper organizational structure are strategy, size, environment, and technology.

Strategy Sports and entertainment leaders stress that to succeed one must have a good strategy and must be mentally prepared for success. **Strategy** is an organization's long-term plan for meeting its objectives. Organizational structure can either aid or inhibit strategy implementation. If an organization fails to achieve its goals, it must make adjustments in its strategy. The same is true with its organizational structure. The Los Angeles Dodgers' consistent success is due largely to its superior minor league system and its recruiting of Latin baseball players. Having an organizational structure to locate and sign players from the Caribbean, Mexico, and Central/South America is a strategy that is not developed overnight. As proven by the Dodgers, once the structure is in place, championships follow.

Major League Soccer has reached a deal not only to broadcast its games to U.S. cities but also to reach fans in Latin America. This arrangement is of special interest to advertisers who want to tap into the huge Latino market.

Size There are many ways to measure the size of an organization. Sales volume and number of employees are among the most common measures. Even though many small organizations succeed, large organizational structures tend to be more successful with regard to specialization. Large organizations also benefit from standardization and decentralization. With standardization, decisions are made in similar ways. Decentralization empowers lower-level managers to make decisions.

Environment With respect to organizational structure, environment refers to how work is done. The environment of an organization can be mechanical or organic. In a **mechanical environment**, tasks are specific and top managers primarily make decisions. Communication is narrow and limited. In an **organic environment**, decisions are made through empowerment and networking. Communication flows throughout the organization. Consider the case of planning a high-performance car show. If the show was planned by the National Hot Rod Association (NHRA), it would most likely be the product of a mechanical environment. Show organizers would be given specific work tasks. The show would need to meet NHRA standards. All communication would occur among the NHRA, local car clubs, and the media. If the show was planned by a local car club, it would most likely be created from an organic environment. Show organizers would be given great freedom in designing their own work tasks. The show would take on the personality of the local car club. Communication might be effective or ineffective, depending on the skills of the planners.

Technology If an organization uses many forms of technology, its organizational structure will reflect the technology used. A good example is the San Francisco Giants. The Giants use the team's web site to encourage fan interactivity and to stimulate ticket sales. Managers in the organization are technology-oriented in their planning and communication. This orientation gives managers the ability to change direction quickly and respond to opportunities or crises. Managers can communicate directly with fans or address problems that concern fans.

CREATING DEPARTMENTAL STRUCTURE

Departmentalization is the process of grouping jobs into related work units or activities. The units may be related based on work function, product, geography, or customer.

Functional departmentalization means that the department's work or activities are grouped around basic functions like production, marketing, finance, or human resources. The primary advantage to this form of departmentalization is that it allows for specialization within functions. An example is a local nonprofit organization that sponsors a 100-mile bike race. Functional departmentalization would divide the work tasks by function. One group consists of those who will physically set up the course and monitor its progress. A second group is those who sell tickets, promote the race, and award prizes. A third group includes those who collect the funds. A fourth group is those who hire workers or enlist volunteers. A disadvantage of functional departmentalization is that one work group does not always know what another work group is doing.

© GETTY IMAGES/PHOTODISC

Product departmentalization includes all the activities necessary to produce and market a product or service, usually under a single manager. The advantage of this method is that it allows employees to identify with a specific product or brand. Loyalty is high in this structure. However, competition among various product groups can become a problem. There often is duplication of facilities and equipment.

Geographic departmentalization refers to organizations that are physically spread out over several states or countries. Using local people is an advantage, and service can be high with this approach. However, this is a costly method if there are too many geographic regions.

Customer departmentalization focuses on customers and their needs. Advantages and disadvantages are similar to the product departmentalization method. The Houston Rockets reconsidered its departmental structure when the organization signed Chinese basketball star Yao Ming. The Rockets now target Asian-Americans with a special sales staff that is bilingual and culturally sensitive to this growing customer group.

INTERMISSION

What are four ways to departmentalize an organization?

____

____

WHO IS IN CHARGE OF THE ORGANIZATION?

Authority is the right to make decisions about assigned work and to delegate assignments to others. Delegation is the means by which authority is exercised. A supervisor pushes authority down through his or her employees. Authority can be delegated, but responsibility cannot. Managers must create structures that not only aid the accomplishment of goals and objectives but also hold decision makers accountable for their actions.

In any sports or entertainment organization, managers distinguish between *line authority* and *staff authority*. Examples of line managers are presidents, CEOs, sales managers, event planners, directors, and producers. All of these individuals are authorized to issue orders. Staff managers have different responsibilities and authority. These managers do not issue orders. Instead, they assist and advise line managers. Sometimes a manager's authority changes with respect to line and staff roles. A player development manager might have the authority to hire a player but not the authority to negotiate the player's contract. This manager might work closely with scouts and recruiters but might be distant from day-to-day operations.

© BRAND X PICTURES

There is always the danger of conflict between line managers and staff managers. Often a line manager feels that the advice or assistance from the staff managers is poor or insufficient. Staff managers, on the other hand, often feel that line managers do not listen and that they make poor decisions. If an event manager fails to act on information provided by staff managers, poor strategy is often the end result.

INTERMISSION

What is the difference between line authority and staff authority?

____

____

UNDERSTAND MANAGEMENT CONCEPTS

Circle the best answer for each of the following questions.

1. Which of the following is not a key factor in determining organizational structure?

a. geography **c.** strategy
b. size **d.** technology

2. ___?___ are responsible for providing assistance and advice rather than issuing direct orders.

a. Line managers **c.** CEOs
b. Staff managers **d.** Sales managers

THINK CRITICALLY

Answer the following questions as completely as possible. If necessary, use a separate sheet of paper.

3. Research Select a recent entertainment event that appeared on television. Describe the event. Who sponsored the event? Who was in charge of the event? Based on these answers, what can you say about the event's organizational structure?

____

____

____

4. Assume that you have been put in charge of the event selected in Question 3. What would you do to make the event better? How would you change the event's organizational structure to implement your ideas?

____

____

____

____

5. Technology Describe and illustrate how technology impacts an organization's structure.

____

____

____

IMPLEMENTING AND CONTROLLING

OPENING ACT

The Annual Kodak Albuquerque International Balloon Fiesta is the most photographed event in the world. The fiesta attracts people from over 50 countries. As a result of its popularity, the Balloon Fiesta demands a high degree of management control to achieve success. The number of balloons each year at the fiesta continues to grow. Recently, the Balloon Fiesta Committee limited the total number of balloons. According to officials, fewer is sometimes better. The committee is wondering whether photographers, the media, and visitors will agree.

Work with a partner. Make a list of the reasons that the Balloon Fiesta Committee might need to control the total number of balloons at the fiesta. What other controls also might be important to the committee? Explain your answer.

Explain the activities of the implementing function.

Describe the management control process.

List and describe the three steps for efficient control.

THE IMPLEMENTING FUNCTION

Implementing involves guiding employees' work toward achieving the company's goals. To implement successfully, managers must complete several activities designed to encourage employees to achieve company goals. These activities include effective communication, employee motivation, development of efficient work teams, and operations management.

EFFECTIVE COMMUNICATION

Communication is an essential part of implementing. Communication is much more than telling employees what to do. In fact, if employees believe managers are being too directive, they will likely not work as effectively as they could. Important communication skills for managers include listening to employees and involving them in decision making.

EMPLOYEE MOTIVATION

Motivation is a set of factors that influence an individual's actions toward accomplishing a goal. Managers use rewards and penalties to encourage employee motivation toward pursuing company objectives. A key to motivation is knowing what employees value and giving them these rewards for achieving company goals.

© GETTY IMAGES/PHOTODISC

EFFICIENT WORK TEAMS

Employees seldom complete all of their work alone. Most employees are part of a work group and rely on cooperation from others to perform their tasks. To develop efficient teams, managers must help to organize the team and develop needed team skills. Managers must also create a supportive work environment and help the group resolve problems.

OPERATIONS MANAGEMENT

Operations are the major ongoing activities of a business. When completing the implementing function, managers are ensuring that employees are performing these business activities as planned. Effective planning and organizing are important parts of operations management. If problems occur in the operations of a business, managers should examine the plans and organization of the work.

INTERMISSION

What does implementing involve?

____

____

WHY SHOULD MANAGERS PRACTICE CONTROL?

Control means knowing what is occurring in comparison to preset standards or objectives. If corrections are necessary, they must be made for the control process to be complete. Like planning, control addresses several pertinent questions.

1. Where are we now?
2. Where do we want to be?
3. How can we get there from here?

Although control can be preventive (occurring before anything happens), most control occurs after actions have been taken.

THE MANAGEMENT CONTROL PROCESS

To effectively control a sports or entertainment event, a manager must devise a simple model that illustrates the control process. In this model, the manager acts as a regulator who handles information input such as reports or communication on activities. Through information channels, such as memos, e-mails, or verbal conversations, the manager assesses whether plans or objectives are being met. **Standards** serve as points of reference for judging the company's performance. The method of assessing standards tells the manager if the plans or objectives are on track or need to be adjusted.

The management control process matches inputs (information) to outputs (results) through a **feedback system**. Feedback is a vital part of the manager's control process. Feedback allows all members of the organization to feel that they are empowered to affect decision making. This characteristic is evident in successful sports and entertainment management organizations.

Assume that you are in charge of planning a whitewater rafting trip for 20 members of your class. You have drawn up your plan and asked several friends to help you. Now it is time to devise a control process. You construct a model that shows what types of reports you would like to receive. These reports include travel arrangements, lodging reservations, and insurance signups. An information channel funnels these reports through you and any designated assistants. Standards are based on other trips that you have taken and rules mandated by the school system. As the trip develops, you must submit reports to sponsors indicating the success of the venture. If deviations or problems occur, they must be dealt with using ideas from your plan. At the end of the trip, you would be wise to do a follow-up to see if everyone enjoyed his or her experience. This feedback system will allow you to plan for the next adventure.

The International Organization for Standardization (ISO) is the world's largest developer of standards. ISO's principal activity is the development of technical standards. ISO standards also have important economic and social impacts. Compliance of products and services to ISO standards provides assurance about their quality, safety, and reliability. ISO standards make a positive difference, not just to engineers and manufacturers for whom they solve basic production and distribution problems, but to society as a whole.

THINK CRITICALLY

1. **Visit the ISO's web site. According to the web site, why do standards exist?**
2. **What would happen if there were no standards for products and services?**

INTERMISSION

What is a standard and what does it do?

____

____

The Monterey Jazz Festival in Monterey, California brings together 500 jazz greats. Their music is presented on seven stages spread over a 20-acre fairground. Artists and lovers of jazz come from around the world to experience this unique musical event. The festival is increasingly attracting high school jazz artists who win awards and scholarships from the event. The festival prides itself on being the discovery place for many future jazz superstars.

THINK CRITICALLY

1. **Why is the Monterey Jazz Festival an example of an event that embraces diversity?**
2. **Why would the Monterey Jazz Festival encourage young high school jazz musicians?**

REQUIREMENTS FOR EFFECTIVE CONTROL

Sports and entertainment managers follow three basic steps to ensure that their organization's control processes are efficient.

1. Establish standards.
2. Monitor results and compare them to standards.
3. Correct for any deviations.

In sports and entertainment management, standards normally measure worker performance, quality of service, revenue, or other indicators of meeting goals and objectives. For example, if a manager has a goal of making $100,000 for a sporting or entertainment event, then the standard of performance is $100,000. Evaluation and control will determine if this standard is too high or too low.

It is often the role of financial managers in sports and entertainment organizations to monitor results and compare them to standards. Monitoring is often thought of as being the same thing as controlling. However, it is only one part of the control process. By gathering data, managers can predict problems and can determine where these problems might occur. Timing is critical. The manager must recognize a problem in time to correct it.

In sports and entertainment management, it is often easy to set goals or objectives. It is much more difficult to ensure that the goals or objectives will be met. For control processes to be effective, sports and entertainment managers must solve long-range problems. Otherwise their organizations will eventually suffer because of their lack of foresight.

Potential reasons for not meeting goals or objectives are

- Faulty planning
- Poor communication
- Lack of training
- Poor motivation
- Failure to recognize changes in the environment

INTERMISSION

List the steps to ensure an efficient control process.

UNDERSTANDING MANAGEMENT CONCEPTS

Circle the best answer for each of the following questions.

1. A set of factors that influence an individual's actions toward accomplishing a goal is known as

a. communication
b. motivation
c. control
d. operations

2. Knowing what is occurring in comparison to preset standards or objectives is called

a. planning
b. organizing
c. feedback
d. control

THINK CRITICALLY

Answer the following questions as completely as possible. If necessary, use a separate sheet of paper.

3. Like planning, control addresses several pertinent questions. What are these questions?

____

____

____

____

4. You are an events planner for a local entertainment organization. List five factors that would motivate you to pursue your company's objectives. Which of these factors do you value most?

____

____

____

____

5. You are the director of your school prom. Describe several standards that you could use to control the event and ensure that your plans and objectives are being met.

____

____

____

CHAPTER 5 REVIEW

REVIEW MANAGEMENT CONCEPTS

Write the letter of the term that matches each definition. Some terms will not be used.

a. departmentalization	**g.** motivation
b. descriptive plan	**h.** organic environment
c. feedback system	**i.** organization
d. formal plan	**j.** specialization
e. informal plan	**k.** standards
f. mechanical environment	**l.** strategy

____ **1.** An environment in which decisions are made through empowerment and networking

____ **2.** Points of reference for judging the company's performance

____ **3.** People whose specialized tasks are coordinated to contribute to the company's goals

____ **4.** A set of factors that influence actions toward accomplishing a goal

____ **5.** An environment in which tasks are specific and top managers primarily make decisions

____ **6.** The process of grouping jobs into related work units or activities

____ **7.** The management control process that matches inputs to outputs

____ **8.** A loose collection of thoughts about how to do something

____ **9.** A plan that states what is to be achieved and how

____ **10.** Occurs when work is given to those people who can best accomplish the tasks

____ **11.** An organization's long-term plan for meeting its objectives

Circle the best answer.

12. The use of an organization allows people to
- **a.** always make a profit
- **b.** reduce marketing and other costly efforts
- **c.** use power and authority more effectively
- **d.** eliminate forces in the environment

13. If an organization's departments are grouped around basic functions such as marketing, finance, or human resources, the method of grouping is called
- **a.** product departmentalization
- **b.** functional departmentalization
- **c.** geographic departmentalization
- **d.** customer departmentalization

THINK CRITICALLY

14. Discuss with a classmate which external forces would have the most impact on a sports team's organization. Make a list of these forces. Compare your list with others in the class.

15. You have just been given the assignment of reorganizing the live entertainment department of Walt Disney World. In the past, this department has been responsible for live broadcast events and concerts on Disney properties. Which of the departmental structure methods described in the chapter would be best for your reorganization? Explain your answer.

16. Explain how conflict could occur between line managers and staff managers. How would diversity issues affect this conflict?

17. What are the differences among descriptive, strategic, and operational plans?

18. You have just been hired by the *Survivor* television show. Your job is to construct an initial plan to bring the next *Survivor* show to Mt. Kilimanjaro in Africa. Using the Internet, create an initial plan to investigate Mt. Kilimanjaro as the next *Survivor* site. Explain what you would do.

MAKE CONNECTIONS

19. Management Math You are the financial manager for a professional women's beach volleyball league. The league plays 10 games a week. Each game brings in receipts of $20,000. The average ticket price is $10. The league is considering raising ticket prices to $13.50. How many fans attend an average game? What would be the increase in revenue for an individual game from this proposed ticket price increase? What would be the impact of the increase on weekly league games?

20. Technology Use the Internet to find information about how professional sports teams plan. What types of plans did you find? How did you find the information? What additional information would you like to have found?

21. Communication You are the promotions manager for a local radio station. The station is sponsoring a "golden oldies" rock and roll concert in three weeks. Write a brief letter to a local hot rod club indicating how you would like them to participate. Support your letter with a plan for the proposed involvement.

22. Production Management Your class is organizing a call-a-thon to raise money for a local charity. Devise a control process for administering the collection of the anticipated funds. How can you ensure honest accounting practices and guarantee that the funds get to the right parties?

23. Management Responsibilities You are concerned that your school's community service program is not working well. Many projects lack substance, and a number of projects remain unfinished. Propose a reorganization of the school's community service program. Include discussions of the best way to organize the program, critical factors to watch for, and a plan for implementing your suggestions. Design a control mechanism to determine if the goals or objectives of the reorganization are being met.

24. Communication You are the event manager for a local hot-air balloon festival. You would like to model your event after the Albuquerque International Balloon Fiesta. What types of standards should be used from the Albuquerque event? Write a brief one-page memo to your event board that explains how you will use these standards to make this year's event the best ever.

25. Technology Thanks to the donation of a wealthy alumnus from your school, this year's senior trip will be to Cabo San Lucas, Mexico. Search the Internet for information on Cabo San Lucas that could be used in developing a plan for the senior trip. Categorize the data as related to either planning, organizing, implementing, or controlling. Which category of data was the easiest to find? Which category of data was the most difficult to find? Could you plan your trip from this data? Explain your answers.

CASE STUDY

DECA PREP

WAR ANXIETY PUTS LIFE ON HOLD

The war in the Middle East had a definite impact on consumer behavior in the United States. The uncertainty of war has the greatest psychological effect on the economy. People tend to go into a cautionary mode, similar to precautions taken for natural disasters like hurricanes, blizzards, or tornadoes.

Consumers shun shopping, travel, and even Disney World during times of uncertain peace. Consumers put off buying the SUVs they are so accustomed to seeing in their driveways. Even extremely low-priced travel specials outside of the United States receive little consumer attention. Rooms at Florida hotels can be rented for as little as $42 a night.

Americans seem to be immobilized by fear of the unknown. War puts a lot of uncertainty into the general mood of consumers. People don't know if the war will last three days or if it will have a lingering price tag for the next two generations.

Most people who face uncertain times will postpone making any major financial decisions. Marketers don't know whether to advertise, and retailers don't know whether to stock merchandise. Financial advisors can't convince clients that any move is the right move.

Effect on Travel

A war can paralyze the economy and can cost the nation billions of dollars. No industry is hit harder by war anxiety than travel. The Air Transport Association projects that air travel will drop 8 percent during a year of uncertainty. Predictions are that airlines face $11 billion in losses as a result of this drop.

Room occupancy in the Orlando area was down 5.5 percent during the first two months of 2003, according to the Orange County Convention and Visitors Bureau. Four of Epcot's eight general admission turnstiles were closed on a Sunday, typically its busiest day. Visitors experienced no waits for rides, and many of the park's plazas were empty. Florida tourism industry officials reported that the drop in travel was statewide.

War in 2003 caused Air Jamaica to put off indefinitely its plans for a second daily flight from Los Angeles to Jamaica. Contingency plans called for canceling many Air Jamaica flights and temporarily closing several resorts.

Effect on Car Buying

Even though travel feels the most pain, it is hard to find a business that does not suffer from the uncertainty of war. Incentives of more than $3,000 per vehicle could not sell more General Motors' vehicles in 2003. Both Ford and General Motors responded to the decrease in sales by cutting production. A car is a purchase that can be put off until the world and economy become seemingly better. Many people opt to service their used vehicles instead of buying new automobiles.

Businesses that trim their workforce and production are not likely to expand immediately after a war ends. The long-term direction of the economy depends largely on how long a conflict lasts.

Think Critically

1. **Why are consumers hesitant during times of international uncertainty?**
2. **Why would a period of uncertainty be a good time to take a vacation within the United States?**
3. **What types of promotion should automobile manufacturers implement to stimulate car sales in a time of war anxiety?**

SPORTS AND ENTERTAINMENT MARKETING MANAGEMENT TEAM DECISION MAKING

You are on the management team for Disney Theme Parks in Orlando. Due to unstable international affairs, Florida's tourism industry has taken a dramatic drop. Room occupancy rates within Disney Theme Parks are down by 6 percent. Attendance at the parks is down by 12 percent.

You must come up with fresh marketing strategies to bring more people to the Disney Theme Parks in Florida. Your marketing themes must promote the parks as an excellent family vacation spot. Security has become a major issue for many people, so you must assure guests that they will be safe at the parks. You must devise a strategy to sell more hotel rooms and theme park packages by introducing theme celebrations such as graduating seniors' weekend, Memorial Day specials, and Fourth of July specials. Popular entertainers who will perform at the park should help to increase attendance.

You will present your marketing strategies to the CEO and other managers of Disney Theme Parks.

Performance Indicators Evaluated

- Define the challenges facing the Disney theme parks, and create strategies to overcome them.
- Describe new theme celebrations to increase sales.
- Explain the parks' target markets and how they will be reached with the appropriate promotions.
- Explain the strategy to ease tourists' fears.

Go to the DECA web site for more detailed information.

1. What major ideas will you include in your marketing strategies to increase attendance at the parks?
2. What special events will you promote to gain the attention of large target markets like graduating seniors and holiday travelers?
3. What special hotel/park admission packages will you offer to families?
4. How will you assure the safety of park guests?
5. Outline your advertising and promotional strategies.

www.deca.org/publications/HS_Guide/guidetoc.html

CHAPTER 6

Decision Making

© GETTY IMAGES/PHOTODISC

6.1 HOW MANAGERS MAKE DECISIONS
6.2 GROUP DECISION MAKING
6.3 KNOWLEDGE MANAGEMENT

© GETTY IMAGES/PHOTODISC

© GETTY IMAGES/PHOTODISC

© GETTY IMAGES/PHOTODISC

WHERE THE WEST BEGINS

For many years, Ft. Worth, Texas was a sleepy, mid-sized city. It was more comfortable showcasing its cattle and ranching heritage than making its mark in today's high-tech world. That is no longer true. City planners assumed the difficult task of moving Ft. Worth into the twenty-first century. To accomplish this feat, difficult decisions were made.

The city undertook a massive venture to transform itself into a popular entertainment spot to rival any other city in Texas. The Ft. Worth-area Chamber of Commerce, local businesses, and entrepreneurial business leaders contributed to the effort. The most critical decision made was to build on the city's strength—its western heritage.

In times past, cattle drives began in Ft. Worth. Today, the old cattle drive stockyards are a focal point for many entertainment activities in the city. Billy Bob's of Texas provides song and dance. The Fort Worth Herd runs a daily cattle drive. The Tarantula Excursion Train welcomes visitors aboard. A variety of restaurants build on the western theme. Large events such as rodeos and conventions are attracted to the venue.

Decision makers found that problem solving was possible with the use of creative management principles, dedication, timely funding, and a spirit of cooperation. Increased revenues and business expansion have proved that the decisions made were not only sound but also well executed.

THINK CRITICALLY

1. What entertainment decisions did the business leaders of Ft.Worth make to lead their city into the twenty-first century?
2. Why were the Ft. Worth stockyards chosen as a focal point for the city's transformation?

HOW MANAGERS MAKE DECISIONS

Discuss the types of decisions made by managers.

Describe the conditions faced by a manager when making a decision.

OPENING ACT

In January 2000, media giant Time Warner Inc. agreed to be acquired by the popular Internet service provider America Online Inc. So far, the results of the merger have been far less than spectacular. In the first three years of the merger, AOL Time Warner's stock value dropped from $284 billion to $61 billion. Dick Parsons, CEO and Chairman of AOL Time Warner, is the first African-American to head a major media group. Parsons, though rich in managerial experience, will need to make some creative decisions to put AOL Time Warner back on top in the entertainment industry. He also will have to deal with powerful personalities, including AOL's former CEO Steve Case, in order to return the media giant to a profitable path. In Parsons' view, AOL Time Warner does not need radical surgery. Parsons' plan includes selling AOL Time Warner's "noncore" businesses, such as book publishing and CD manufacturing. His plan carries him into uncharted waters.

Work with a partner. Discuss other ideas that Dick Parsons could consider for making AOL Time Warner profitable again. Choose your two best ideas and present them to the class.

IS IT DECISION MAKING OR PROBLEM SOLVING?

Exactly what is decision making? **Decision making** is the process of creating and choosing alternatives to reach a goal or objective. This is similar to, but not exactly like, problem solving. **Problem solving** is the process of choosing actions to combat or resolve a problem. All problem solving involves decision making. However, not all decision making entails problem solving. For example, if a food and beverage manager at a sports facility chooses the types of drinks to sell, that manager is making a decision. However, the manager is not really solving a problem.

Sports and entertainment managers must learn how to effectively separate decision making from problem solving. Decision making is a learned skill that managers often practice. Problem solving frequently can be delegated to employees. If employees solve problems successfully, decision making becomes much easier for the manager.

DECISIONS—PROGRAMMED OR NONPROGRAMMED

Do you plan your decisions or just let them happen in a natural way? Most managers do both.

Programmed Decisions **Programmed decisions** are carefully thought out. They use some form of procedure that probably has been used before. Most routine, repetitive, or automatic decisions are reached in this way. For example, if the coach of a high school track team gives a water break every 30 minutes during intensive practices, the coach is following a programmed decision process. The reason for the automatic water breaks could be due to climate, safety, school policy, or coaching experience. Or it could be just the way the coach has always approached track practice.

© GETTY IMAGES/PHOTODISC

As many as nine out of ten decisions made are programmed decisions. This means that many managers have reduced decision making to automatic responses. They often do not recognize when a situation has changed and might require a new way of making a decision. What if high humidity or poorly conditioned athletes dictate that water breaks should occur every 15 minutes? The coach using the programmed approach might fail to recognize the need for this change and make a poor decision.

Nonprogrammed Decisions Managers make **nonprogrammed decisions** when they have no prior history, guidance, process, or system for making the decisions. This process often is called *creative decision making* or *judgment decision making*. Managers usually consider nonprogrammed decisions more difficult and risky. To aid managers faced with the problems brought on by nonprogrammed decision making, several approaches are suggested. Each approach has merits and difficulties.

The **intuitive approach** is used when sports or entertainment managers make decisions based primarily on guesses, hunches, or intuition. This method is closely associated with how a manager feels about the decision. The intuitive approach is probably the poorest of all the decision-making methods. There is a strong likelihood that an emotional manager will make a mistake. Managers using this approach often are considered "old style" in their decision-making approach. For example, for many years sports administrators assumed that female athletes could not effectively compete in sports that required extreme physical conditioning, high stress, or physical contact. This assumption has proved to be wrong. Some of the most popular and heavily merchandised women's sports are the ones that "old style" administrators believed could never exist. Merchandising packages for women's professional basketball and soccer rival many packages devoted to men's sports.

The NBA experienced a 0.5 percent decline in attendance for the first time in many years during its 2002–2003 season. This decline was attributed to poor decisions made with respect to ticket sales and the movement of several franchises to new cities.

The **optimizing approach**, unlike the intuitive approach, is a rational method of decision making. Using time-tested methods, managers determine the need for making a decision and weigh decision criteria. They decide the best way to make the decision and gather pertinent facts. Next, the managers devise possible ways to approach the decision. They evaluate these alternatives and pick the best one. This "scientific" approach is deemed by many managers to be among the best decision-making methods. The process removes many of the risks associated with nonprogrammed decision making. Sports and entertainment managers who are responsible for producing a product or service often use the optimizing approach. Managers can use this method to make decisions regarding inventory, merchandise, revenues from licenses, and salaries based on productivity of the athletes or entertainers.

The **satisficing approach** occurs when managers set a minimum standard of acceptance. The managers then select the first decision alternative that meets that minimum standard. Assume that you are going to the movies on a Friday night, but you have no particular movie in mind. You approach the box office at 7:30 P.M. The next movie is showing at 7:35 P.M. followed by another movie at 8:10 P.M. Your minimum standard is that you don't want to wait more than 15 minutes for a movie. Therefore, you select the 7:35 P.M. movie because it is playing soon. Obviously, selecting a movie based on time of performance rather than the movie itself can be risky. This example points out the fundamental weaknesses of the satisficing approach to decision making. Information gathering is limited and sometimes biased. Information also may not be as relevant as it should be. Managers who are time-pressured often use this method of decision making. They sometimes pay a price for giving in to that pressure.

© GETTY IMAGES/PHOTODISC

DECISION-MAKING STYLES

There are many decision-making styles among managers of sports and entertainment organizations. One method is called **autocratic decision making**. The manager makes decisions alone without consulting anyone. A second method of making decisions is called **consultative decision making**. The sports or entertainment manager shares problems and opportunities with employees. The manager calls on many others to share in the decision-making process. Consultative decision making empowers employees and holds them accountable for decisions made within the organization. The third method of making decisions is **group-oriented decision making**. A group of employees, consultants, or other managers is called upon to make decisions for the organization. All three decision-making styles are used with varying degrees of success by sports and entertainment organizations.

CHOOSING THE RIGHT ENVIRONMENT FOR DECISION MAKING

To make effective decisions, a manager must create an environment that is favorable to decision making. The manager should recognize that four factors influence the decision-making environment.

1. The personality of the manager (How experienced is the manager?)
2. The organization itself (Is the organization designed for decision making?)
3. Groups in the organization (Do groups support decision making?)
4. Relationships in the organization (How do managers and employees communicate?)

INTERMISSION

What is the difference between programmed decision making and nonprogrammed decision making?

____

____

CONDITIONS IMPACT DECISION MAKING

Managers often face conditions that alter decision making. The importance of a decision becomes clear only after events occur. Conditions that affect and alter decision making often are not under the control of the decision maker. Although some conditions are barriers to effective decision making, good managers meet these challenges head-on.

© GETTY IMAGES/PHOTODISC

COMMON DECISION-MAKING CONDITIONS

A wide range of conditions can alter the sports or entertainment manager's decision-making ability. Common conditions are (1) degrees of certainty or uncertainty, (2) the element of risk, (3) individual differences in the manager, (4) shortcuts to decision making, (5) how the manager thinks about the decision itself, and (6) barriers from within the organization. Helpful areas within the organization from which a manager can obtain advice on how to handle these conditions are the strategic development department and the human resources management department. These departments specialize in fostering good decision making.

ETHICS in Action

Title IX, which balances attention and funding devoted to male and female collegiate sports, is now 30 years old. This gender-equity law revolutionized athletics in colleges. Title IX still is hotly debated in legal, academic, and athletic circles. Perhaps it is all a question of programmed, or even intuitive, decision making. Prior to the implementation of Title IX, most decisions with respect to college athletics ignored the possibility that women's sports could be profitable. Doubt ran high that the sporting public would demand women's athletic programs. This has not proven to be the case. As the number of female athletes has grown on college campuses, the desire to watch them play also has increased. On most college campuses today, there are as many female sports programs as there are male sports programs. Expenditures for women's collegiate sports are only about one-third of those spent on men's athletics. However, the trend toward increased spending on women's athletics is favorable.

THINK CRITICALLY

1. **How are ethics involved when making decisions related to Title IX?**
2. **What do you think the future will bring for Title IX?**

Degrees of Certainty The first condition that can alter a manager's decision-making ability is whether the decision is being made in a state of certainty or uncertainty. If the manager knows exactly what will happen, then the decision is being made in a state of certainty. If the manager does not know exactly what will happen, then the decision is being made in a state of uncertainty. Most managers face conditions of uncertainty if they do not have good information about the decision. For example, if an entertainment manager of an outdoor concert knows that the sun will set at exactly 8:25 P.M., the manager can plan a fireworks show for 8:45 P.M. with the certainty that it will be dark. However, the manager will not be as certain about the weather conditions.

Risk A second condition that is commonly faced in decision making is the element of risk. If the manager, because of inadequate or incomplete information, is in doubt about a decision's outcome, then the manager is taking risk in decision making. Most managers seek to reduce or eliminate risk. This can be difficult to accomplish.

Individual Differences Because all managers perceive a decision situation differently, they may act on information about the decision situation differently. Gaining information is not always a plus. *Information overload* occurs when managers receive so much information that they become confused, hesitant, or even reluctant to make a decision. One way to understand individual differences is to have a manager chart his or her decision-making style. Is the manager's style structured and logical or intuitive and spontaneous? Style can greatly impact how managers view situations and consequences of decisions.

Shortcuts At one time or another, almost all managers take shortcuts in their decision making. These shortcuts are called *rules of thumb*. What is the rule of thumb in the following example? Most people attending a local baseball team's games begin leaving the ballpark after the seventh inning. A sports manager of concession operations decides to close soft drink and food stands after the seventh inning of each game. How did the sports manager make this decision? Was the decision based on statistical facts or observations? What if the game was against an archrival, had a close score, or went into extra innings? Would the manager's rule of thumb hurt food and beverage sales? Shortcuts, while convenient, are not always the best decision-making method.

What Managers Think Managers often "frame" decisions. In other words, each manager defines a decision in a particular way. Some managers see a decision situation as being a serious problem while others see it as minor. A manager's attention to detail and ability to see the big picture increases or decreases decision-making effectiveness. A manager's personal feelings and accountability for actions also impact decision making. Framing decisions is overcome by realizing the impact of small decisions on the outcome of bigger, future decisions.

Barriers The last condition faced by managers when making decisions is barriers within their own organization. Does the organization stimulate decision making? Does the organization reward quick and decisive decision making? Are managers afraid to make decisions because of consequences? Are organizational politics a barrier that often cannot be overcome? Answers to these questions will indicate whether the organization limits its managers' decision-making ability.

INTERMISSION

What six conditions affect a manager's decision-making ability?

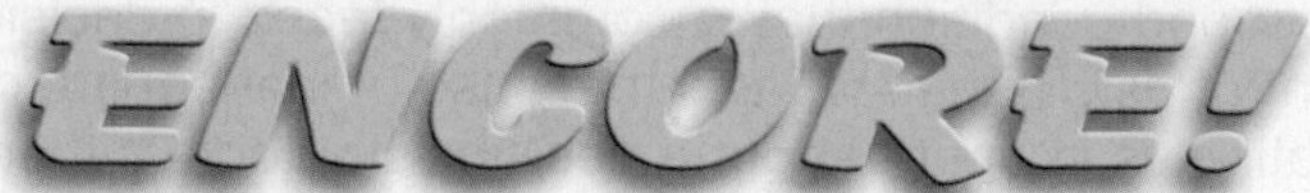

UNDERSTAND MANAGEMENT CONCEPTS

Circle the best answer for each of the following questions.

1. The best example of a rational decision-making approach is
a. the intuitive approach
b. the optimizing approach
c. the satisficing approach
d. all of the above

2. When a manager "frames" a decision, he or she
a. posts the decision on a wall
b. draws a picture of the decision process
c. assigns the decision to a subordinate
d. defines the decision in a particular way

THINK CRITICALLY

Answer the following questions as completely as possible. If necessary, use a separate sheet of paper.

3. Define decision making.

4. Marketing Management How is a programmed decision different from a nonprogrammed decision in the area of marketing management? Provide an example to illustrate your answer.

5. Illustrate a situation in which a sports manager uses the satisficing approach to make a decision. Explain your example.

6. How can organizations create barriers that prevent managers from making effective decisions?

GROUP DECISION MAKING

OPENING ACT

In many sports, the individual athlete makes decisions that impact the outcome of the game or event. However, group decision making also is important in sports. The game of rugby, for example, is dominated by group decisions. In rugby, players constantly move and interact with one another. Each player depends upon the decisions made by other team members for the ultimate success of the group. When watched from above, rugby looks like one continuous offensive and defensive decision in progress. Team members contribute to the play and make decisions to move an offensive player across the goal line. In this sport, as in many others, the win or loss is a group effort.

Work with a partner. Make a list of other sports or events where group decision making is important to the overall success. Discuss these in class.

Explain the advantages and disadvantages of group decision making.

Identify techniques for improving group decision making.

TWO HEADS ARE BETTER THAN ONE

Group decision making is important to the success of sports and entertainment management. A **group** is two or more persons who interact for some specific purpose. In the process of interacting, they influence one another. Being part of a group is different from just associating with people. A group is generally cohesive—something attracts its members. Members follow rules to be in the group. Individuals who violate group rules usually leave the group, either voluntarily or at the request of other members.

Being in a group often is not easy. You must be willing to make sacrifices beyond your personal needs. In return for these sacrifices, you can gain wisdom, friendship, and goal completion. Think about the times that you have seen group decision making in action in sports and entertainment management. Do you remember seeing a head football or basketball coach surrounded by assistant coaches? Do you remember seeing the director of an entertainment event being fed information and suggestions about camera angles and lighting? These situations were group decision making in action.

Managing sports and entertainment teams and events is a complex process. Decisions are rarely made by just one individual. Group performance is generally superior to individual performance. Groups tend to generate more ways to solve problems.

Major League Soccer's Dallas Burn has invested heavily in Spanish language broadcasting to increase its share of the Hispanic audience in Texas. This has attracted the sponsorship of a large, local car dealership. Shared goals are characteristic of effective group decision making.

ADVANTAGES AND DISADVANTAGES OF GROUP DECISION MAKING

Every successful manager needs to know when group decision making is called for and when it is not. Two heads are better than one unless the two heads want to go in opposite directions. Responsible managers must know when to encourage group initiative and when to encourage individual ambition. There are many advantages of group decision making.

- A problem is seen from several perspectives.
- More knowledge is brought to the solution process.
- Members of the group tend to take ownership and responsibility for the decision once it is conceived.
- Group members understand the decision better because they were part of the decision process.

The X Games is an extreme-sports event aimed at a late-teens and early-20s target audience. When McDonald's agreed to become a significant sponsor of the X Games, critics believed that the move would bring disappointment and disaster. Because the decision process included groups from several levels of the company, the organization presented a united front to critics. The resulting popularity of the X Games boosted McDonald's market share with the event's target audience.

Just as there are advantages to group decision making, there also are disadvantages. To illustrate these disadvantages, think about the last time you participated in a group decision-making effort. This could have been when you worked with a group on a school project. It could have been when you worked with a group to put on an event or when you made a group decision in a team sport. Regardless of the group decision-making situation, problems may have occurred.

© GETTY IMAGES/PHOTODISC

- In every group, there is usually a "bossy" individual who tries to dominate the decision-making process to suit his or her own needs.
- When groups make decisions, there is often pressure to conform to the group's decision even if you disagree.
- It is common for each group member to promote his or her own solution to a problem, even if the solution is a poor one.
- Groupthink can occur. **Groupthink** happens when group members try so hard to agree with one another that they ignore an individual member's point of view.
- Group decisions take longer to make and implement.

A good example of the problems associated with group decision making occurred in the golfing world. Female golfer Annika Sorenstam ranks among the top female golfers in the world. When she signed to play in the PGA Bank of America Colonial golf tournament in 2003, she set off a firestorm of controversy. According to tradition and rules, the PGA is for men and the WPGA is for women. Sorenstam crossed the line with her entry to play in the Colonial. Traditionalists from the PGA immediately gave hundreds of reasons why Sorenstam should not be allowed to play. Even members of the WPGA were not sure that her play in the event would be good for their sport. The PGA is an influential group with rigid rules for membership and play. Few in the group were willing to publicly disagree with tradition. However, Sorenstam played in the tournament. Though she did not make the final cut for championship play, she played well. To her credit, Sorenstam made golfing history. She challenged consensus, groupthink, and tradition. Her play in the PGA tournament influenced the golfing world to review its standards of play.

> **the Global Manager**
>
> David Beckham is not only a world-famous soccer player but also a great entertainment manager. He has made a movie to woo female soccer fans and has signed licensing deals that would make Michael Jordan proud. Beckham's soccer team, Real Madrid, is a billion-dollar enterprise that complements his merchandising and entertainment talents. Beckham earns about $80 million per year. He hopes to increase this amount by smart management of his assets and merchandising potential. Beckham is a key figure in the attempt to increase soccer's popularity in the United States. He understands that the merchandising opportunities in this country are endless.
>
> **THINK CRITICALLY**
>
> 1. How has David Beckham increased his merchandising potential?
> 2. What dangers might there be in a player or entertainer managing his or her own career?

GOOD GROUP DECISION MAKING RESULTS IN GOOD TEAMS

Unlike a typical group, a **team** defines the roles of members with respect to expectations and positions. It often even defines members' roles with respect to decision making. Managers who study group decision-making ability recognize that the positive aspects of group decision making can be transferred to teams.

The New York Yankees is not only a highly successful team but also a lucrative marketing organization. Controversial owner George Steinbrenner would agree that group decision making contributes heavily to team performance on the field and in the business office. Steinbrenner surrounds himself with business experts just as he surrounds his baseball operation with seasoned professionals. Although some people doubt

Steinbrenner's commitment to team decision making, results and success of the operation indicate otherwise. If you were to examine a list of the management team members in the Yankees' dugout or business office, you would see a "who's who" of success. The Yankees organization is the wealthiest and most profitable team in Major League Baseball. It also has accumulated more victories that any other MLB team. Simply put, the New York Yankees consistently make great baseball and business decisions.

INTERMISSION

List the advantages of group decision making.

____

____

TECHNIQUES FOR IMPROVING GROUP DECISION MAKING

Managers must foster a creative atmosphere for individuals and groups. To improve group performance, sports and entertainment managers should understand several decision-making tools. These tools are tied to the creative process necessary for a successfully run organization. If mastered, these techniques can solve many of the natural problems associated with group decision making. The five most popular group decision-making tools are

1. Brainstorming
2. The nominal group technique
3. The Delphi technique
4. Brainwriting
5. The synectics methods

Brainstorming exposes a group of people to a problem and then allows them to generate ideas for a solution. All ideas are considered. These ideas stimulate other ideas from the group. This method builds on collective thinking and makes problem solving fun. Several solution alternatives usually emerge from the use of brainstorming.

The nominal group technique, unlike brainstorming, reduces group interaction. Group members work separately in the early phases to solve the problem. They share discoveries at the end of the process. Using the nominal group technique, each group member writes proposed solutions to the problem and offers these solutions to the group. Group members vote on the best solutions and discuss the outcome of the vote. A final vote produces a solution. This method works well for groups in which interaction is awkward or difficult to achieve.

The Delphi technique is similar to the nominal group technique, but it does not include voting. Using the Delphi technique, a problem is identified. Group members then offer possible solutions by answering questionnaires about the problem. The group examines the questionnaires and reaches a consensus on a solution. A drawback to the Delphi technique is that it assumes each group member has some expertise that lends itself to problem solving.

Brainwriting asks group members to review a problem situation and write ideas for a solution on a piece of paper. Members anonymously exchange papers within the group and then build on the ideas. Brainwriting assumes that all group members can clearly express their ideas in written format.

The synectics method coaxes group members to "make the familiar strange and the strange familiar." Group members are asked to view problems using personal analogies (placing themselves in the role of a related object), symbolic analogies (viewing the problem in terms of symbols), and fantasy analogies (creating a perfect solution or best-case scenario). The synectics method is perhaps the most creative of the five group decision making techniques. It also is one of the most difficult to administer effectively.

Once group members become familiar with the various approaches to group decision making, the manager will be able to identify the technique that seems to best fit the group's personality and composition.

Have you ever been to the World Grits Festival in St. George, South Carolina? This annual spring event celebrates grits—a traditional southern dish—and the people who love them. The World Grits Festival has extended its reach and appeal by expanding its promotion to the Internet. By linking descriptions of this festival to popular search engines, travel sites, entertainment venues, and commercial transportation advertisements, the festival now is able to reach consumers outside the southern U.S.

THINK CRITICALLY

Use the Internet to find three other festival sites. Compare these sites to the World Grits Festival site for information and ease of use. Report your findings.

INTERMISSION

Why is it important for managers to understand the tools for group decision making?

____

____

UNDERSTAND MANAGEMENT CONCEPTS

Circle the best answer for each of the following questions.

1. Disadvantages of group decision making include all of the following except
  a. the tendency for "bossy" individuals to dominate the group
  b. the pressure to conform to the group's decision
  c. the lack of ownership in a group decision
  d. the likelihood of groupthink

2. A tool for enhancing group decision making that "makes the familiar strange and the strange familiar" is called
  a. the synectics method
  b. brainstorming
  c. brainwriting
  d. the Delphi technique

THINK CRITICALLY

Answer the following questions as completely as possible. If necessary, use a separate sheet of paper.

3. Technology You are in charge of designing a web site for a local festival. Which of the five group decision-making tools would you find most useful for stimulating new ideas for the web site? Explain your answer.

4. Marketing Management Form a small group. Devise a strategy for promoting one of your school's athletic teams. Your goal is to increase game attendance.

5. How can brainstorming be used to solve a problem in sports or entertainment management? Give an example.

KNOWLEDGE MANAGEMENT

OPENING ACT

Can winning records in business be transferred to winning records in sports management? AOL Time Warner executive Ted Leonsis is betting the answer is yes. Several years ago, this successful Internet and entertainment manager invested heavily in the National Hockey League's Washington Capitals. At the time of the investment, business was going poorly for the Capitals. Leonsis is now the Capitals' chairman and majority owner. He brings a variety of knowledge from AOL Time Warner to the sports business. Leonsis' challenge is to use marketing and knowledge-management techniques that worked well in the entertainment field to turn around a failing NHL franchise. His goal is to win a Stanley Cup. Only time will tell if Leonsis' knowledge and dedication are being applied correctly to the operation of the Washington Capitals.

Work with a partner. Make a list of points of knowledge from AOL Time Warner's entertainment business that might be useful in developing a winning NHL franchise. Explain your list.

Describe the concept of knowledge management.

Explain how knowledge communities can benefit sports and entertainment managers.

WHAT IS KNOWLEDGE MANAGEMENT?

Knowledge is wasted if it cannot be extracted or used during critical decision-making periods. This situation often happens in sports and entertainment management. Sports and entertainment managers attempt to make decisions by themselves, using their own knowledge exclusively rather than using the collective wisdom of the organization or industry.

© GETTY IMAGES/PHOTODISC

Knowledge management is the ability of a manager to understand what is known in his or her organization and to use that knowledge effectively. The manager must understand that there is a difference between information and knowledge. Information is simply data. Knowledge involves applying information for a useful purpose.

WHAT KNOWLEDGE DOES AN ORGANIZATION HAVE?

Knowledge can relate to tangible or intangible resources in an organization. *Tangible knowledge resources* can be licenses, such as a contract, and brands, such as the team name or event name. Tangible knowledge resources also can be database information on customers or competitors or even time-tested ways of solving problems. *Intangible knowledge resources* might be employee experiences, traditions, or the results of brainstorming sessions. When both of these knowledge resources are summarized, a sports or entertainment manager may use the knowledge to create a "best practices" portfolio to aid in making decisions.

The reason that an organization collects knowledge is to make decisions or to take action. Knowledge is constantly reviewed and revised. To be useful, knowledge should be applied to something. For example, if you have an understanding of mathematical relationships but never apply the information, this factual knowledge eventually fades and is not used to make daily decisions.

Organizations constantly struggle with the cost of obtaining information or gaining knowledge that already may be present within the company. Purchasing knowledge can be expensive. Once it is obtained, it must be used again and again.

In the past, the Miss America pageant was stereotyped as a "fluff" event made up of beautiful women in bathing suits. Pageant organizers decided that this image could be changed. They collected information that disputed the stereotype and then acted on that information. The organizers found that contestants were knowledgeable and intelligent. They also discovered that contestants were primarily interested in the scholarships offered by the event. The pageant is now built around this new knowledge.

THINK CRITICALLY

1. **How could pageant organizers use the information they found to change the pageant's stereotype?**
2. **How could the information be converted into knowledge?**

KNOWLEDGE CAN BE GENERATED

Sports and entertainment organizations use several methods to generate knowledge. First, knowledge can be bought or acquired. If country singer Faith Hill hires a songwriter who is experienced in the pop and R&B music fields, she has just acquired knowledge that might allow her to create music in these areas.

Second, we can sometimes rent knowledge. A consultant could be hired to solve a problem. This form of knowledge generation is often short-term.

Third, there can be a designated knowledge function within the organization. This function is often called research and development, or R&D. R&D commonly is used in sports organizations with scouting departments that assess new talent or follow competitive teams. Maintaining this form of knowledge generation can be expensive.

Fourth, organizations can meld one part of the business with another. If Pixar, the developer of the movie *Toy Story*, brings its computer animators together with its story development department, new ideas and knowledge about animation may result.

Fifth, knowledge is constantly growing and changing. Fostering change can generate new knowledge. Sports teams that are constantly reinventing themselves or their sport use this form of knowledge generation.

Finally, knowledge communities can be formed using the Internet and other computer technologies. This new form of network is a key ingredient in knowledge generation in the twenty-first century. Solving problems in an open format will eventually emerge as one of the best knowledge generation formats.

© GETTY IMAGES/PHOTODISC

INTERMISSION

What is knowledge management?

____

____

KNOWLEDGE COMMUNITIES

Knowledge communities can be everything from informal hallway or water-cooler conversations to formalized groups or networks on the Internet. Collective thinking usually is better than individual thinking when it comes to solving large organizational problems.

Knowledge communities create, capture, share, and maximize the use of knowledge about a particular subject. These communities provide trust, reflection, judgment, passion for learning, and exploration of the unknown. Although this may sound impressive, most communities are simple in concept. Do you often visit Internet chat rooms? If you do, you are probably part of a knowledge community. You share ideas, opinions, thoughts, complaints, likes and dislikes, and to some extent virtual friendship.

In sports and entertainment management, knowledge communities can occur within the organizations or the trade. They also can include the interested public. Many mid-level baseball executives participate in fantasy baseball leagues that are popular on the Internet. Leagues share information and knowledge about the daily problems faced by baseball managers. Executives often learn creative solutions to problems that would not have been discovered independently. Effective listening and dialogue are often the keys to successful information sharing within the knowledge community.

Public chat rooms often discuss popular television shows and other entertainment events. These discussions become springboards for new ideas. Many experts believe that the original ideas for the currently popular reality television shows came from public chat rooms.

KEYS TO SUCCESSFUL KNOWLEDGE TRANSMISSION

Knowledge is of little value to an organization if it is not used. Knowledge must be transmitted, absorbed by individuals, and used to solve problems. Successful sports and entertainment organizations have many of the following characteristics in common with respect to knowledge management.

- The organization includes an internal and external information system. The system provides appropriate tools for acquiring knowledge.
- The organization's senior managers believe in knowledge acquisition and knowledge management.
- The organization has an enlightened view toward gathering and sharing knowledge. It supports the idea that "two heads are better than one."
- The organization believes in change and pursues it by creating links between knowledge and the overall organizational mission.
- The organization encourages opportunities for learning and gaining knowledge. Employees constantly are challenged to learn new things.

INTERMISSION

Define knowledge communities and give three examples.

Lead the Way

AMERICAN IDOL

One of the most popular entertainment events of recent years is the Fox Network's *American Idol*. This unique program uses the "star search" venue to find and showcase musical talent. Although three animated and often critical judges review talent in the early phases, the national audience votes for the American idol in the latter phases of the competition. This participation process has helped to make the program a ratings success. Although critics have said that the voting process is flawed, the audience doesn't seem to be concerned.

Will *American Idol* and its unique format continue to be popular? With a television audience of nearly 40 million and auditioners in excess of 50,000, the answer appears to be yes!

THINK CRITICALLY

1. **What does *American Idol* do to involve the audience in the program?**
2. **Why do you think *American Idol* is so popular with its audience?**

UNDERSTAND MANAGEMENT CONCEPTS

Circle the best answer for each of the following questions.

1. ___?___ knowledge resources can be licenses, brands, or database information on customers or competitors.
a. Tangible
b. Intangible
c. Circular
d. Extracted

2. The reason that an organization collects knowledge is to
a. prove how smart it is
b. fulfill a government requirement
c. meet the public's need for knowledge
d. make decisions or take action

THINK CRITICALLY

Answer the following questions as completely as possible. If necessary, use a separate sheet of paper.

3. Make a list of knowledge communities that you belong to at school or at work.

____

____

4. Management Math Adding a research and development department to your organization will cost $500,000. Failure to add it will result in a $2 million shortfall in sales. What will be the net gain by adding the R&D department?

____

____

5. Technology Use the Internet to research knowledge management. List three useful web sites that explore the field.

____

____

____

6. Communication Compose a letter that supports the addition of a knowledge community to your school's web site.

____

____

REVIEW

REVIEW MANAGEMENT CONCEPTS

Write the letter of the term that matches each definition. Some terms will not be used.

____ **1.** The process of choosing actions to combat or resolve a problem

____ **2.** The ability of a manager to understand what is known in his or her organization and to use that knowledge effectively

____ **3.** Happens when group members try so hard to agree with one another that they ignore an individual member's point of view

____ **4.** Groups that create, capture, share, and maximize the use of knowledge about a particular subject

____ **5.** The process of creating and choosing alternatives to reach a goal or objective

____ **6.** Two or more persons who interact for some specific purpose and, in this interaction process, influence one another

____ **7.** Decisions that are carefully thought out and use some form of procedure that probably has been used before

____ **8.** Used when managers make decisions based primarily on guesses, hunches, or intuition

____ **9.** Occurs when managers set a minimum standard and select the first decision alternative that meets that standard

____ **10.** A group that defines the roles of members with respect to expectations and positions

____ **11.** A decision-making style whereby a manager makes decisions alone without consulting anyone

a. autocratic decision making
b. consultative decision making
c. decision making
d. group
e. group-oriented decision making
f. groupthink
g. intuitive approach
h. knowledge communities
i. knowledge management
j. nonprogrammed decisions
k. optimizing approach
l. problem solving
m. programmed decisions
n. satisficing approach
o. team

Circle the best answer.

12. Decision making is
- **a.** an inherited trait
- **b.** a skill that can be learned
- **c.** only for a chosen few
- **d.** almost always intuitive

13. If a manager has no guidance in making a decision, the decision is
- **a.** a programmed decision
- **b.** a rational decision
- **c.** a nonprogrammed decision
- **d.** none of the above

THINK CRITICALLY

14. Use the Internet to illustrate how a sports or entertainment manager could use the optimizing approach to make a decision. Explain any assumptions that the manager might make.

15. After reviewing common decision-making conditions discussed in this chapter, design a plan for making a good decision with respect to a planned school talent show. Be specific with your planning steps and the decisions you must make.

16. You are the promotions manager at a major university that is planning its 100-year anniversary. Explain how you might use a knowledge community to aid in your planning efforts.

17. Visit the web site for The Institute for the Future, and research the services offered for enhancing your knowledge. Apply this knowledge to forecast the future of a sports event or an entertainment event.

18. The members of your Student Council are exhibiting signs of groupthink in decision making. Compose a brief letter to the Student Council about the dangers of groupthink. Explain why the group should consider individual expressions.

MAKE CONNECTIONS

19. Management Math Voting in the 2003 *American Idol* talent competition's finale totaled 37 million votes. The final tally separated the two finalists by only 165,000 votes. What was the winning percentage margin for the finalist who won the competition? Given the nature of voting by telephone or via the Internet, would this margin of victory be of concern to you as a manager of the event? If so, what would you do about the problem in the future?

20. History Use the Internet to find information about the history of knowledge management. Write a one-page paper about your findings. Comment on what you perceive to be the future of the knowledge management field.

21. Communication Visit the web site for *Knowledge Management Magazine.* Using the magazine's contact method, ask the editors three questions about knowledge management. Report your findings.

22. Marketing Management Your school is starting a campus radio station and has been granted a PBS license. Design a format outlining what you will broadcast for your station's six-hour broadcast day. What promotional materials would be best to announce your school's new station to the public? Design a logo for the new station. Share the logo with your class.

23. Marketing Management Your community has just been granted an "A" league baseball franchise. An "A" league is the lowest level of professional baseball franchises and is generally a learning league for young players. Name the team, and design a logo. Identify the materials that would be best suited for promoting the new team locally. Briefly explain how the new team could use the Internet to enhance ticket sales during its first season in the community.

24. Management Math Plan a budget for implementing a Web-based knowledge community in your school. Review the equipment needed, the organizational structure for such a community (such as the usage of an intranet), costs of promotion, and any maintenance expenses.

25. Research Two popular female-oriented web sites are iVillage and the Oxygen network. Visit one of these web sites and research how the web site treats sports and entertainment for females. What information could be used from your research that would apply to other sports or entertainment audiences?

26. Marketing Management Professional sports are making strides in attracting ethnic audiences. Choose a professional sport. Describe in detail how this sport has made decisions that have led to increased involvement or interest by ethnic groups. Critique those decisions.

FEW CAN AFFORD MEMBERSHIP IN PRIVATE GOLF CLUBS

A primary barrier that prevents women and minorities from joining private golf clubs is cost. A 2003 *USA Today* survey found an average initiation fee of $48,900 for the 78 host courses on the LPGA, PGA, and Champions tours.

Monthly dues and fees, plus operating and capital expenses, can add up. The initiation fee at Trump International Golf Club in West Palm Beach, site of the LPGA's ADT Championship, is $350,000 with yearly dues of $13,000.

The 2000 census reveals that few women and minorities are able to afford such membership fees.

- Households with incomes of $100,000 or more a year are 87% Caucasian, 5% African-American, and 5% Asian. The remaining 3% are spread among "other race" categories.
- Males make up 83% of the individuals earning $100,000 or more a year.

A second barrier to female and minority membership is lack of connections. Research indicates that 67% of the private golf clubs hosting professional events require at least one existing member to sponsor a new member. Private golf club members tend to sponsor new members from among their friends.

The LPGA would like to see the game of golf grow in terms of participation, interest, fan retention, and fan creation. Old barriers and hard feelings continue to hinder progress. Some minorities are not willing to join country clubs due to a history of discrimination.

The Reverend Joseph Lowery, president emeritus of the Southern Christian Leadership Conference, was instrumental in diversifying Shoal Creek, the site of the 1990 PGA Championship. He believes that many African-Americans can afford to join country clubs. However, membership is not a high priority for them. Most minorities do not believe that it is a good investment to pay a $100,000 initiation fee to an organization where other members may not accept them.

Other Options

Private golf clubs are owned by members, corporations, or limited partnerships. A private club is not open to the public. Only members or their guests can play it.

A semiprivate club is a golf club that has private memberships. It is open to the public on specific days at specific times or for specific greens fees. Semiprivate clubs must observe all public accommodation laws.

Public golf courses are completely open to the public. Resort courses are located at a hotel or resort and are open to the public. Golfers pay daily greens fees to use the courses. Hotel or resort guests are frequently given preferential tee times and lower greens fees.

Think Critically

1. Why are women and minorities not joining private golf clubs?
2. What type of public relations campaign must take place to turn around the stereotype about golf clubs?
3. What strategy can be used to attract more fans to golf?

SPORTS AND ENTERTAINMENT MARKETING MANAGEMENT TEAM DECISION MAKING

The PGA has hired you to develop a strategy that will interest more people in golf. The purpose of your campaign is to increase female and minority memberships at private clubs. You realize that high initiation fees and annual dues are the biggest barriers to joining private clubs. Also, a history of discrimination has decreased the interest of minorities and females.

You must devise a plan to increase high school students' interest in golf. You also must develop a new type of membership plan for Highland Country Club to gain a wider variety of members, including females and minorities. Current initiation fees for Highland are $45,000, and annual fees are $12,000. You must create membership packages that are more flexible and reasonably priced.

You also are challenged to plan several events that will attract more minorities, women, and youth to Highland Country Club.

You will present your plan to the CEO of the club.

Performance Indicators Evaluated

- Understand why minority, youth, and female memberships are low for the golf club.
- Design financial packages that are more flexible for the target markets.
- Explain how the new financial packages will affect the overall budget.
- Describe special events to increase membership for the target markets.
- Explain how discriminatory stereotypes will be eliminated.

Go to the DECA web site for more detailed information.

1. What special packages will you offer to gain membership from new target markets?
2. What stereotypes will you need to break down? How will you accomplish this task?
3. What special events will you hold during the year to get new people interested in the club?
4. Outline your advertising and promotional strategies.

www.deca.org/publications/HS_Guide/guidetoc.html

CHAPTER 7

Management Strategies

© GETTY IMAGES/PHOTODISC

7.1 THE BUILDING BLOCKS OF STRATEGY
7.2 THE PROCESS OF STRATEGIC MANAGEMENT
7.3 STRATEGIC PLANNING TOOLS

© GETTY IMAGES/PHOTODISC

© GETTY IMAGES/PHOTODISC

© GETTY IMAGES/PHOTODISC

WINNING *Strategies*

ONLY THE TOUGH SURVIVE

Are you tough? If you think you are, you can enter the Grand Floridian Triathlon. Soon you will find out how tough you are. This annual event consists of a 2.4-mile swim, a 112-mile cycle, and a 26.2-mile run. These challenges almost double the distances required for Olympic competition.

The event attracts rugged individuals and teams from around the world. The Grand Floridian Triathlon separates participants into five-year age categories to ensure that the competition is fair and equal. Entrants must be at least 18 years of age to compete. The event coordinators believe that the spirit of competition and decision-making experiences are great practice for the participating athletes.

Entrants say that the challenge of competition, the ability to develop and implement strategy, and the need to prove oneself are all great reasons for competing. Most participants claim that the thinking, planning, and discipline portion of the triathlon is much more difficult than the physical portion of the event. Poor strategic decision making leads to poor performance and loss. In the Grand Floridian Triathlon, the best strategists win!

THINK CRITICALLY

1. List the various strategic decisions that a participant in the Grand Floridian Triathlon might have to make.
2. Do you think children under the age of 18 should be allowed to participate in the Grand Floridian Triathlon? Why or why not?

LESSON 7.1

THE BUILDING BLOCKS OF STRATEGY

Describe three levels of strategy.

Discuss the advantages and risks of strategic management.

OPENING ACT

Michelle Kwan is probably one of America's most famous female figure skaters, even though she has never won an Olympic gold medal. Kwan began her skating career in 1993. Since then, she has won the World Championship five times and the U.S. National Championship six times. She also has received silver and bronze medals in Olympic Games. Kwan's practice and performance strategy is to learn from every competition and work hard until a goal is met. She may never receive an Olympic gold medal, but Kwan's planning and work ethic have impressed all who follow figure skating. Kwan always tries something new in performances. This strategy has allowed her to succeed in almost all of her endeavors. The Olympic gold medal, however, is still out there. Michelle Kwan is determined to make it hers.

Work with a partner. Discuss what types of strategies a figure skater might need to employ to become successful in the sport of figure skating. Are these strategies primarily mental or physical?

THE ROOTS OF STRATEGY

Strategy is a concept that has a long and rich history. The ancient Greeks first coined the phrase more than 2,000 years ago to describe the art and science of managing military forces and military conflict. Today, *strategy* refers to the basic steps a manager must take to reach objectives or to accomplish plans. Strategies for reaching objectives and accomplishing plans are often varied and creative. Good managers learn as many strategies as possible, so that when confronted with decision-making opportunities they are prepared to act decisively.

© GETTY IMAGES/PHOTODISC

Strategic management is a process for identifying and furthering an organization's mission. Strategic management occurs when the organization matches its internal processes with its external environment. The external environment includes the forces over which the organization has little control. Strategic management is action- and goal-oriented.

THREE LEVELS OF STRATEGY

Any sports or entertainment organization can use three distinct levels of strategy. These levels address various challenges and opportunities faced by the organization. The three levels of strategy are corporate strategies, business strategies, and functional strategies. Human resources managers must know how to match the skills of managers, supervisors, and employees to each of these strategy levels.

Corporate strategies address the broad needs of the sports or entertainment organization. When CBS decides how resources will be allocated for the next budget period, managers formulate corporate strategies. These strategies are long-range in nature and are formed at the highest levels of the organization. They control the overall direction of the organization and generally are tied to the organization's mission statement.

Managers in sports and entertainment organizations generally implement four specific corporate strategies. *Growth strategies* help the organization decide the amount and direction of growth. For example, when game giant Nintendo first began operations, it focused only on video games for growth. Today, Nintendo has branched out into many other entertainment areas.

Stability strategies are used when the organization is satisfied with its performance. Stability strategies can sometimes result in indifference and loss of competitive edge. Even the best sports teams sometimes fall into the "stability trap."

Organizations often feel threatened by risk and find it necessary to use *defensive strategies*. When Disney was confronted by a growing number of entertainment competitors such as Nickelodeon, MTV, and Sesame Street, it retreated into what it knew best—cartoons and family programming. Retreat is seldom a wise long-term strategy, however, as competitors usually advance.

Organizations can use a *combination* of these strategies. For example, a Major League Baseball team could give up the idea of building a new stadium—a defensive strategy. At the same time, it could expand resources devoted to developing a four-star web site as a growth strategy.

The Internet has provided an excellent way for Disney to compete on its animation strengths. Creative programming on the Disney web site has opened the eyes and hearts of a new generation to the Magic Kingdom. Disney is once again on top of the children's entertainment market.

THINK CRITICALLY

1. **Use the Internet to locate the Disney web site. What do you think of the animation graphics? What interactive features are present on the web site?**
2. **Describe three strategies you think Disney uses to reach the children's market. Describe two strategies it uses to reach the parents' market.**

Many sports stadiums are trying out a new strategy to impress technologically oriented fans. In 2003, DirecTV began providing high-definition televisions and programming in sports stadiums.

Business strategies are narrower in scope than corporate strategies. These strategies focus on a specific business such as the licensing division of a professional sports team. Some time-tested business strategies are

1. **Cost Leadership** Deliver the product or service more cheaply than competitors.
2. **Differentiation** Be unique in product or service delivery.
3. **Focus** Concentrate on a particular market segment and surround it with a quality product or service.

Sports and entertainment organizations typically use differentiation and focus as primary business strategies. These two strategies are usually easier for the organizations to control. Costs are not as simple to control.

An illustration of how organizations have combined differentiation and focus comes from the world of sci-fi comics. Sports teams such as the Dallas Cowboys and the Boston Red Sox have asked *Spawn* creator Todd McFarlane to bring his sci-fi toy-making skills to the sports toy market. Sports teams hope that combining sound differentiation strategies with a new market focus may be just what is needed to produce more revenue from the teen market.

Functional strategies govern an organization's day-to-day operations. These strategies relate to the functions of a business, such as marketing, production, and finance. Functional strategies are directly tied to the strategies constructed at the corporate level and the business level.

Functional strategies are focused on short-term events, usually of less than one year. Functional strategies also are called *operational plans* or *tactical plans.* Because of the need for timeliness and flexibility, functional strategies are among the most important strategies.

Functional strategies are tied to corporate strategies and business strategies. For example, NASCAR made the decision to focus on the entertainment component of stock car racing as well as on the sport itself. First, NASCAR opened an office in Los Angeles to be close to entertainment opportunities. Second, NASCAR signed short-term entertainment contracts with Fox Television. This strategy ensured that NASCAR stars would have a production company to aid with brand recognition. Third, NASCAR developed specific entertainment products such as the Fox series *Fast Lane* and movies for IMAX theaters. These NASCAR functional strategies have made NASCAR drivers into national celebrities.

BRAND X PICTURES

List the three levels of strategy and give an example of each.

____

____

USING STRATEGIC MANAGEMENT

As history has shown, organizations that use strategic management are more likely to succeed in accomplishing organizational goals and objectives. However, strategic management is not always without shortcomings.

ADVANTAGES OF STRATEGIC MANAGEMENT

Managers in sports and entertainment organizations have found that five basic advantages are gained by using a strategic management approach to running their businesses.

1. *Use of strategic management prevents problems before they happen*. The entire management structure of the organization is aware of the goals and objectives necessary for success. Managers can then prevent problems before they occur.
2. *Strategic management reinforces the strength of group decision making*. Group problem solving is generally a better approach.
3. *Managers and employees tend to become empowered with decision-making opportunities*. Line managers and staff make quick decisions that allow the organization to be flexible.
4. *Strategically managed firms usually do not have glaring weaknesses*. Managers of these firms do not forget details that could cause problems in the long run.
5. *The entire organization tends to react more rapidly to new opportunities and environmental changes*. Sports teams want players to adapt quickly to changing conditions. Sports and entertainment organizations should do the same. Strategic management aids the change and reaction process.

the Global Manager

Swatch™ Group Ltd., the giant Swiss watch company, recently became one of the International Olympic Committee's worldwide sponsors. This sponsorship cost the company approximately $65 million for the 2008 Olympics. Swatch invested this lofty sum to beat out rival Seiko, a previous Olympic sponsor, for world attention and prestige. Swatch previously sponsored the 1996 and 2000 Summer Olympics with great success. Swatch's strategy for the 2008 Olympics will be to have high visibility for Swatch products. The strategy will include advertisements and plenty of Swatch-brand athletic wearables. This strategy may be a key to winning instant brand recognition.

THINK CRITICALLY

1. Why would Swatch risk $65 million to sponsor the 2008 Olympics?
2. What types of strategies will Swatch use in its promotional efforts for the 2008 Olympics?

RISKS OF STRATEGIC MANAGEMENT

Risk is something that every sports and entertainment manager must live with on a constant basis. The same is true for the manager who adopts strategic management practices. In sports and entertainment organizations, strategic management risks generally fall into one of three categories.

1. *The discipline involved in implementing strategic management may not be easy to accomplish*. For example, athletic teams often are resistant to a new way of approaching strategy in their sport.
2. *Strategic managers must be cautious of making extravagant promises*. Statements such as "we will win this year" or "we will be champions" can be difficult to fulfill. Success, like change, takes time.
3. *Managers and employees may expect immediate rewards for their roles in the strategic management process*. Even if an entertainment management team puts together a winning television series in its first year of operation, a long-term contract may not result. Success must be measured over time.

If strategic managers can control risk and manage problem solving, their organizations tend to become successful, and real change results. Patience, successful risk management, employee empowerment, and flexible problem solving sustain these organizations through most challenges.

University of Arizona softball ace Jennie Finch is helping to bridge the gap in equality between male and female athletes of the same sport. In a recent season, Finch pitched thirteen no-hitters and six perfect games. Her pitches have been clocked in excess of 70 miles per hour. Individual accomplishments such as this probably will not bring about equity in sports in the near future, but may help to even the playing field in years to come.

THINK CRITICALLY

1. **How can athletic accomplishments such as the one described above help bring about equity in sports?**
2. **Can accomplishments such as the one described above discourage equity in sports? Explain your answer.**

INTERMISSION

Why must a strategic manager understand risk?

____

____

UNDERSTAND MANAGEMENT CONCEPTS

Circle the best answer for each of the following questions.

1. A process for identifying and furthering an organization's mission is called
   a. short-term management **c.** strategic management
   b. tactical management **d.** operational management
2. Cost leadership and differentiation are examples of
   a. functional strategies **c.** corporate strategies
   b. business strategies **d.** none of the above

THINK CRITICALLY

Answer the following questions as completely as possible. If necessary, use a separate sheet of paper.

3. **Production Management** Research the history of the PGA (Professional Golfers' Association). How does the PGA produce new members for its tours? Which of the three levels of strategy would apply to this process?

   ____

   ____

   ____

4. **Marketing Management** You are in charge of developing a strategy for ensuring that graduating seniors avoid alcohol on their graduation night. Outline your strategy and how you would promote it.

   ____

   ____

5. **Technology** Design an electronic presentation for attracting a major cycling event to your city. Premier cyclist Lance Armstrong has agreed to race in the event should you be able to attract one. Your presentation must convince the event organizers that your city can use strategic management to ensure the event's success. Demonstrate your strategic management ability by designing a sound strategy for the proposed event. Be creative with your presentation.

   ____

   ____

   ____

THE PROCESS OF STRATEGIC MANAGEMENT

Identify the steps in strategic management.

Explain the development phase of the strategic management process.

Describe the action and review phases of the strategic management process.

OPENING ACT

There is a new game in town, and it is about to become big. SlamBall is played four-on-four on a full court similar to the one used in basketball. The difference is that hockey-style contact rules make dribbling in the traditional sense difficult. Innovations in moving the ball up the court are encouraged. SlamBall courts are enclosed in Plexiglas to ensure that the ball stays on the court. Players use trampolines that surround the goal and extend play up to 17 feet in the air above the court. Fans seem to love the aerial excitement and full contact. At present, there are six professional SlamBall teams. This number is expected to grow as publicity reaches potential fans.

Work with a partner to discuss the future of SlamBall. What strategies should franchise owners consider for expanding the growth of the sport? What problems will they face? How can they overcome these problems?

HOW DO MANAGERS PLAN?

Sports and entertainment managers plan by using the strategic management process. This process directs the actions of managers, employees, and the organization. The purpose of this planning effort is to reach goals and objectives that have been outlined by the organization's leaders. The strategic management process usually includes five steps.

1. Formulate the organization's mission or purpose.
2. Describe the business market that the organization will pursue.
3. Set objectives for meeting the needs of this market.
4. Create and implement strategies to address market needs better than competitors.
5. Develop contingency (backup) plans for any needed adjustments.

The steps in the strategic management process do not all happen at once. Generally, the strategic management process is made up of three major phases—development, action, and review. From these phases, managers plan strategies for success in the sports and entertainment markets.

INTERMISSION

List the steps in the strategic management process.

____

____

DEVELOPMENT

In the development phase of the strategic management process, the initial strategic plan is developed. In this phase, sports or entertainment managers develop corporate strategies and business strategies. To begin the development phase, managers must *formulate the organization's mission*. The mission of an organization reveals its purposes for being.

Forming a mission is often a difficult managerial responsibility. Most sports and entertainment organizations have business-related missions. Additionally, these organizations may be concerned with such areas as diversity, social responsibility, and fairness and truth. Consider Ben & Jerry's Ice Cream™. This company's mission could be as simple as, "We are in the business of making ice cream." Instead, the company believes that it has a social mission to aid mankind, an ecological mission to protect the Earth, and a shareholder mission to protect the money invested in the firm. Regardless of how the mission is defined, it is critical that the organization has one.

Once the mission is formulated, the managers review past and present strategies and performance. By examining what has happened and what is happening, the organization is better prepared to *describe the business market* and *set objectives*.

© GETTY IMAGES/PHOTODISC

© GETTY IMAGES/PHOTODISC

Objectives are statements that reveal the priorities of the organization. Objectives must be consistent with the organization's mission. Objectives can reveal short-term priorities of less than six months or long-term priorities of more than six months. Typical objectives address profits, service, employee relationships, and growth. An objective of a minor league hockey team such as the Houston Aeros could be to win the Calder Cup, minor league hockey's championship. However, by winning, many of the organization's players might be called up to the major league. The result would then be a rebuilding year as the reward for team success. As you can see, objectives often conflict with one another. Managers must resolve these conflicts.

POLICIES, PROCEDURES, AND RULES

To help explain the objectives of the organization to employees, a manager can use policies, procedures, and rules to provide guidance. **Policies** are guidelines established to make decisions regarding specific, recurring situations. Policies should be tied to achieving objectives. For example, the famous Title IX provisions are policies that are intended to prevent discrimination and inequality in college-level sports.

Policies are not always needed to guide an organization's direction. Procedures and rules often can be used. A **procedure** is a list of steps to be followed for performing certain work. The key to a procedure is that there is some order to the steps. If the steps are followed, a specific result will occur. Policies often lack details. Procedures add these details.

Rules are a prescribed direction for conduct. Rules leave little to the imagination and often constrain decision making. "No running in the hallway" means no running in the hallway. Rules can be random since they do not have a sequence of steps to follow. To be useful, rules must be organized, or they will be forgotten. Remember that the primary purpose of policies, procedures, and rules is to provide guidance and direction.

ENVIRONMENTAL ANALYSIS

Managers have developed specific tools for assessing the environments they confront as they attempt to make decisions. These tools can be applied to the study of the external environment or the internal environment.

External Environment The **external environment** is characterized as being everything that lies outside an organization's control. A sports manager must be aware that government regulations, the economy, competition, technology, global affairs, and society at large are beyond the organization's control. However, by analyzing what is going on in these external environments, the sports manager can be better prepared to meet any unforeseen challenges. For example, Major League Baseball has suffered a drop in attendance in recent years, due in part to a sluggish economy. The Commissioner of Baseball and team owners must be aware of this environmental threat when meeting to address pricing, league expansion, labor practices, or skyrocketing franchise fees. Entertainment managers face similar external environmental conditions.

A manager of an entertainment event must be aware of local legal policies, broadcast or Internet regulations, the economy, and competition. Society's view toward the event, cultural or moral standards of conduct, and public pressure groups can also impact the entertainment organization. Organizers of the Mrs. America pageant face different external environmental conditions than do those of the Miss America pageant. In fact, any broadcast pageant cannot be considered to have the same external environment. The Mrs. America pageant appeals to a different audience, attracts different sponsors, and has different competitors. The Mrs. America pageant also comes under the eye of different public interest groups than other talent, beauty, or scholarship contests.

Internal Environment The **internal environment** concerns factors that are under the control of the organization. Managers must continually assess the internal environment for changes in performance, adherence to standards, accomplishment of objectives and goals, and good business practice.

Internal assessment is often a difficult task for managers. The organization may not have a system for analyzing its internal environment. Reports may not be completed, data may go uncollected, falsifications may occur, or employees simply may not care.

Assume that an event was held at your school honoring the accomplishments of females in the senior class. Based on ticket sales, the event was deemed a success. However, upon reflection, organizers might not be so sure of this. If an internal assessment of the event was completed, it might reveal that honorees were from a select class of students. Therefore, the event did not reflect the accomplishments of all females in the senior class. A negative impact on the event could have been caused by a lack of racial diversity or a lack of balance between honorees (for example, all were athletes or members of the student council). Flawed measurement standards (only grade point average or school popularity was considered) or judging bias (the selection committee was small and unaware of all possible recipients) could also negatively impact the event. Although the event was thought to be successful, many students might have felt left out. Without correction, the success of future events might be in jeopardy. Constant internal assessment is a valuable tool to prevent organizational failure.

© GETTY IMAGES/PHOTODISC

COMPLETING THE DEVELOPMENT PHASE

The development phase is essential to good strategic management. This phase of the strategic management process involves

- Formulating the organization's mission
- Reviewing past and present strategies for success and failure
- Using strategic tools to assess the organization's external and internal environments

Sports and entertainment managers agree that time spent in the development phase can identify, if not prevent, problems that could jeopardize success in later strategic management phases.

INTERMISSION

Explain the differences among policies, procedures, and rules.

ACTION AND REVIEW

After the development phase of the strategic management process is completed, sports and entertainment managers are ready to *create and implement strategies*. Once the corporate strategies and business strategies are developed to help the organization reach its goals and objectives, it is time to take action. Implementing the strategies often is one of the hardest tasks imposed on managers. Best-laid plans often go astray, making implementation difficult to achieve.

Several NBA teams are experimenting with a new strategy for rewarding fans—team "swipe cards." Fans who swipe their team cards at kiosks when they attend games receive bonuses and discounts.

ACTION PHASE

Three events normally take place in the initiation of action. First, an appropriate organizational structure must be present. Second, short-range goals or objectives must be constructed and implemented. Long-range goals and objectives then are more likely to be achieved.

Finally, functional strategies must be constructed in critical areas such as accounting, marketing, production, promotion, pricing, distribution, and information systems. Each of these areas needs to adapt its particular function to the overall goals and objectives of the organization. Managers must watch for consistency among these functional levels. For example, if promotion promises great service but production delivers something less, then the sports fan or entertainment customer will begin to doubt the sincerity of the organization.

REVIEW PHASE

Review, evaluation, and control help to ensure that all significant goals and objectives are met. Progress measurement is the key to accomplishing strategies. This process helps to identify those strategies that have worked and those that have not. Additionally, managers can discover the causes behind poor performance. Managers learn from success and failure. Both measures are important. Good sports and entertainment managers are proactive. They anticipate problems, develop contingency (backup) plans, and meet the obstacles head on.

Athletes and entertainers constantly assess their individual and team performances. Managers of sports and entertainment organizations must do the same. The ultimate purposes of strategic management are to

- Continuously evaluate and respond to external and internal environmental changes
- Examine strategies for correct direction and successful results
- Organize people in the most effective and efficient manner

Significant competitive advantages can be achieved if the strategic management process is completed successfully.

INTERMISSION

Why is the review phase important to the strategic management process?

___

___

Lead the Way

ARTURO MORENO

Arturo (Arte) Moreno is the owner of the California Angels. This Hispanic-American businessman bought the baseball franchise from the Walt Disney Company for a reported $180 million. Moreno expects that his ownership of an MLB team will signal that ownership of major sports franchises by minorities is long overdue. The NFL and MLB have lagged behind the NBA in minority ownership.

Moreno was one of the original investors in the Arizona Diamondbacks. With a background in marketing and outdoor advertising, he is aware of the power of communication for accomplishing goals, objectives, and strategies.

Moreno hopes that his understanding of the Hispanic community will help the Angels increase its fan base among this market. Moreno plans to hire bilingual ticket takers and ushers for Angels home games to assist with the anticipated increase of Hispanic fans. He also plans to make changes in the front office that will enhance the team's appeal to the Hispanic market. However, Moreno pledges not to forget that baseball is for all markets.

THINK CRITICALLY

1. **What impact is Arte Moreno likely to have on Major League Baseball?**
2. **What strategies might Moreno use to increase fan support?**

UNDERSTANDING MANAGEMENT CONCEPTS

Circle the best answer for each of the following questions.

1. The first phase of the strategic management process is the
a. action phase **c.** tactical phase
b. review phase **d.** development phase

2. Statements that reveal the priorities of the organization are called
a. procedures **c.** objectives
b. policies **d.** strategies

THINK CRITICALLY

Answer the following questions as completely as possible. If necessary, use a separate sheet of paper.

3. Marketing Management Assume that you are the marketing manager for an NBA franchise. Develop a policy for licensing your team's merchandise.

____

____

____

4. Technology Using the Internet, locate the management rosters of an NFL, NBA, and MLB team. Count the number of women who could be considered in top management positions. List these female managers. Comment on which team is doing the best job of balancing the management workforce.

____

____

____

5. Communication You are a newly hired publicist for the Seattle Mariners baseball team. You have been given the assignment of publicizing the achievements of the team's Asian and Hispanic baseball players in the hopes of increasing attendance among these minorities at home games. What external environmental factors would you research to determine if this would be a sound marketing strategy for the team? Explain your answer.

____

____

____

STRATEGIC PLANNING TOOLS

Describe the major strategic planning tools available to managers.

Explain how sports and entertainment managers may achieve strategic fit.

OPENING ACT

There are few entertainment managers who are as successful as Oprah Winfrey. This dynamic talk-show host and actress also is chairman of Harpo Productions, which includes studios, film production, print, and video businesses. Winfrey is the wealthiest and most successful of all African-American female businesswomen. However, wealth and power are not what make her a successful manager. Winfrey excels at identifying problems and developing creative solutions to solve those problems. Through the years, she has learned to use many managerial tools to aid in planning efforts for her companies. Winfrey was among the first entertainment managers to see the value of a multimedia approach to her industry. She also was among the first to embrace the power of the Internet as a new entertainment medium. Her Oxygen Network is among the most popular female-oriented web sites today.

Work with a partner to discuss how Oprah Winfrey has achieved success in entertainment management. Characterize Winfrey's management style. What planning tools do you think she uses to manage her enterprises?

THE PLANNING TOOL BAG

Effective managers must be able to see the future of the organization and react to it in decisive ways. Managers are not fortunetellers. However, they do use specific planning tools to help them reveal what will most likely happen in the future.

Successful sports and entertainment managers recognize that some futures are more predictable than others. They know that strategic planning tools can be used to improve predictive powers. There is usually not just one future. In reality, several futures are possible depending on what actions a manager takes.

© GETTY IMAGES/PHOTODISC

Though many planning tools are available to managers of sports and entertainment organizations, four specific tools are significant. These tools are environmental scanning, SWOT analysis, benchmarking, and scenario building.

ENVIRONMENTAL SCANNING

Managers are confronted with two environments—the external environment and the internal environment. For strategic planning purposes, the external environment presents the greatest challenge because of its many unknowns. **Environmental scanning** is a strategic planning tool that helps managers identify critical events from the external environment that will have a direct impact on decision making. These critical events may be known or unknown at the time of environmental scanning. Environmental scanning also can be seen as an information discovery process.

The sports and entertainment industries have six major external environments that might create opportunities for or pose threats to future planning efforts. The external environments are

1. Demographic trends
2. Economic trends
3. Political trends
4. Competitive trends
5. Technological trends
6. Cultural and lifestyle trends

Demographic trends show how market forces are changing. For example, Americans are aging, there are more women than men in the U.S., the Hispanic-American population has surpassed the African-American population in numbers, and people are living longer. By themselves, these trends may just be interesting facts. However, when the trends are applied to specific sports or entertainment problems and opportunities, planning aids may result. NASCAR discovered several years ago that the number of female fans was increasing at a higher rate than the number of male fans. NASCAR acted on this fact by creating more services for female fans, including more restroom facilities at raceways.

Economic trends indicate the general state of the economy and how this state might influence decisions made by sports and entertainment managers. These trends might affect ticket prices, wages and salaries of employees, and the cost of resources. They also might determine whether business expansion is justified.

Cereal companies have long been sponsors of major athletic and entertainment events. The logic of this strategy is simple for the cereal companies. They find health-oriented or active consumers and make a product pitch to a captive audience. This formula has worked for a number of years. However, some people have started to question the fit between cereals, a healthy lifestyle, and sports and entertainment events. Cereal companies may not be producing products that really match these intended audiences' needs. Some of the most popular and widely advertised cereals today are those that come with freeze-dried fruits. These "healthy lifestyle" products often have as much as ten times the sugar of fruit-free versions. Is this really the path to a healthy lifestyle?

THINK CRITICALLY

1. **What is the ethical issue in this story?**
2. **Are cereal companies good sponsors for sports and entertainment events? Explain your answer.**

© GETTY IMAGES/PHOTODISC

Political trends are reported almost daily in the media, but managers need more information than is provided by the national press. Sports and entertainment organizations, like all businesses, are regulated to some extent. If possible, the organizations would like to have an impact on that regulation. For this reason, managers are wise to stay abreast of political changes and trends.

Competitive trends are critical to the success of an organization. Most sports and entertainment managers know who their main competitors are and what they are doing. Analyzing secondary competition also has become important. In some instances, a sports franchise's main competitor may not be another sports franchise. It may be the local movie theater. Successful managers develop means to constantly scan competitors.

Technological trends impact the sports and entertainment industries in profound ways. Fans now demand technological services at sporting venues and other places where entertainment events take place. Viewing standards change yearly. Big-screen viewing and instant replays, whether at a ballgame or at a concert, are now standard.

Cultural and lifestyle trends of the marketplace must be tracked. Television show producers have learned, sometimes painfully, that tastes and preferences among viewers do change. Today's hit is tomorrow's flop. Successful organizations have specific plans for assessing cultural and lifestyle changes.

SWOT ANALYSIS

SWOT analysis is a strategic planning tool for analyzing the **S**trengths, **W**eaknesses, **O**pportunities, and **T**hreats of an organization. Honesty is a key to the successful use of this tool. When used correctly, SWOT analysis can be a valuable strategic planning aid.

In the strengths category, a manager might list player or entertainment talent, popularity with fans, flexible decision making, and employee loyalty. If these areas are real strengths, the organization can build upon these strengths when developing strategies.

In the weaknesses category, a manager might list personnel problems, falling revenues, weak market image, or poor management decisions. The organization must address weaknesses and fix them. If weaknesses cannot be fixed, planning must compensate for the weaknesses.

© GETTY IMAGES/PHOTODISC

In the opportunities category, a manager might list the power of the Internet, licensing opportunities, global expansion, or improvements in the general economy. The manager should be ready to capitalize on opportunities.

Finally, the manager must list perceived threats to the organization. These threats could be aggressive competition, lawsuits, labor troubles, or declining popularity with fans. Plans should be constructed to meet threats.

BENCHMARKING

Successful companies often can learn from other successful companies, even if they are competitors. **Benchmarking** is a planning process whereby an organization learns from "best practices" within its industry or from other successful companies. The benchmarking process should follow four simple guidelines in order to be effective.

1. Have a specific problem in mind that should be compared to other organizations.
2. Make sure that the correct "best practices" or benchmarks are identified.
3. Do not expect too many answers from sensitive areas such as pricing, revenues, or managerial discipline.
4. Keep the data received confidential to ensure that strategies can be built upon the information.

Benchmarking is used when athletes learn from competitive counterparts, when coaches copy and modify successful plays of competitors, and when entertainers match the styles of industry leaders.

SCENARIO BUILDING

How many times do you say "what if" when making plans? Or maybe you say, "Well, under the best-case scenario, I would do this." Most sports and entertainment managers do the same thing when preparing to make decisions. This process is called **scenario building**. Building a scenario involves creating a hypothetical situation that is then used to aid decision-making efforts. The scenario often reveals alternatives that would have gone unnoticed under other decision-making models.

The military and law enforcement agencies use scenarios to practice responses to events that have not yet happened. Sports managers do the same thing in spring training and endless practice sessions. The question "What do you do when. . .?" is a form of scenario building.

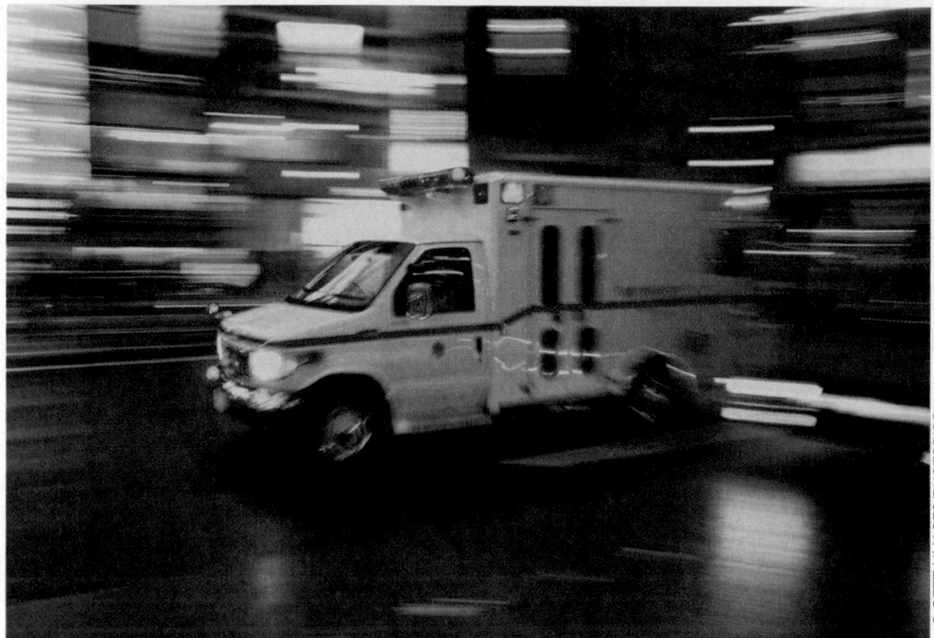
© GETTY IMAGES/PHOTODISC

Scenario building forces strategic managers to think creatively. The result prepares managers to face difficult problems and provides a means of testing managerial response to those difficult situations. For example, every entertainment event manager must be prepared for the worst-case scenario. This could be an accident, a fire, an act of terrorism, or a death. Merely having emergency medical service facilities available is no longer the only responsibility of the entertainment manager. The good manager tries to predict the unknown and devises a plan for dealing with it.

USING THE TOOL BAG

Various techniques are available to sports and entertainment managers who wish to improve their strategic planning efforts. Managers know that experience is a valuable guide. Experience must be shared so that future managers can profit from successes and mistakes that came before them. Strategic planning will significantly improve if managers

- Use strategic planning tools
- Keep abreast of changes in technology
- Discuss strategies with peers on a daily basis
- Remain receptive to new ideas about how to make decisions

In most cases, practice does improve managerial performance. Follow the advice of successful managers—practice, practice, practice!

INTERMISSION

How is benchmarking different from scenario building?

____

____

A GOOD FIT

Experienced sports and entertainment managers have found that devising a plan is not enough to ensure success in meeting organizational goals and objectives. It also is necessary to match those plans to all of the organization's activities. The manager must strive for consistency and continuity in planning and strategic efforts. The goal is known as **strategic fit**. Strategic fit, however, can be elusive.

Consider the following problem involving the lack of strategic fit that might be faced by a sports manager. The merchandising and licensing department of a sports franchise has developed an excellent growth strategy. This new strategy will achieve merchandise sales growth by licensing the franchise symbol to regional and national merchants. Unless this strategy can be matched with previous strategies or with strategies from other departments, strategic fit will not be achieved. Overall performance will be less than adequate.

How could misfit or mismatch occur? If we assume that previous merchandising and licensing strategies included local merchants, the proposed growth strategy might hurt these existing relationships because of new competition. Since many of the local merchants might be involved in ticket sales to the public, jeopardizing relationships with them may be a poor strategy. These merchants may decide to reduce efforts directed toward ticket sales. They may feel that the sports organization failed to show loyalty toward the local merchants with the proposed growth strategy. Because of these conflicts, the sports manager may find that the new merchandising and licensing strategy actually achieves less sales growth than the previous strategies. Strategic fit is not achieved, and organizational goals suffer.

TYPES OF STRATEGIC FIT

Three general types of strategic fit are possible for most sports and entertainment organizations. First, market-related strategic fit can be achieved. Common ways to achieve this form of strategic fit would be to

- Share sales force activities with other departments
- Share after-sale service responsibilities
- Allow the organization's brand name to be matched with other brand names
- Share advertising and promotional activities among departments
- Find common distribution channels that can be used by more than one element of the organization
- Share order processing and purchasing responsibilities

Second, a strategic fit can be achieved among operational departments within the organization. For example, departments can commit to purchasing via the Internet whenever possible. They also can use common suppliers to achieve volume discounts, share shipping vendors, and split the administrative costs for operations.

The U.S. Olympic Committee has authorized only two companies to sell tickets to the 2004 Summer Games in Athens. This plan may lack strategic fit with the committee's objective to raise attendance to the Games. Because of high demand, a fan might have to spend as much as $20,000 to guarantee a front-row seat throughout a popular event such as basketball or gymnastics.

© DIGITAL VISION

Finally, management itself becomes part of the strategic fit goal. Managers can offer advice and experience to other departments or units that could benefit from such assistance. Many entertainment organizations require that middle- and upper-level managers work in other departments for a short time each year. This practice helps the managers see problems as others see them. It also acquaints each manager with a sense of the whole organization. This practice not only makes strategic fit a goal but also helps to make it a reality.

BENEFITS OF STRATEGIC FIT

There is logic to why sports and entertainment managers should strive for strategic fit within the organization. Among the most visible reasons are

- Reduced conflict between marketing and sales functions
- Balance in communication and promotional efforts
- Maximum utilization of equipment
- Efficient utilization of the workforce
- Harmony with suppliers and distributors
- Regulation and sequencing of ordering and inventory cycles
- Direction for support services

Management also is able to transfer its knowledge, experience, and ideas to other managers within the organization.

Strategic fit is a worthy goal because it is a great competitive weapon. Most sports and entertainment managers find that many organizations in their industries never achieve strategic fit. Organizations that recognize the benefits of strategic fit have a real edge over competitors.

INTERMISSION

What are the three common types of strategic fit available to sports and entertainment managers?

____

____

ENCORE!

UNDERSTANDING MANAGEMENT CONCEPTS

Circle the best answer for each of the following questions.

1. ___?___ deals primarily with examining demographic, economic, political, competitive, technological, and cultural and lifestyle trends.

a. Environmental scanning
b. SWOT analysis
c. Benchmarking
d. Scenario building

2. The "S" in SWOT analysis stands for

a. survey
b. strategy
c. strengths
d. sports

THINK CRITICALLY

Answer the following questions as completely as possible. If necessary, use a separate sheet of paper.

3. Technology Use the Internet to find three articles that discuss how sports managers develop strategies. What are the main points covered in each article? Write a paragraph for each article.

4. Management Math You are a purchasing manager for a theater. You must purchase costumes from one of two companies. Company A is willing to sell the needed costumes for $20,000, but it offers no discounts. Company B sells the costumes for $22,500, but it offers an 11 percent discount if the account is paid within 30 days. Which firm offers your theater the better deal? Explain your answer.

5. Research Use the Internet to research benchmarking. Write a one-page paper on this strategic planning tool. Cite specific examples of companies that are commonly benchmarked.

REVIEW MANAGEMENT CONCEPTS

Write the letter of the term that matches each definition. Some terms will not be used.

____ **1.** Consistency and continuity in planning and strategic efforts
____ **2.** A planning process whereby an organization learns from "best practices" within its industry
____ **3.** Everything that lies outside an organization's control
____ **4.** A process for identifying and furthering an organization's mission
____ **5.** Guidelines established to make decisions regarding specific, recurring situations
____ **6.** Long-range strategies that are formed at the highest levels of the organization
____ **7.** Factors that are under the control of the sports or entertainment organization
____ **8.** Strategies that govern an organization's day-to-day operations
____ **9.** A strategic planning tool for analyzing the strengths, weaknesses, opportunities, and threats of an organization
____**10.** The process of creating a hypothetical situation that is then used to aid decision-making efforts

a. benchmarking
b. business strategies
c. environmental scanning
d. external environment
e. functional strategies
f. corporate strategies
g. internal environment
h. policies
i. procedures
j. rules
k. scenario building
l. strategic fit
m. strategic management
n. SWOT analysis

Circle the best answer.

11. Which of the following is not a characteristic of a corporate strategy?
a. long-range in nature
b. formed at the highest levels of the organization
c. relates directly to the functions of the organization
d. controls the overall direction of the organization

12. The strategic management process normally begins with
a. setting objectives
b. formulating a mission
c. creating strategies
d. developing contingency plans

13. Time-tested business strategies include
a. differentiation
b. focus
c. cost leadership
d. all of the above

THINK CRITICALLY

14. Describe the three levels of strategy. Demonstrate these levels by applying them to a goal of forming a DECA club at your school.

15. Describe which of the three business strategies described in Lesson 7.1 would be most appropriate for a sports league that wished to expand operations to Japan, China, and Korea. Explain your choice.

16. Discuss the advantages and the risks of implementing strategic management in an organization.

17. Search newspapers, magazines, or the Internet to find articles about how the external environment impacts your favorite sports team. Be specific in your comments.

18. Design a collage or poster with pictures that demonstrates an environmental scan of forces that might impact your favorite band's admission into the Rock and Roll Hall of Fame.

MAKE CONNECTIONS

19. Management Math You are in charge of buying press gifts for the reporters covering a news conference to introduce the latest Jennifer Lopez film. You could choose a Sony Walkman for $19, a Nokia picture phone for $89, or a small hand-held tape recorder for $35. Which press gift would be best? Justify your choice and the cost of the item.

20. Technology Use the Internet to find the mission statements of three entertainment organizations. Compare the three mission statements and point out the similarities and differences.

21. Communication You are a talent scout for a new reality television show that follows students during their freshman year of college. The show will focus on relationships, classes, and dorm life. Write a memo to your supervisor outlining specific activities that you would like to film and explaining what you wish to communicate with these scenes.

22. Marketing Management You are in charge of convincing your city's civic leaders, business leaders, and citizens that your city would be a great location for the annual H.O.G.S. convention for Harley-Davidson motorcycle owners. This would primarily be an open-air event in a local park for approximately 25,000 bikers. Create an electronic presentation designed to accomplish the goal of gaining approval for the event.

23. Marketing Management You are the promotions manager for a local charity benefit concert. The event has been cancelled twice in the past year due to bad weather and illness of the band's lead singer. Devise a promotional strategy to encourage ticket sales and restore confidence among fans. What would you do if the concert were cancelled again?

24. History Investigate famous female drivers in auto racing by using an Internet search engine to acquire information about these daring women. Write a one-page paper detailing your discoveries.

25. Production Management You are impressed with the growing success of the new sport SlamBall. You would like to develop another game that would combine elements of existing sports with new, more action-oriented features. You also want to focus on attracting the teenage and young adult markets. Describe your proposed new sports game. What strategic planning tools did you use to develop your plan?

26. Communication You have been hired as a strategic planner for a newly proposed professional water polo league. Considering what you have learned about the strategic management process, outline a plan for bringing this new league to the public. Use the Internet to conduct research on water polo before you begin your planning efforts.

CASE STUDY

DECA PREP

CREATING A SUCCESSFUL SITCOM

What has happened to the blockbuster sitcoms that used to fill the television networks? Each year since 1994 when *Friends* debuted, major networks have promised that the next big sitcom hit was just a season away.

When sitcoms dominated the television schedule, viewers were told that there were too many shows diluting the audience and the talent supply. Today, sitcoms are in shorter supply. Networks claim that there are not enough time slots, so writers aren't given a chance to develop their talents. The television audience has become splintered, the competition has increased, and the best creative talents seem to be more interested in dramas.

The fall of sitcoms has been dramatic. At the end of *Seinfeld's* final season in 1998, six sitcoms were ranked in the top ten shows being watched. During 2003, only two sitcoms had reached that level—*Friends* and *Everybody Loves Raymond.* The only time in history when sitcoms have fared worse was in 1983 when *Kate & Allie* was the only comedy to hit the top-ten list.

The Cosby Show revived sitcoms in 1984. *The Cosby Show* was an old-fashioned, family sitcom with loving parents who were in control. This show gave respect to the African-American middle class, which had been overlooked in shows like *Good Times* and *The Jeffersons.*

Successful sitcoms write about life in a humorous way. *Seinfeld* was the highest-ranked show from 1990 to 1998. Sitcoms like *Cheers* create great characters. Even people who can't remember the details of any *Cheers* episode probably can tell you something about Sam, Diane, Carla, Coach, Norm, and Cliff.

Some sitcoms have specific political messages, like *Designing Women,* which had things to say about the treatment of American women. Others are centered around past eras or historical events. *Happy Days* took us back to the 1950s, a time of bobby socks, leather jackets, and youthful innocence. *M*A*S*H* relived the experiences of medical military personnel in the Korean War.

Winning sitcoms take risks, like *All in the Family* (1971–1983), the highest-ranked sitcom ever. This show was not afraid to take on every difficult '70s social issue. It addressed racial bigotry at a time when racial tensions were at their height.

The Golden Girls was a big hit because it valued experience. *The Golden Girls* attracted audiences of all ages with the life experiences of its characters and the work experience of a heavyweight cast.

Successful sitcoms like *The Mary Tyler Moore Show* are patient. The show was not an instant hit and did not soar until its characters had time to deepen. Sitcoms like *I Love Lucy* know how to be funny. The writing and supporting cast for this long-term success story were superb.

By watching the ratings, good sitcoms like *The Dick Van Dyke Show* (1961–66) know when to call it quits. Although ratings had gone down, the quality of *The Dick Van Dyke Show* had not diminished when the show ended its run.

Creating a sitcom is not easy, but it may be time to return to the basics. Numerous television viewers are turning to cable stations to view reruns of old sitcoms. Success may depend upon taking cues from previous sitcom hits.

Think Critically

1. **List the characteristics for sitcom successes.**
2. **Why are sitcoms not so popular today?**
3. **Do sitcoms have a chance to make a big comeback today? Why or why not?**

SPORTS AND ENTERTAINMENT MARKETING MANAGEMENT TEAM DECISION MAKING

A major television network has hired you to put together a promotional package that advertises "The Greatest Sitcoms." The shows will air every weekday during the last week in February. You must first choose at least two sitcoms for each night of the week. Then you must create television, newspaper, and other promotions to attract large television audiences. The purpose of this week-long sitcom series is to rekindle television viewers' interests and to develop new sitcoms that will be equally popular. You are trying to move away from fads like reality television.

Performance Indicators Evaluated

- Describe the target markets for this project.
- Define the overall purpose of this promotional campaign.
- Explain the rationale for the television shows chosen.
- Describe special promotions and how they will reach the largest possible target markets.
- Explain the mindset you are trying to develop in television viewers.

Go to the DECA web site for more detailed information.

1. Devise at least five creative strategies to increase audience interest in the week-long marathon of old sitcoms.
2. What variety of sitcoms will you show each night? Why?
3. How will you measure audience feedback to this special promotion?
4. Outline your promotional and survey strategies.

www.deca.org/publications/HS_Guide/guidetoc.html

CHAPTER 8

Organizing and Staffing

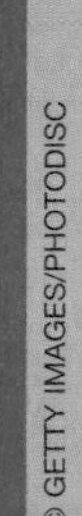

8.1 COORDINATING FOR SUCCESS
8.2 NETWORKING AND DELEGATING
8.3 MANAGEMENT CAREERS IN SPORTS AND ENTERTAINMENT

© GETTY IMAGES/PHOTODISC

WINNING Strategies

A MOVING EXPERIENCE

Carol "Gil" Gilson began his career in the entertainment industry in the early 1960s. His first opportunity was a job offer from Disney. A later break to work with commercials marked the start of his career in the film industry. He continued to work on commercial sets for three years.

Gilson eventually switched from working on commercial sets to "driving" dressing rooms for television shows and movies. In the 1960s, television and movie stars were transported from set to set in small motor homes.

In late 1970, Gilson became a captain of transportation on the set of the television show, *Streets of San Francisco*. As captain, Gilson met daily with the director to read over the script. He had to pay close attention to the scenes involving stunt cars, drivers, or anything transportation-related. He was the person responsible for locating a particular make, model, and color of a car for specific scenes. He managed all transportation-related aspects of the show.

Gilson retired in 1989. He still has many great memories of the entertainment business. Gilson's career allowed him to see the cowboy country of West Texas, the mountains of Georgia, and many other scenes across the United States.

THINK CRITICALLY

1. What are the benefits and drawbacks of working on location in the entertainment industry?
2. What qualities are needed to be a captain of transportation?

LESSON 8.1

COORDINATING FOR SUCCESS

Define human resources management and identify human resources management activities.

Describe the procedure to recruit and hire the best personnel.

Explain why coordinating and giving feedback are important responsibilities of human resources management.

OPENING ACT

True Value Hardware was losing its share of the home-improvement market. To gain more visibility, the company undertook an ambitious marketing strategy from 1996 through 1998. True Value realized the importance of relationship marketing. It took advantage of the popularity of sports to restore its position in the hardware market. True Value Hardware paid each NFL team $150,000 for the right to undertake a unique project. NFL quarterbacks dipped helmets and footballs in paint and threw them against a canvas. The resulting works were sold as True Value "art." True Value also became the official sponsor of opening day for Major League Baseball (MLB). It provided each MLB stadium with 30,000 to 50,000 balls containing facts about each team. Fans were excited to receive the collector's item at the end of the game.

Discuss with a partner other ways that a company like True Value can become more visible.

MANAGING HUMAN RESOURCES EFFECTIVELY

A business is only as good as the people it employs. **Human resources management** consists of all activities that are involved with hiring, developing, and paying the individuals responsible for doing the organization's work.

Satisfied employees are more likely to contribute to a successful team effort. Many factors influence employees' productivity, performance, and years of employment. These factors include salary, benefits, training, and work environment. Company loyalty often depends upon the trust that the employee will have future job security. Layoffs and reductions in the workforce diminish that loyalty.

HUMAN RESOURCES ACTIVITIES

Human resources activities include recruiting, hiring, and training the best employees. The organization must ensure that employees feel a part of the team. The company also must supply workers with the equipment and resources necessary to meet the organization's goals. These resources include job descriptions, policies, and company procedures.

WHAT'S IMPORTANT TO EMPLOYEES?

Financial security is a big issue for most people. Salaries and benefits for employees make up a large portion of every company's budget. Employees' salaries are based upon what competitors are paying as well as the area's economy. For example, the cost of living is much higher in Los Angeles than in Kansas City, Missouri. The higher cost of living results in higher pay in Los Angeles.

Benefits are equally important to workers. **Fringe benefits** are items in addition to pay that employees receive in exchange for their labor. Full-time employees are more likely than part-time employees to receive fringe benefits. Health insurance is an important fringe benefit because health care can be expensive. Paid vacations and personal leave are additional fringe benefits provided to full-time employees. Sports and entertainment management positions often include the fringe benefits of attending events and socializing with celebrities.

TIME OUT

Suppose you make a salary of $40,000 in Kansas City, Missouri. You would need to make $45,900 in Los Angeles to have the same spending ability, due to the higher cost of living.

INTERMISSION

How can the human resources department increase employee loyalty?

____

____

HIRING THE BEST PERSONNEL

All activities required to maintain an adequate number of qualified employees for the company are collectively known as **employment**. Employment involves matching people with the best skills for each job. Training and development programs for a new employee are costly. Selecting the best match for a job is financially important for a company.

MONEY AND TIME

Sports and entertainment businesses are no different from other companies that operate under tight budgets. A manager must prove a need for a new employee. This proof helps persuade financial planners to include the cost associated with the new hire in the budget. The manager works with the human resources department to complete the hiring process. A job description is written to list the basic tasks of the job. A **job specification** is also written that lists all qualifications a worker needs to successfully complete the job.

© GETTY IMAGES/PHOTODISC

The sports and entertainment industry is highly competitive. Many individuals get their foot in the door by taking part in internships. These experiences allow ambitious people to prove that they are dedicated workers. Employees must be willing to put in the necessary hours to successfully produce a big event. Managers of professional sports, theme parks, and other entertainment venues work long hours. Sixty- to eighty-hour workweeks are common during the busiest seasons. Productive and enthusiastic interns are often rewarded with full-time positions. The company does not want to lose them to a competitor.

RECRUITING APPLICANTS

Future employees are recruited through recommendations from current employees, employment agencies, and applications. Colleges have placement offices that help graduates find jobs. Advertising is commonly used to attract applicants. Ads are no longer just included in newspapers and professional publications. Numerous web sites list job openings and descriptions.

Sports and entertainment management is a highly competitive field. It is not unusual for some of the more popular positions to attract hundreds of applicants. To select the best candidate for the position, the human resources department reviews all applications. A detailed job specification makes it more likely that only qualified individuals will apply for a position.

Job applicants must understand the importance of the resume and cover letter. A *resume* is a summary of an applicant's previous and current job experiences. A *cover letter* explains why the applicant is qualified for the position and requests an interview. It is important that the resume and cover letter are well written. A candidate who sends a resume and cover letter containing errors is usually not considered for the job.

INTERMISSION

Why is the job specification so important?

____

____

IMPROVING EMPLOYEE PERFORMANCE

The human resources department provides training and development programs to raise work performance to a higher level. Employees constantly learn in a dynamic business environment. They must be willing to improve their skills and master new concepts.

Orientation is initial training to make new workers feel comfortable with their jobs and the organization. Technology, new management, and productivity may require employees to take part in additional staff development activities. Staff development should be upbeat and well organized.

Flattened organizations with fewer managers are becoming increasingly popular. Businesses are counting on employees to work as a team. The teams are expected to take more responsibility for their work and to make more decisions. Human resources departments are accountable for preparing these employees for their new responsibilities.

MATCH MAKING

Each person hired by a company has strengths that should be fully utilized. **Coordinating** involves matching the best employees with the tasks that must be completed.

Coordinating an effective workforce is difficult when the economy slows. Human resources departments are faced with employee cutbacks and department eliminations. The best organizations try to find new positions for employees who have contributed to the companies' past success.

Employee relations is a critical piece of the human resources puzzle. The human resources department assures effective communication and cooperation between employees and management. *Labor unions* often represent the sports and entertainment industries. The unions bargain with management for their members' wages, hours, and working conditions. Human resources managers assist in negotiating the labor contract with the union.

PERFORMANCE COUNTS

Performance, or employee output, is evaluated in relation to a company's mission. Managers evaluate performance to determine if it is meeting expectations. Performance problems may indicate a need for training.

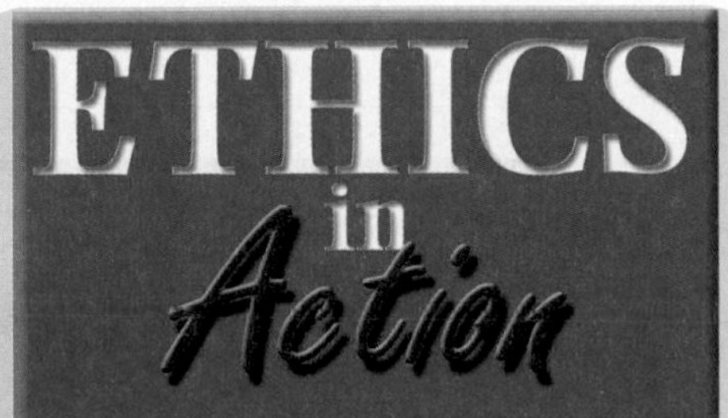

The first decade of the 21st century has endured economic ups and downs. Company layoffs and closings are common. Job security is a thing of the past for many people. While many people are just happy to have a job, athletes are asking for greater salaries and new sports arenas. The average fan struggles to afford the price of attending a professional sporting event. Even many college sports are pricing devoted fans out of the ballpark.

THINK CRITICALLY

1. **Should athletes reconsider their requests for multimillion-dollar contracts when the economy is down? Explain your answer.**
2. **Why are new stadiums and arenas being built during uncertain economic times?**

Managers must evaluate the employees they supervise and work to improve performance. Feedback gives workers a better understanding of their strengths and needs for improvement. The **360-degree feedback** system evaluates an employee based upon information from a range of people who have contact with the employee. The people may be from inside or outside the company. Peers, customers, and suppliers may all contribute to the employee's evaluation. Most employees appreciate a 360-degree feedback system. They believe the people they work with every day have a better understanding of their contributions to the organization.

Promotions are based upon outstanding employee performance. Sports and entertainment managers must be willing to put forth the extra effort necessary to gain a promotion.

INTERMISSION

What is 360-degree feedback? Why is it valuable?

____

____

Lead the Way

DENISE DEBARTOLO YORK

Denise DeBartolo York has worked more than 25 years in the fields of sports management and real estate. DeBartolo York currently serves as chairperson of the DeBartolo Corporation. She oversees the corporation's many businesses, including the San Francisco 49ers football team. The DeBartolo Corporation was ranked in the top 50 of 2002's *Working Woman* Top 500 woman-owned businesses in the country.

DeBartolo York began her career with the DeBartolo Corporation after graduating from St. Mary's College at Notre Dame. After the death of her father, Edward J. DeBartolo, she was named chairperson of the DeBartolo Corporation.

DeBartolo York generously gives her time and resources to charities and community organizations. She recently contributed $500,000 to the women's athletic programs at Youngstown State University.

THINK CRITICALLY

1. **Do you think Denise DeBartolo York's success is due mainly to her management skills or mainly to her family name? Defend your answer.**
2. **Locate the list of *Working Woman* Top 500 woman-owned businesses for the current year. Choose two of the businesses and write a one-page report on each of the companies.**

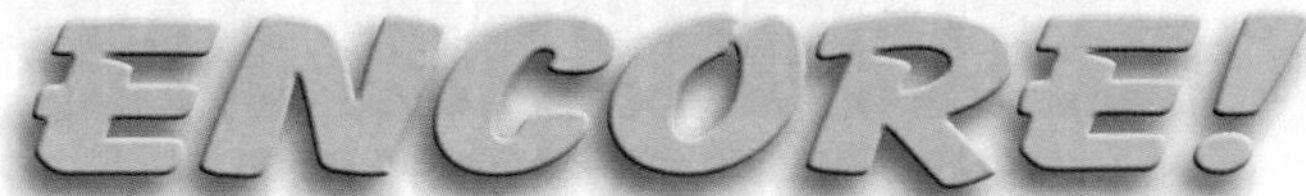

UNDERSTAND MANAGEMENT CONCEPTS

Circle the best answer for each of the following questions.

1. Internships
   a. provide a valuable learning tool for employees seeking future management positions
   b. are always paid
   c. usually require a 20-hour workweek
   d. both a and b

2. A flattened organization
   a. has fewer managers
   b. makes each individual more responsible for his or her work
   c. works more as a team
   d. all of the above

THINK CRITICALLY

Answer the following questions as completely as possible. If necessary, use a separate sheet of paper.

3. You are the ticket sales manager for a company that promotes popular musicians. Your company uses a 360-degree feedback system for performance evaluation. Who should contribute to your evaluation? Why?

____

____

____

4. Make a list of what is important to employees. Rank these items according to how much they cost the employer. The highest-priced item should be ranked number 1.

____

____

____

5. **Communication** Write a job description and a job specification for your dream job.

____

____

____

NETWORKING AND DELEGATING

Define delegation of duties.

Explain the latest trends in the sports and entertainment industries.

Describe the skills needed by employees in today's workforce.

OPENING ACT

Successful companies such as Nordstrom and Wal-Mart empower employees to make decisions. Their workers are prepared to take on company responsibility and carry out the organizations' missions. More companies are looking for employees eager to learn. Employee success depends upon seeking information instead of counting on others for answers. Companies are changing from the traditional manager–employee structure. Teams are expected to accomplish organizational goals. Flattened organizations require project teams and close-knit internal networks for success. Employers are looking for self-reliant employees with a good work ethic. Organizations need individuals who can think and make decisions on their own.

Discuss with a partner the characteristics needed to work in an organization that has cut back on management. How can schools help develop these necessary skills?

CHANGING BUSINESS CULTURE

The U.S. economy has shifted from producing physical goods like cars to producing services and information. In 2000, the percentage of workers employed in industries producing physical goods dropped below 20 percent. This level was the lowest since 1850. The sports and entertainment industries reflect this trend.

Manufacturing has moved overseas to benefit from cheaper labor. Families are spending a smaller portion of their income on food, clothing, and shelter. Two-income families are opting to spend their extra money on entertainment, dining out, and information technology.

Most organizations believe that customers' needs take priority. There is greater emphasis on personal responsibility and management participation. Leadership is no longer about rank, command, or status. Success depends upon encouraging, enabling, and empowering every employee in the organization.

PASS IT ON

Delegation is passing duties to another employee or team member with the expectation that the individual will fulfill the responsibility. Employees who delegate tasks must trust that the persons to whom they delegate will follow through on the tasks.

Trust becomes stronger with a flattened organization that has few layers of management. Employees and managers must work as teams to accomplish the organization's mission. Everyone must understand the importance of delegation and commitment to completing all tasks correctly.

When leaders delegate tasks, they understand the risk they are taking. Managers realize that even delegated tasks are ultimately their responsibility. Workers who are assigned delegated tasks must feel empowered to complete the tasks with the support of management. Employees must also feel the appreciation of a job well done. Effective managers give positive feedback and recognition to team members who carry out delegated tasks.

The service industry gives individuals only one chance to establish a long-term relationship with customers. The services offered must leave a positive impression with customers in order to attract repeat business. Employees who have been delegated tasks are counted on to provide customers with a great experience.

TIME OUT

Sixty-four of the top 100 companies on the 2002 *Fortune* 500 list were service companies.

INTERMISSION

Why is delegation important in today's business?

____

____

THE LATEST TRENDS

To keep their company competitive, managers must stay informed about current business trends. Globalization, technology, diversity, and networking all present new challenges for sports and entertainment managers.

Globalization means taking business beyond the borders of the country where the company is located. Professional sports teams and musicians realize the value of global popularity. Many companies have foreign operating divisions. The foreign divisions customize services and products to the local cultures. International divisions have management teams that operate both separately from and cooperatively with corporate headquarters.

Advanced computer technologies allow workers to operate "virtual offices." Online services, cell phones, and personal digital assistants make these offices accessible 24 hours a day. The increased speed of business makes fast decision making necessary. There is no longer time for decisions to travel through layers of management for approval. Companies also no longer want to spend a lot of time training employees on new technologies. They expect employees to contribute to the company from the moment they are hired.

Today's workforce is taking on a more diverse look. Organizations must be aware of the changing demographics of their employees, customers, clients, and investors. Sports and entertainment managers must be sensitive to the needs of a diverse workforce. Awareness of diversity is necessary to recruit and retain effective employees. As target markets expand, it is important for sports and entertainment managers to know about and respect other cultures.

THINK CRITICALLY

1. **Why should organizations pay attention to changing demographics?**
2. **How should companies change their recruiting strategies in response to increased workforce diversity?**

Success in the sports and entertainment industries depends upon the application of critical knowledge through efficient communication. Successful companies like Wal-Mart expand sales while minimizing costs through information technology. Wal-Mart has a powerful computer system second only to that of the U.S. government.

Diversity in the workplace is frequently related to race and ethnicity, but diversity also includes differences in lifestyle, age, nationality, physical abilities, religion, geographic background, position in an organization, and social and economic status. According to a recent study, 85 percent of new entrants into the workforce of the 21st century will be women, minorities, and immigrants. Successful companies appreciate the potential offered by a more diverse workforce.

Networking involves creating and maintaining relationships that are beneficial to all participating parties. Effective networking takes place when individuals learn more about their business associates and respect the uniqueness of each person. Networking is no longer just the "good old boy" system. A diverse workforce must learn how to effectively build and maintain profitable relationships. Business leaders network with key individuals and maintain strong relationships within their professional environment. Marketing managers in sports and entertainment understand the importance of networking with major sponsors. These sponsors pay thousands of dollars to advertise in a stadium, ballpark, or arena.

Sports and entertainment management is all about building and maintaining relationships. Fans, sponsors, television networks, entertainment venues, and the general public all contribute to the company's success.

INTERMISSION

Explain why networking is so important in today's workplace.

___

___

WHAT SKILLS DO EMPLOYEES NEED?

Today's employers want employees who have a strong work ethic and can act on their own. *Self-direction* is increasingly important in organizations where workers have different areas of specialty. Employees are held accountable for everything within the boundaries of their authority. Success no longer depends upon employees' knowledge. Success is measured by the ability to find information, process it, and use it.

EFFECTIVE COMMUNICATION SKILLS

Success depends upon the ability to communicate laterally, upward, and downward in the organization. The flattened organization has replaced top-down communication with shared information and more problem-solving discussions.

Communication must be clear, accurate, and well organized. Written communication must have correct grammar, spelling, and punctuation to make a positive impression. Nonverbal communication skills also are important for business leaders. Managers must have the ability to respond to body language and other nonverbal cues.

© GETTY IMAGES/PHOTODISC

DECISION-MAKING SKILLS

More evenly distributed power in a flattened organization requires workers to make more decisions. Critical thinking goes beyond completing an assigned task. The ability to plan and project is part of the critical-thinking process. Managers of an outdoor concert must use their critical-thinking skills to consider all possible scenarios. They must go well beyond selling tickets and making sure the musicians are hired for the event.

TEAMWORK IS KEY

The ability of employees to work effectively as a team is increasingly important for business success. A flattened organization may count on teams to create goals for the company's mission and strategic objectives. **Focal point teams** are charged with working on each of the goals to accomplish the mission and strategic objectives of the organization.

INTERMISSION

Explain why teamwork has become increasingly important in business organizations.

____

____

UNDERSTAND MANAGEMENT CONCEPTS

Circle the best answer for each of the following questions.

1. ___?___ involves maintaining positive relationships with other leaders.

a. Networking **c.** Delegation
b. Globalization **d.** Diversity

2. ___?___ involves assigning responsibilities to others.

a. Networking **c.** Delegation
b. Globalization **d.** Diversity

THINK CRITICALLY

Answer the following questions as completely as possible. If necessary, use a separate sheet of paper.

3. Why has the U.S. economic environment shifted from primarily manufacturing firms to a majority of service organizations?

____

____

____

____

4. Explain how the sports and entertainment industries have become more global in nature.

____

____

____

____

5. List three major skills you must possess for success in a management position. Explain why each skill is important.

____

____

____

____

____

MANAGEMENT CAREERS IN SPORTS AND ENTERTAINMENT

Define a career development program.

Describe various career levels in sports and entertainment management.

Explain the importance of a career portfolio.

OPENING ACT

Professional athletes and entertainers realize that their high-profile careers require more than playing a game or performing a concert. Luis Gonzalez is a popular baseball player. Gonzalez has served on the board of directors for a chapter of the American Cancer Society. He was also the spokesperson for Life Gift organ donations. Gonzalez established the "Kids Going Gonzo" program for youth, while also working closely with the Make-A-Wish Foundation.

Work with a partner to list other ways that popular athletes and celebrities can network with the public to maintain a positive image.

CAREER DEVELOPMENT PROGRAMS

Forward-thinking sports and entertainment organizations devise plans for meeting future employment needs. What jobs will be available in the future? How many people will need to be employed in each of these jobs? What knowledge and skills will be essential for successful employees? These questions are answered with a long-term career development program.

GET WITH THE PROGRAM

A **career development program** is a long-term organizational plan that includes a career path, effective performance reviews, career counseling, and training and development.

Career paths guide employees through a series of related jobs with increasing skill requirements and responsibility. These paths become the roadmap to a management position.

Performance reviews let employees know their greatest contributions to the organization and the areas in which they need growth. Effective managers carefully evaluate performance and regularly review the information with employees.

Career counseling identifies jobs that are part of an employee's career path and ultimately results in a career plan. A **career plan** helps an employee gain a better understanding of the training and development needed to advance along a chosen career path.

Training and development prepares employees in the skills needed for a dynamic career field such as sports and entertainment management.

INTERMISSION

Explain the importance of career counseling.

The Internet is a great place to find a job or an employee to fill one. Web sites help employers and prospective employees find a good career match.

THINK CRITICALLY

1. **What advantages might searching the Internet for a career position offer?**
2. **What limitations does an online job search pose?**

STARTING A CAREER

Students interested in a sports and entertainment management career should seek job observation opportunities or internships. Most management positions require either an undergraduate or a master's degree.

Internship programs give students a taste of the sports and entertainment profession. Ambitious interns who make a positive impression are often considered for future positions.

Entry-level occupations involve routine activities. Ambitious employees usually hold entry-level jobs for a short period before they are promoted.

Career-level jobs allow employees to control some of their work and make some decisions. Career-level employees view work as more than a job and want to move up within the organization.

Specialist occupations require a variety of skills in one or more business functions. Specialists are the most skilled experts in their field.

Supervisors are the first level of management in an organization. These individuals have a high level of knowledge in the areas of the company that they oversee. Supervisors must be effective decision makers and have strong leadership skills.

Executives perform all tasks necessary for managing a major function, a work unit, or the entire company. Executives set the standard for the entire organization and serve as role models for employees.

INTERMISSION

List the progression of career levels within an organization.

THE IMPORTANCE OF CAREER PLANS

To earn a management position in sports and entertainment, you should develop a career plan that involves the following steps.

1. **Develop an understanding** of business concepts and careers in your chosen field. In-depth study of sports and entertainment management careers may involve an internship.
2. **Complete a self-assessment** of your knowledge, skills, and aptitudes as related to those needed in a sports and entertainment management career. Determine if you have the personality necessary for a career that requires long hours during nights and weekends.
3. **Discuss your education and experience** with individuals currently working in your field of interest. Talk to high school and college counselors. Determine which courses will best prepare you for a sports and entertainment management career.
4. **Develop a career plan** that includes the necessary knowledge and skills for your chosen career. Include a strategy to develop your skills through a combination of education and experience. Your career plan will help you determine the best college to attend and the requirements necessary to meet your career goals.

U.S. companies spend $50 billion to $60 billion each year on formal training programs. Most of these programs are designed to improve the productivity of employees. Informal training, such as learning on the job, self-study, and coaching, costs an additional $200 billion.

CAREER PORTFOLIO

A **portfolio** is an organized collection of information and materials developed to tell a story about you. The portfolio should include clear descriptions of your achievements and career preparation. Portfolios can even include descriptions of hobbies related to your career ambitions. Active involvement in organizations like DECA (Distributive Education Clubs of America) and FBLA (Future Business Leaders of America) will strengthen a portfolio. The portfolio should be kept up to date. The best portfolios allow you to add and remove items. You can scan pictures and printed materials to create and add to a portfolio. A portfolio is useful for conducting self-assessment and for selling your qualifications to prospective employers.

QUALIFICATIONS FOR SPORTS AND ENTERTAINMENT MANAGEMENT CAREERS

Sports and entertainment managers must possess many qualities. Good communication skills, knowledge of various management responsibilities, and outstanding organizational skills are important for success.

Music production managers must have many talents to be successful. These energetic individuals must be familiar with sound, staging, lighting, venues, and talent searches. They also must be able to master complex productions that come in under budget and creatively solve production problems. Music production managers supervise large groups of workers with varied specialties and often handle big-name personalities.

Sports camp organizers must have outstanding organizational skills to manage all details from pre-registration to camp check-out. Financial management skills are necessary to pay bills on time, collect amounts owed by sponsors and camp participants, and prepare profitable budgets.

Athletic directors for universities must have strong budgeting skills. They must observe trends from past years to make current decisions about finances. A variety of sports programs vying for funds makes budget planning a challenging process for athletic directors.

College coaches must have excellent time management and planning skills. They must be aware of all NCAA rules. During the recruiting season, coaches often schedule their own flights, rental cars, and hotel rooms.

Sports agents must have knowledge of contracts and other legal matters. Agents must be willing to work hard for the players they represent. Eric Bieniemy is an assistant football coach at the University of Colorado. Prior to coaching, Eric played professional football for the San Diego Chargers, Cincinnati Bengals, and Philadelphia Eagles. As a professional football player, Eric learned the importance of selecting the best agent for representation.

the Global Manager

Weng Xianding runs a $120-million investment company near Hong Kong. Among the projects of his New China Industries Investment Company are a laser vision surgery clinic, several high-tech start-ups, and a sports club with racquetball courts and bowling lanes.

Xianding has linked ability, education, performance, and networking to reach his present position. Xianding scored so well on a university entrance exam that he was admitted into the master's program at the Chinese Academy of Social Sciences. There, he met students who later attained government positions and with whom he networked to build his company.

THINK CRITICALLY

1. What skills do you think Weng Xianding has to be a successful manager and business owner?
2. Does a manager in a foreign country need different skills than a manager in the United States? Why or why not?

INTERMISSION

Give three characteristics for success in sports and entertainment management.

___

___

ENCORE!

UNDERSTAND MANAGEMENT CONCEPTS

Circle the best answer for each of the following questions.

1. ___?___ let employees know their strengths and the areas in which they need improvement.
   a. Career plans
   b. Growth plans
   c. Performance reviews
   d. Career maps

2. ___?___ involve routine activities and are usually held for a short period of time.
   a. Entry-level occupations
   b. Specialist occupations
   c. Career-level jobs
   d. Management positions

THINK CRITICALLY

Answer the following questions as completely as possible. If necessary, use a separate sheet of paper.

3. What items would you include in your career portfolio? Why would you include these items?

____

____

____

____

4. Communication You are a sports camp organizer. Work with a partner to develop a one-page form to be used to evaluate the performance of the camp staff.

____

____

____

____

5. Why are many highly paid athletes and celebrities involved with charities and special causes?

____

____

____

____

REVIEW MANAGEMENT CONCEPTS

Write the letter of the term that matches each definition. Some terms will not be used.

____ **1.** Activities involved with hiring, developing, and paying the individuals responsible for doing the organization's work

____ **2.** Items in addition to pay that employees receive

____ **3.** All activities required to maintain an adequate number of qualified employees for the company

____ **4.** Matching the best employees with the tasks that must be completed

____ **5.** Organized collection of materials

____ **6.** Initial training for new employees

____ **7.** Evaluates employees based upon information from a range of people

____ **8.** Lists all qualifications a worker needs to successfully complete the job

____ **9.** Passing duties to another employee

____**10.** Responsible for working on goals to accomplish the mission and strategic objectives of the organization

a. 360-degree feedback
b. career development program
c. career plan
d. coordinating
e. delegation
f. employment
g. focal point teams
h. fringe benefits
i. human resources management
j. job specification
k. orientation
l. portfolio

Circle the best answer.

11. Most individuals get their foot in the door of a sports and entertainment organization through
a. entry-level positions
b. internships
c. career-level jobs
d. specialist positions

12. Delegation
a. is becoming increasingly popular in flattened organizations
b. transfers responsibility to another individual
c. releases all personal responsibility for the tasks you give others
d. both a and b

13. Flattened organizations
a. have eliminated some management positions
b. require more teamwork
c. require employees to take on more responsibility
d. all of the above

THINK CRITICALLY

14. List three responsibilities of a company's human resources management department. Give a creative example of what human resources management can do for the effective training and development of employees.

15. Survey ten adults with full-time employment to learn what they consider the most important values of a job. Examples might include pay, stability, health insurance, company car, paid vacations, and so forth. You may want to include a list of items for the surveyed individuals to rank. Be sure to include an "other" category. What were the results of your survey?

16. Give three reasons why organizations are becoming more flattened.

17. What are the best sources for recruiting qualified employees? Give rationale for each of your answers.

18. You have delegated tasks to other employees within your company. What will you do to ensure that those workers follow through with the tasks? How will you reward good performances?

MAKE CONNECTIONS

19. Management Math Many companies lose large sums of money each year due to employee sick leave. Companies are realizing that employees sometimes use the days for personal leave rather than sickness. One company estimates that it costs the organization $500 each day that an employee is absent from work. Suppose a company hires 100 employees who each have eight days of sick leave per year. The company estimates that the employees will use 60 percent of their sick leave days. Each day an employee is absent costs the company $500 for that employee. How much will sick leave cost the company in one year?

20. Technology Use the Internet to locate articles about labor disputes. Find three articles and indicate the major disputes between labor and management.

21. Communication Employee absences due to used sick leave are costing your company large sums of money. Design an incentive package for employees who do not use their sick leave during the year. Write a memo to employees telling them about the incentive program.

22. Technology Search the Internet to locate information about Equal Employment Opportunity laws. Write a one-page paper explaining why managers need to understand and follow these guidelines when recruiting candidates for a position.

23. Human Resources Management As the new human resources manager for your organization, you are responsible for conducting orientation sessions. You are putting together the material that you will present at your first session. What information will you provide to new employees to help them feel comfortable in their job and in the organization?

24. Management Responsibilities You are the manager of a successful sports camp. Your camp plans to offer three individuals the opportunity to work as paid interns during the summer months. You have received more than 20 applications for these internship positions. How will you select the three interns? On what criteria will you base your decision?

25. Communication You are the vice president of corporate sponsorships for a professional sports team. You are in charge of establishing and maintaining corporate sponsorships for your organization. You have expressed the need to hire a new employee in your department. This employee will actively contact corporations and negotiate sponsorships. Write a job description and job specification for this new position you want to create.

26. Human Resources Management You are the human resources manager of a major organization in the entertainment industry. You have been asked to speak to a group of high school students about the skills necessary to successfully compete in a global marketplace. What will you tell them? What skills and abilities will you suggest they develop?

WHEN BELIEFS CONFLICT WITH ENTERTAINMENT

Dan Shannon is a former New England Patriots fan who has decided that he has watched his last professional football game. Shannon has a fond passion for the sport, but he calculates that it takes 3,000 cows to supply the NFL with one year's worth of footballs. The Super Bowl alone requires 3.8 steers to sacrifice their hides.

As an animal lover, Shannon also no longer supports college football. Once the mascot for the University of South Carolina Gamecocks, he now refuses to support a team that has a cockfighting bird with spurs as sharp as razor blades for a mascot.

Shannon also boycotts hockey because he finds it distasteful to have octopi thrown on the ice at Red Wings games.

Shannon is the sports campaign coordinator of People for the Ethical Treatment of Animals (PETA™). As coordinator, he persuaded the NCAA to abandon the use of leather basketballs in favor of synthetic balls for the Men's and Women's NCAA Tournaments. Shannon is even turned off by leather athletic shoes and catcher's mitts. He believes the animals that end up as baseballs and soccer cleats suffer confinement, branding, tail docking, dehorning, and cruel treatment during transportation.

Many people believe that PETA members are obsessed with their cause. Civilization has had multiple uses of the Earth's resources, including animals, since the beginning of time. While PETA members have a right to their opinion, they should not automatically condemn athletic equipment manufacturers that make use of animal byproducts. The issue becomes even stickier when PETA members take their cause to the streets and confront individuals who do not have the same beliefs.

Think Critically

1. **Should PETA have the right to give negative publicity to sports that use leather balls and other athletic equipment? Why?**
2. **Should professional and college sports be required to use synthetic sports equipment? Why?**
3. **How would farmers who raise livestock respond to the PETA cause?**
4. **Can sports organizations reach some type of happy medium on the leather issue without alienating any group of fans? How?**

PUBLIC RELATIONS PROJECT

Your city offers professional and college sports as well as other entertainment venues. Athletic teams at your suburban school are successful, but attendance at sporting events is low. In teams of three, you must develop strategies to increase attendance, implement the strategies, and record the results.

A starting point might be a survey to discover why students and adults do not attend high school sporting events. The final product will be a written paper limited to 30 double-spaced pages. You will have ten minutes to present your project. The judges will have five minutes to ask questions. The following information must be covered in your paper.

I. EXECUTIVE SUMMARY
One-page description of the project
II. CAMPAIGN THEME OR FOCUS
   A. Description of the issue
   B. Rationale for selecting the issue
   C. Description of the target population
III. LOCAL MEDIA AND OTHER PROMOTIONS
   A. Local print and broadcast media
   B. Other promotional activities
   C. Media mix and rationale for media and other promotional activities
IV. CAMPAIGN ORGANIZATION/IMPLEMENTATION
   A. Organizational chart, member involvement, and job description
   B. Description of the campaign
   C. Estimated impact on target population
V. EVALUATION AND RECOMMENDATIONS
   A. Evaluation of the process
   B. Future campaign recommendations
VI. BIBLIOGRAPHY
VII. APPENDIX

Performance Indicators Evaluated

- Describe your target market.
- Describe the local competition for entertainment and how you will win consumer dollars.
- Explain the survey you will use to find out more about your target market.
- Describe special promotional strategies to increase attendance at games.
- Explain the financial commitment necessary for your plan.
- Explain projected results from your efforts.

Go to the DECA web site for more detailed information.

1. What is the purpose of your public relations campaign?
2. Why is it important to first conduct a survey?
3. How will you use the information gathered?
4. What special promotions are necessary to increase attendance at games?

www.deca.org/publications/HS_Guide/guidetoc.html

CHAPTER 9

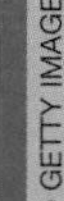
© GETTY IMAGES/PHOTODISC

Leaders in a Changing Environment

9.1 CHARACTERISTICS OF LEADERS
9.2 HOW DO LEADERS MOTIVATE?
9.3 AGENTS OF CHANGE

© DIGITAL VISION

© GETTY IMAGES/PHOTODISC

© GETTY IMAGES/PHOTODISC

WINNING *Strategies*

THE HARD ROAD TO SUCCESS

Gloria Estefan grew up in a Cuban ghetto in Miami. While her mother was making a living for the family, Gloria cared for her invalid father, Jose. She found comfort in her guitar and spent hours in her room singing the Top 40 tunes of the day.

Gloria's big break into the music industry came in 1975. Her mother urged Gloria to sing at a wedding where the Miami Latin Boys were performing. The band leader, Emilio Estefan, was so impressed by Gloria's smooth alto voice that he asked her to join his band. Gloria reluctantly agreed to sing on weekends. With the addition of a female vocalist, the band was renamed the "Miami Sound Machine."

The Miami Sound Machine rose to fame. By 1983, the group was well known throughout Central and South America. Emilio convinced record executives to release an English-only album in 1984 to the U.S. and European markets. "Dr. Beat" (the first single) became a huge hit on the dance charts. A second single hit, "Congo," became the only song in history to appear on *Billboard*'s Pop, Latin, Soul, and Dance charts all at the same time.

Tours, awards, fame, and fortune continued to flow freely for the Miami Sound Machine. But good luck ran out on March 20, 1990, when Gloria suffered a broken back in an auto accident. The delicate surgery that followed required two 8-inch rods to be placed on either side of Gloria's spine.

Gloria was performing again within one year of the operation. During a time of excruciating pain, Gloria received thousands of letters, telegrams, and floral arrangements from well-wishers. She returned the favor in 1992 by organizing a benefit concert, "Hurricane Relief," which raised $3 million for victims of Hurricane Andrew.

THINK CRITICALLY

1. What is unique about Gloria Estefan's success?
2. Give three examples of how Gloria Estefan is a leader.

CHARACTERISTICS OF LEADERS

Define leadership and list leadership characteristics.

Identify ways that managers influence employees.

Describe important human relations skills.

OPENING ACT

Leadership opportunities are everywhere. Organizations have difficulty finding leaders who qualify for demanding positions at the top of the ladder. Some individuals are promoted to positions that are beyond their level of competency and climb no further. Some individuals do not like the politics necessary to move into leadership positions and opt for pure management roles. Other individuals become so valuable that competitors lure them away. The leadership shortage is real in all aspects of society. Excellent leaders and successful managers have different characteristics. Leaders understand their strengths and maximize their leadership characteristics. Most managers are leaders in only one or two areas. Unfortunately, most people move from management into leadership positions with no roadmap for success. However, more emphasis is being placed on leadership training within all types of organizations.

With a partner, discuss how your DECA chapter or other school organization can prepare high school students for leadership roles.

© GETTY IMAGES/PHOTODISC

THE NEED FOR LEADERSHIP

The role of management has changed. Managers can no longer just tell employees what to do and expect the work to be completed. Employees want to be recognized as an important part of the business structure. Managers must value the ideas and work of employees. **Leadership** is the ability to influence individuals to cooperatively achieve goals for an organization. **Leaders** are managers who earn the respect and cooperation of employees to effectively accomplish the organization's work. Leaders must have strong **human relations** skills—the ability to get along within a group due to respect for every individual. Leaders must establish a good human relations environment for the success of a sports and entertainment organization.

CHARACTERISTICS OF LEADERS

Leadership is directly related to the success of a business. Leaders have the ability to create an atmosphere that encourages employees to put forth their best effort. Good leaders create a work environment that employees enjoy. Employees are more productive when their work meets their personal needs as well as the needs of the business.

Leadership characteristics are personal traits and do not necessarily reflect how managers behave within an organization. Basic leadership traits include

- **Intelligence** Leaders use their intelligence to study, learn, and improve their management skills. They also help others to develop and learn new skills.
- **Judgment** Leaders are called upon to make numerous decisions. They must carefully consider all the facts and apply knowledge, experience, and new information in order to make good decisions.
- **Objectivity** Leaders cannot be biased. They must be able to look at all sides of a problem. Leaders value individual uniqueness, not stereotypes or first impressions.
- **Initiative** Leaders are self-starters who have a plan to accomplish personal and organizational goals. Ambition and persistence are two characteristics possessed by leaders.
- **Dependability** Leaders are consistent in their actions, and others rely on them. Leaders do not make promises that cannot be fulfilled.
- **Cooperation** Leaders understand the team concept. They work well with others.
- **Honesty** Leaders possess high standards of personal integrity. They are ethical in decision making and in their treatment of others.
- **Courage** Leaders have the courage to make unpopular decisions and to try new solutions for problems.
- **Confidence** Self-confidence gives leaders the green light to make decisions and expect the highest-quality results.
- **Stability** Leaders cannot afford to be highly emotional. They are a calming influence counted on to reduce conflicts and solve problems.
- **Understanding** Leaders respect the feelings and ideas of others. They try to understand the people they work with and encourage others to share their ideas and opinions.

INTERMISSION

List three characteristics of leaders.

____

____

Leaders in the sports and entertainment industry who have the appeal to become successful public speakers earn large sums of money. Rick Pitino, the University of Louisville basketball coach, receives $20,000 to $25,000 for a one-hour speech.

HOW MANAGERS INFLUENCE OTHERS

Managers are expected to influence people to accomplish the organization's work. Managers who get others to do what they want are not necessarily effective leaders. Managers can influence employees through their power. **Power** is the ability to control behavior. Managers obtain power in different ways. Position power, reward power, expert power, and identity power are four types of power available to managers.

Position power comes from the position the manager holds in the organization. Managers who supervise have the power to give directions. They expect employees to complete the assigned work.

Reward power is based on the ability of the manager to control rewards and punishments. When managers control who receives preferred work schedules, pay increases, or bonuses, they have power over their employees. Power also is present when a manager can penalize employees for unacceptable performance.

Expert power is gained by having superior knowledge about the work. Employees feel comfortable turning to an expert when they are not sure how to perform a task or when they need information to solve a problem.

Identity power is earned when others identify with managers and want to be accepted by them. Employees who want positive recognition will try to please their manager by doing whatever he or she requests. Experienced or dynamic managers have identity power. They can influence the work of others in the organization.

INTERMISSION

List four ways managers influence their employees. Which method would you prefer as an employee?

____

____

DEVELOPING LEADERSHIP SKILLS

Individuals are not born leaders. Training and personal development help individuals improve their leadership skills. People have the ability to learn how to be dependable, take initiative, and cooperate with others.

Leaders must be strong team players. More businesses are using employee teams to plan work and make company decisions. Companies are now evaluating prospective workers for their leadership characteristics. Leaders are called upon to be the role model for employees to work effectively as a team. Well-organized teams have expert power and identity power to accomplish projects.

In order to work well with others, leaders must develop human relations skills. These skills include self-understanding, understanding others, communication, team building, and developing job satisfaction.

Self-understanding involves awareness of your attitudes and opinions, your leadership style, your decision-making style, and your relationships with other people. Employees look to leaders for information and direction. Leaders must be able to make decisions, solve problems, and communicate expectations. Individuals who have a good self-understanding feel more comfortable selecting the best way to work with people and the leadership style to use.

Understanding others is a critical skill for leaders. Each person is unique and has a different background. No two people have the same attitudes, skills, and needs. Leaders realize that they cannot treat everyone the same way. While some people want a great deal of support and communication from their supervisor, others want more freedom and flexibility. Some employees feel that it is important for managers to consult them when making important decisions. Others do not want to be involved in the decision-making process.

the Global Manager

Wolf Trap is America's National Park for the Performing Arts. Catherine Filene Shouse founded Wolf Trap by donating 100 acres of her Vienna, Virginia farmland to the U.S. Government. Shouse funded the construction of a 6,800-seat indoor/outdoor theater at the park. A typical season at Wolf Trap includes a wide array of entertainment. Performances range from pop, country, folk, and blues to orchestra, dance, theater, and opera. Wolf Trap has gained worldwide recognition for its Wolf Trap Opera Company, a summer residency program for young opera singers. This highly selective program provides invaluable experience for young singers at the start of their professional careers. Wolf Trap Opera Company produces some of the finest and most critically acclaimed performances in the country.

THINK CRITICALLY

1. What is the international benefit of a park like Wolf Trap?
2. What characteristics does a manager need to successfully operate Wolf Trap?

Communication with employees is a major factor in becoming an effective leader. Leaders must understand the importance of clear communication, both written and oral. Human relations problems occur when communication breaks down. Leaders must decide what information to communicate and use the best channels for communication. Listening is one of the most important communication skills needed by leaders. Listening allows leaders to identify employees' problems and needs in order to respond to them more effectively.

Team building contributes to the success of the organization. Successful sports and entertainment organizations have strong team structures. Teams feel responsibility and pride for the work that they complete. The team counts on respect, solid communication, and common goals. Individuals must feel that their presence is important and that they can count on team members for support.

Developing job satisfaction is key to helping employees enjoy their work and become more productive. Leadership within an organization can change employees' attitudes toward their jobs. Managers are aware of how each employee is unique. This understanding of uniqueness helps managers devise personalized plans for employee success.

Individuals who are carefully matched with the kind of work they perform will usually have a better attitude toward their job. Head coaches for successful sports teams rely on a staff of specialized coaches who are experts for different parts of the game. Concert tour organizers make sure that all team members have a thorough understanding of their roles to ensure that an ambitious concert tour is successful.

BECOMING A SUCCESSFUL LEADER

While leaders often are seen as decision makers who empower people and build successful teams, managers frequently are viewed as maintenance people for an organization. However, solid management skills are the foundation for good leadership. An individual cannot become an excellent leader without being a good manager. The blend of both management skills and leadership skills equals a winning combination for success.

Leadership involves a state of mind. An individual must want to become a leader before changes can occur. Leadership moves from following decisions to making decisions. Leaders must have the courage to go beyond the familiar comfort zone of routine work. They must surround themselves with strong team members. Leaders must be willing to let go of some of the day-to-day responsibilities.

Training and development can enhance leadership and management skills. While managers realize the importance of leadership, they frequently devote the majority of their time to management matters. Individuals who want to move up in an organization must spend less time on administrative matters and devote more time to leadership.

The director of athletics at a large college views the situation this way: "I'm glad I was a successful coach before I took over this job because I was able to develop most of my leadership skills before I arrived. But I have learned to respect management skills. My transition would have been much easier if I had taken some management courses earlier."

INTERMISSION

How do managers and leaders differ?

____

____

Lead the Way

EWING MARION KAUFFMAN

Ewing Marion Kauffman began his career as a pharmaceutical salesman in 1945. His ambition and outstanding sales techniques allowed him to earn more from commissions than the president of the company. In an effort to stifle Kauffman's success, the president cut Kauffman's commission rate and sales territory.

Frustrated with the political maneuvering, Kauffman started Marion Laboratories in 1950. He led Marion Laboratories from first-year gross sales of $36,000 to sales of $930 million in the last full year before its merger with Merrell Dow Pharmaceuticals in 1989. He developed a profit-sharing program that resulted in 300 of his 3,400 employees becoming millionaires from the success of the company.

In 1968, Ewing Kauffman was motivated to bring professional baseball to his hometown. With no prior experience in professional sports, he and his wife Muriel purchased the Kansas City Royals. To ensure that the Royals remained in Kansas City, Kauffman included a provision in his will stating that local parties must own at least 50 percent of the team. He also left instructions for proceeds from the sale of the team to go to local charities.

Kauffman believed that successful people should give back to the community that created their wealth. The Kauffman Foundation was established in the 1960s with the goal of creating self-sufficient people in healthy communities. Today, the Kauffman Foundation continues to actively promote entrepreneurship education and youth development.

THINK CRITICALLY

1. What type of management power did Ewing Kauffman's original employer use?
2. What rewards did Ewing Kauffman provide to his employees?

UNDERSTAND MANAGEMENT CONCEPTS

Circle the best answer for each of the following questions.

1. Leaders
  a. must earn respect
  b. are automatically rewarded the respect of employees
  c. must have strong human relations skills
  d. both a and c

2. Leaders influence others through each of the following types of power except
  a. threat
  b. position
  c. reward
  d. identity

THINK CRITICALLY

Answer the following questions as completely as possible. If necessary, use a separate sheet of paper.

3. Research Use the Internet to find the biography of a person you consider to be a leader. Print the biography and highlight the main points. What type of power did this person use to influence others?

____

____

____

____

4. List five characteristics of leaders and ways you can develop these traits while you are in high school.

____

____

____

____

5. Why is it important to learn how to be an effective team player?

____

____

____

____

HOW DO LEADERS MOTIVATE?

OPENING ACT

There is some truth to the old saying that "money can't buy happiness." However, money is a strong motivator for many people. Successful leaders determine what motivates employees to perform their duties most effectively for an organization. While paychecks are strong motivators, many other factors also build excitement among employees. Some individuals like to work for sports and entertainment organizations because they are motivated by being able to attend the events. This is a major incentive at successful universities where athletic tickets are scarce. Some companies recognize the employee or team of the month with special incentives. Other organizations split some of the profits from a successful year with the employees who helped achieve the results. Time off, a company car, and positive recognition are all examples of motivators for employees. Perceived status—being associated with a popular professional sports team or a favorite musician or entertainer—also can be a motivator.

With a partner, discuss good motivators for employees and develop a Top Ten List of Motivators.

Explain what motivates individuals to accomplish organizational goals.

Discuss four leadership styles.

Describe strategies that leaders can use to motivate employees.

MOTIVATING TODAY'S WORKFORCE

Today's dynamic workforce is extremely mobile. Individuals no longer enjoy a 40-year career with the same company like their grandparents did. Some people choose to leave organizations because they are not motivated to accomplish company goals. Organizations are challenged to earn the loyalty of employees in a time when layoffs and company closings are not unusual.

HOW MANAGERS' BELIEFS CAN AFFECT PERFORMANCE

Some managers believe that employees will not complete the work correctly unless they are closely managed. This attitude comes from the belief that employees are generally lazy and only work for pay. Managers with this attitude believe that employees will not work any harder than necessary. They do not think that employees will take initiative to complete quality work. Managers with these beliefs are likely to use rewards and penalties regularly to influence worker performance.

A 22-year-old will face an average of six career changes in the next 42 years.

Employees who feel that their manager thinks they are lazy and require close supervision will respond accordingly. Unfortunately, employees working under this type of management become addicted to a system of rewards. They expect bonuses for completing tasks required by their jobs.

A *flexible viewpoint* allows managers to adjust to different circumstances. Every job has some tasks that are more favorable than others. Closer supervision or better incentives must be offered for the less favorable tasks. Leaders influence the attitudes of their team members. Some of the most successful leaders are role models. They are not afraid to complete both favorable and unfavorable tasks with the rest of the team. The community service coordinator for a professional sports team may not enjoy filling 5,000 goodie bags for a 5K run but can encourage employees by helping with the task.

INTERMISSION

How can a manager's beliefs about employees affect employees' work performance?

____

____

TYPES OF LEADERSHIP

The general way a manager treats and supervises employees is called **leadership style**. Leadership style involves how a manager gives directions, handles problems, and makes decisions. Leadership style is influenced by the manager's preparation, experience, and personal beliefs about employees' attitudes toward work. Leadership styles include autocratic, democratic, open, and situational.

© GETTY IMAGES/PHOTODISC

Autocratic leaders give direct orders with detailed instructions. Employees are well aware of what, when, and how work is to be completed. With an autocratic leader, employees generally do not make decisions about the work that they perform. Managers are counted on to handle questions or problems that may arise. One advantage of autocratic leadership is efficiency. Employees are expected to do the work exactly the way the manager has outlined, so there will be no surprises. Autocratic leadership is necessary for tightened security procedures at concerts, theme parks, and other sports and entertainment events.

Many workers resent autocratic leaders because they feel a lack of personal respect. Sometimes autocratic leadership results in a decline in employee performance. Autocratic leadership does not focus attention on preparing others for leadership roles. This type of leadership does not encourage employees to think about better ways to complete their work. The autocratic style is effective in emergencies. Effective leaders choose the autocratic style only when the situation merits it.

Democratic leaders encourage employees to participate in planning work, solving work-related problems, and making decisions. Managers who believe in this style openly communicate with their employees to discuss work-related problems and possible solutions. Democratic managers provide workers with assistance and encouragement. This type of leadership makes employees more responsive to work changes that occur. An athletic director at a major university who uses the democratic style of leadership would expect employees to share ideas at staff meetings.

Many employees prefer democratic leaders who make them feel like active members of a team striving to reach common goals. Employees are more likely to feel like stakeholders for an organization that practices democratic leadership. **Stakeholders** feel ownership or responsibility for the success or failure of an organization's goals.

Dr. Kristen Anderson plays dual roles as a professor of psychology at Houston Community College and as a professional football player for the Houston Reliants. Most people would not expect the petite Dr. Anderson to have a second career as a professional football player. By taking on the unique role of a female professional football player with a completely different daytime occupation, Dr. Anderson serves as a dual example of diversity. This multi-talented individual understands the importance of career flexibility.

THINK CRITICALLY

1. **How can Dr. Anderson effectively relate professional football experiences in her psychology classes?**
2. **How can individuals like Dr. Anderson raise the support for professional women's sports?**

Open leaders give little or no direction to employees. Employees clearly understand the work that needs to be completed. They decide the methods, details, and decisions for accomplishing the tasks. Open leadership works best with experienced workers and in routine situations. Employees who are experts with specific tasks can effectively complete their work with open leadership. Most sports and entertainment organizations do not use open leadership.

Situational leaders understand the strengths of their employees and adjust their leadership style to different situations. They use open leadership when they have a highly experienced team assigned to a task. The autocratic style is put into action when a number of new employees are assigned a task. Democratic leadership is used when the leader wants employees' suggestions on how to solve a company problem.

INTERMISSION

List four styles of leadership. Which type of leadership style would be the most pleasant for employees?

____

____

WHAT DO EMPLOYEES WANT?

Most people work to pay for their needs and wants. Employees are more likely to be loyal to an organization that provides good motivators. All individuals want to be shown respect. Successful leaders respect all people and recognize the strengths of individuals. Successful managers adjust their style of management to the characteristics of the people they supervise and to different situations.

EMPLOYEES WANT CONSISTENCY

Effective management is more concerned with human motivation to reach goals than with efficiency and control. Employees enjoy working for managers who

- Encourage employee participation and suggestions
- Keep employees informed

© DIGITAL VISION

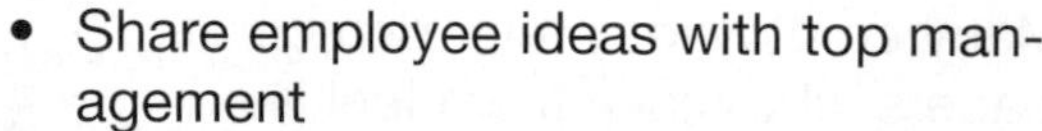

- Share employee ideas with top management
- Work to build and maintain morale among employees
- Are easy to talk to and readily available
- Support employee training and development
- Communicate openly with employees
- Are considerate of the ideas and feelings of others
- Are not afraid to make changes when needed
- Support employees who are doing their best even when mistakes happen
- Show appreciation and provide recognition for good work

Employees expect managers to be consistent with work rules. **Mutual Reward Theory (MRT)** is based on the premise that both parties come out ahead. MRT contends that a relationship between two people or groups is enhanced when there is a satisfactory exchange of rewards between the parties involved. People who want to lead must have followers. Followers support people who provide rewards. Therefore, people who want to become leaders must provide rewards. Employees provide leaders with the reward of accomplishing company goals. Accomplishment of organizational goals can lead to promotion for the manager in charge. Empowered employees are rewarded with greater decision-making power, more responsibility, and less supervision. Most rewards are psychological. Typical psychological rewards include a sense of accomplishment and pride, self-esteem, and greater status. The best reward a leader can provide a follower is good leadership. The best reward a follower can provide a leader is productivity.

DETERMINING THE BEST EMPLOYEE REWARDS

Leaders must be outstanding listeners to discover the right rewards for employees and to achieve organizational goals. The timing of a reward also is important to achieve the proper impact. Leaders must determine what rewards make the most sense in view of the situation. Leaders must constantly monitor and improve their reward system according to the changing needs of their followers.

Personal rewards are given to either a single follower or to a small group of followers. Examples of personal rewards include one-on-one conversations, special attention, and individualized forms of recognition. Rewards that are more valuable should be saved for limited circumstances. The ultimate goal of a reward system is to motivate employees, not to manipulate followers in an unfair way.

Over-the-counter herbal drugs containing ephedrine supplement are being banned by college sports, the Olympics, the NFL, and minor league baseball. Ephedrine is sold over the counter as a weight-loss aid and energy booster. When Baltimore Orioles pitcher Steve Bechler died from heatstroke, the medical examiner cited the use of a controversial ephedrine supplement as a contributing factor to his death. To fight fatigue and weight gain during a 38-week season of long hours and few days off, some NASCAR crew members are turning to dietary supplements containing ephedrine. One team's athletic trainer estimates that up to 80 percent of NASCAR crews have tried ephedrine. NASCAR gives random drug tests, but it does not check for ephedrine.

THINK CRITICALLY

1. **Why are more athletes using supplements containing ephedrine?**
2. **Do you think the FDA (Food and Drug Administration) should regulate herbal supplements? Why or why not?**

INTERMISSION

What is the ultimate reason for an employee reward system?

____

____

UNDERSTAND MANAGEMENT CONCEPTS

Circle the best answer for each of the following questions.

1. Employees are becoming less loyal to companies due to
a. large severance packages
b. the increasing number of layoffs
c. large salaries
d. a wide array of fringe benefits

2. __?__ leadership works well for emergencies.
a. Democratic
b. Open
c. Autocratic
d. Situational

THINK CRITICALLY

Answer the following questions as completely as possible. If necessary, use a separate sheet of paper.

3. List four types of leadership styles and a situation for each style.

____

____

____

____

4. What is Mutual Reward Theory? Give an example of Mutual Reward Theory for an employee and manager of a professional sports team.

____

____

____

____

5. Why must organizations be cautious with the number of rewards they distribute to employees?

____

____

____

____

____

AGENTS OF CHANGE

OPENING ACT

Numerous nightclub tragedies over a period of several decades have led to reforms aimed at making such disasters less likely. When improved safety rules aren't enforced or observed, the individuals who inspect, operate, and patronize nightclubs are doomed to learn painful lessons. Lax enforcement of existing safety laws and a recklessness of the industry are major problems. Twenty-one people died in a stampede at a Chicago nightclub that did not follow an earlier court order to close it down. A fire in a Rhode Island nightclub that killed 97 people was ignited by the illegal use of fireworks during a rock show. The club had passed a safety inspection six weeks prior to the event. Both clubs were overcrowded. Although fire and smoke are lethal, in many cases the worst killer is the crowd. Five people pushing with all of their might can exert a force of 700 pounds or more.

With a partner, discuss why nightclubs take risks to entertain people and how far-reaching the negative results can be.

Explain why people resist change.

Discuss the steps in an effective change process.

List the characteristics of enlightened leaders.

EVERYTHING CHANGES

Change is a constant in the sports and entertainment industry. Customers of sports and entertainment organizations are unpredictable, and it is challenging to meet their changing needs. In addition, sports and entertainment event planners must be constantly aware of changing laws, safety codes, tightened security, liability issues, and legal contracts. Reasons for change can include downsizing, mergers, shift in public perception, and moving teams to different cities.

Many people are not comfortable with change. Moving, adhering to new procedures, and dealing with potential disasters are challenges faced by individuals in the sports and entertainment industry. Employees usually will resist change when they feel their jobs are threatened or when they do not understand the reasons for the change. Resistance also occurs when employees are uncertain about how a change will affect them or when they do not trust the people implementing the change. Employees resist change the most when it occurs suddenly and catches them off guard. Leaders must become *agents of change*, working to overcome resistance and making transitions or changes as comfortable as possible for the employees affected.

Individuals can expect to change their knowledge base and skill set several times throughout their lives, according to Donald Tapscott, author of *The Digital Economy*.

ASKING INSTEAD OF TELLING

When leaders tell people what to do and how to do it, there is a tendency for employees to resist. People are more likely to support ideas that they have helped develop. A negative message is conveyed whenever management tells someone how to do something differently. Defensiveness results when workers are told that the way they have been performing is wrong or not good enough.

Workers are more likely to buy into change when they are asked for their input. Employees are then more likely to use their creativity for the benefit of change. The real experts within an organization are the employees. Management is challenged to tap into this wealth of knowledge available within the organization.

SIGNS OF CHANGE

Most organizations deal with symptoms of problems instead of dealing with the real causes. Nightclubs that have faced tragic situations make exits more visible and hire additional people for crowd control. However, the root of the problem is the risk involved with performers using fireworks or the facilities taking in more people than they can hold.

The symptoms, known as **hard issues**, may include questionable economic conditions, rowdy crowds rushing the playing field, or fans behaving irresponsibly at entertainment events. While these symptoms certainly are problems, they are actually indicators of **soft issues** that include attitudes, mindsets, and states of mind. Soft issues are human issues that are difficult to measure, but they must be considered for change to occur.

The most sophisticated processes implemented for change can be severely limited without the cooperation and support of the people affected by the change. The collective attitude of people within an organization becomes the real issue when dealing with change. Organizations must be prepared to deal with soft issues that can hinder change. Many organizations put all of their energies into the structures and process of change and ignore the attitude that can spell defeat for the change.

© GETTY IMAGES/PHOTODISC

During every stage of life, people base their actions on attitudes and personal experiences. Change requires leaders to modify the ways people think, behave, and manage. Leaders are ultimately required to shift attitudes from change-resistant to change-friendly. The ability of an organization to move forward with change depends upon how much productive energy people are using while moving toward the organization's objectives. Successful organizations must nurture and grow the company's most important assets and resources—its people.

INTERMISSION

What is the difference between hard issues and soft issues when determining changes within an organization?

____

____

STEPS FOR EFFECTIVE CHANGE

Leaders who successfully and effectively implement change follow five important steps.

1. **Carefully plan** for the change.
2. **Communicate with people** to decrease the element of surprise.
3. **Involve people** to make them feel like they are part of the change.
4. **Educate people** for a better understanding of the change.
5. **Support people** who are expected to accept change.

HUMAN RESOURCES MANAGEMENT

Leaders should be careful not to move too quickly to make changes. Change should take place if it will improve the organization. Leaders should gather information, identify and study alternatives, and determine the results of change. A well-organized plan will assure the best results and gain the support and confidence of those affected by the change.

KEYS TO SUCCESSFUL CHANGE

Communication is important for successful implementation of change. Sometimes managers make the mistake of believing it is best not to say anything to employees about possible changes until a final decision has been made. They believe that early information will lead to confusion and misunderstanding. Agents of change recognize that it is almost impossible to conceal information about future changes. Limited and informal communication will lead to rumors and panic within an organization. People who feel that they have been misled or have not been fully informed will usually resist the change. Open, two-way communication between management and employees is needed for an effective change process.

People are more likely to support what they have helped to create. Managers must recognize employees as a good source of ideas for practical solutions. An effective change process involves the people who will be affected in gathering information, considering alternatives, and testing solutions. Although it is not always possible to involve everyone in all parts of the change process, employees will be more supportive when they feel that they have input.

Music discovery sites on the Web are experiencing dramatic increases since MTV opted to show fewer music videos in favor of full-length programs. Yahoo! Music's Launch web site streamed 100 million music videos a month in 2003 compared to 15 million a month in 2002. Rival AOL Music on the America Online service streamed 80 million videos in March 2003, up from 20 million the previous year.

AOL Music is the top music destination, attracting 11 million U.S. users in February 2003. Both AOL Music and Yahoo! Music's Launch offer extensive Internet radio stations, music news, and free libraries of music videos.

THINK CRITICALLY

1. **What is controversial about music and music videos offered online?**
2. **How should radio and television respond to the cyber competition?**

Change within an organization does not just evolve. Individuals must receive training for new procedures, new technology, or redesigned jobs. Managers must be attentive to the needs of individuals who will be the most affected by the changes. Meetings and training programs should be set up to prepare employees for the required changes.

Most individuals resist change because they are uncertain of the end result. People who feel that they will receive support from their organization are more willing to accept change. All change involves some risk, and organizations cannot guarantee success. Individuals who face change want assurance from management that there will be support available to adjust to the change. Management must provide feedback on how employees are performing during changing circumstances. They also should be less critical of mistakes early in the process. Counseling, training, and additional information are methods of support that make employees feel more comfortable.

REDUCTIONS IN THE WORKFORCE

Downsizing occurs when an organization reduces its number of employees. This type of change is difficult for managers to implement and for employees to accept. Some companies try to help people affected by downsizing by providing training for other positions available in the company. Some organizations offer training in new skills to help workers gain employment in other companies.

Sometimes change is negative for employees, especially if they are terminated from their jobs, asked to take a reduction in pay, or required to move to a less desirable location. Companies may offer **severance packages** that provide terminated employees with full or partial salaries for several weeks or months. Severance pay allows the unemployed individuals some time to look for new jobs. Good organizations also provide personal training and career counseling to help with job-seeking skills.

INTERMISSION

What can companies do for employees who lose their jobs due to downsizing?

____

____

LEADERSHIP NECESSARY FOR SUCCESSFUL CHANGE

Change requires *visionary leadership*, which can be defined as individuals who have a vision of the future. Most leaders are uncomfortable with this definition due to its limited implications. Having a vision is not enough to bring about successful organizational change. **Enlightened leadership** requires individuals to have the vision for change and the ability to get members of the organization to accept ownership of that vision. Ownership results in a strong commitment to follow through on the change. Enlightened leaders should encourage their employees to be creative with a vision and empower them to make the vision a reality. Enlightened leadership means bringing out the best in people. Change can be implemented more quickly when employees' mindsets are dealt with before or during the change.

© GETTY IMAGES/PHOTODISC

LEADERSHIP SKILLS

The dynamic nature of organizations provides numerous opportunities for leaders to emerge. Leadership is marked by making things happen. Teams have become increasingly important for many organizations. Leadership passes back and forth among team members as different phases of projects are completed. Leadership is more than the ability to develop a strategy and get things done. Leadership instills a sense of direction and confidence to successfully complete tasks. Leadership requires an understanding of people and the ability to motivate them. Role models, job-based experiences, and student organizations provide the means for leadership development.

© GETTY IMAGES/PHOTODISC

EMPOWERMENT

Successful change occurs when leaders tap into team members' deepest needs to feel empowered. Most people have a "What's-in-it-for-me?" attitude, and successful managers tune in to this soft issue. Effective questions are probably the most valuable empowerment tool within a changing organization. Leaders must be masters at asking effective questions and using effective listening to determine what the answers to the questions really mean. Effective questions must balance the critical aspects of nurturing people and creating organizational results. Effective questions for change must help individuals or teams find their own solutions.

THE RIGHT EQUATION FOR CHANGE

Dynamic sports and entertainment organizations and leaders understand that there is a need for a clearly understood purpose or mission. The mission must inspire the members of the team or organization. Team members must buy into the organization's mission. A shared purpose and vision must come from the heart of the organization. Outstanding organizational performance and personal satisfaction work together and reinforce each other to bring about change.

Leaders must act as role models for team members. They must promote their own willingness to change. Enlightened leaders realize that the key to effective change is the collective attitude of team members. Employees will serve customers to the extent that they feel served by the organization and its leadership.

INTERMISSION

What is enlightened leadership?

UNDERSTAND MANAGEMENT CONCEPTS

Circle the best answer for each of the following questions.

1. ___?___ occurs when companies or organizations reduce the number of employees.
a. Feedback
b. Severance pay
c. Downsizing
d. Mutual reward

2. The sports and entertainment industry has
a. remained relatively stable
b. been very dynamic
c. not been affected by changing laws and regulations
d. not been affected by public perception

THINK CRITICALLY

Answer the following questions as completely as possible. If necessary, use a separate sheet of paper.

3. What are the steps that should be followed for change within an organization? Why should organizations follow these steps?

____

____

____

4. Why do people resist change?

____

____

____

____

5. Why must enlightened leaders pay attention to soft issues when making changes within an organization?

____

____

____

____

____

____

REVIEW MANAGEMENT CONCEPTS

Write the letter of the term that matches each definition. Some terms will not be used.

	a. downsizing
	b. enlightened leadership
	c. hard issues
	d. human relations
	e. leaders
	f. leadership
	g. leadership style
	h. Mutual Reward Theory (MRT)
	i. power
	j. severance packages
	k. soft issues
	l. stakeholders

_____ **1.** The ability to control behavior

_____ **2.** Managers who earn the respect and cooperation of employees

_____ **3.** The general way a manager treats and supervises employees

_____ **4.** Based on the premise that both parties come out ahead

_____ **5.** Employees who feel ownership for the success or failure of an organization

_____ **6.** Requires individuals to have the vision for change and the ability to get members to accept ownership of that vision

_____ **7.** Full or partial salaries paid to employees who are terminated from a company

_____ **8.** Human issues that are difficult to measure but must be considered

_____ **9.** The ability to get along within a group due to respect for every individual

_____ **10.** The ability to influence individuals to cooperatively achieve goals for an organization

_____ **11.** Reduction in a company's number of employees

Circle the best answer.

12. Which kind of feedback should leaders avoid giving employees during changing circumstances?
- **a.** critique on mistakes
- **b.** encouragement
- **c.** support
- **d.** evaluation of job performance

13. Hard issues are an organization's
- **a.** problems
- **b.** highlights
- **c.** symptoms
- **d.** assets

14. A situational leader does not
- **a.** adjust leadership to different circumstances
- **b.** make use of individual employees' strengths
- **c.** understand the importance of flexibility
- **d.** use autocratic style in all situations

THINK CRITICALLY

15. Give examples of hard issues and soft issues at sporting events such as soccer, football, and basketball games.

16. Think about the teachers and principals at your school and explain how each group gains power (position, reward, expert, or identity power) within the school. Explain your answer thoroughly.

17. Discuss the meaning of empowerment. What are the most valuable empowerment tools in a changing organization?

18. Name at least four characteristics that successful leaders possess.

19. Choose one form of entertainment and explain the changes that it has undergone recently. Explain the reasons for the changes.

MAKE CONNECTIONS

20. Management Math You are in charge of downsizing your company. Unfortunately, you have to break the news to five executives that your company will no longer employ them. Each executive makes an annual salary of $240,000. You will offer these individuals three months of severance pay. How much will the gross severance pay for these five executives cost your company?

____

____

____

21. Communication Interview someone in your community whom you consider to be a leader. (You might choose a leader in your school, in a local business, or in a sports or entertainment organization.) Ask about his or her leadership style, strengths and weaknesses as a manager, and methods for motivating employees. Write a one-page paper about this community leader.

____

____

____

____

22. Technology Use the Internet to research a major sports or entertainment event scheduled for the future, such as the Super Bowl, state fair, Final Four, or Bowl Championship Series. Describe the information that is provided on this web site. Would you classify this web site as user-friendly? Why or why not?

____

____

____

23. Human Resources Management More businesses are operating 24 hours a day, seven days a week, requiring sports and entertainment employees to work evenings and weekends. What kinds of rewards should companies offer employees for working unusual schedules?

____

____

____

____

24. Business Management Principles Nightclubs are experiencing more tragedies due to fires and out-of-control patrons. What are the soft issues and hard issues causing problems for nightclubs?

25. Financial Management Popular musicians are becoming increasingly frustrated with lower sales of CDs, records, and cassette tapes due to many people burning songs from the Internet onto CDs. Napster was the first guilty culprit that allowed individuals to illegally copy music from the Internet. Today there are numerous other sources for downloadable music. What is the best solution to this dilemma that decreases the income earned by musicians?

26. Human Resources Management Now is the time to assess your leadership characteristics. What characteristics do you possess that make you a leader? How can you strengthen or acquire leadership skills?

27. Communication You are in charge of implementing a number of new processes and procedures within your organization. Knowing that employees are likely to resist these changes, you have decided to gain their buy-in by asking for their input and involvement. Write a memo to employees telling them about the exciting new changes planned for the company and soliciting their suggestions for implementing the changes.

DECA PREP
An Association of Marketing Students

HOSTING THE BIG EVENT

The Super Bowl brings more than fans, athletes, and media to the host city. This major sporting event delivers close to $300 million to the local economy. Ninety percent of that money will be spent on lodging, food, beverages, and entertainment. The remaining ten percent will be spent with local companies. The National Football League (NFL) and the host city's Super Bowl Host Committee make every effort to invest a percentage of the revenue in minority- and women-owned businesses in the local community.

Opportunity for Businesses

The Super Bowl presents a tremendous opportunity for emerging businesses. Participants learn how to develop new contract relationships with NFL sponsors and affiliates. They also have the opportunity to link with well-known brands across the country.

The Host Committee

The Houston Super Bowl Host Committee for Super Bowl XXXVIII is the liaison between the NFL and local efforts. The committee is comprised of 200 business and community leaders from the Houston area. The group is responsible for transportation, marketing, special events, minority business development, public relations, and volunteer recruitment.

A major objective of the host committee is to prepare Houston to welcome the Super Bowl. Strategies are planned for fulfilling the obligations made to the NFL and its owners in a way that encourages them to award Houston a future Super Bowl.

The host committee plans to take advantage of the local economy's $300 million expansion by creating jobs and administering a business development program. The committee will host seminars to help minority- and women-owned businesses learn more about the requirements and processes necessary to be vendors for the big event. The theme for business involvement—"Get in the Game!"—has positive implications for businesses long after the Super Bowl game is played on February 1, 2004.

The host committee plans to enhance Houston's worldwide visibility and add to the quality of life of the individuals who live, work, and visit the city of Houston and the state of Texas.

Volunteers and Venue

It takes nearly 10,000 volunteers to help with the Super Bowl. Volunteers serve as ambassadors to the host city and play an important role in showcasing it as a great Super Bowl venue.

Houston's state-of-the-art Reliant Stadium also helps promote the city as a great location for the Super Bowl. The climate-controlled stadium, with a retractable roof and 166 luxury suites, provides an attractive facility for this major sporting event.

Sponsors

The Super Bowl is unlike any other experience in sports. The parties, concerts, interactive exhibits, and football game converge to provide the ultimate experience for companies that participate. Sponsors for the Super Bowl receive a four-pronged benefits strategy of

- customized brand marketing and promotional opportunities
- unique and exclusive corporate hospitality programs
- client incentive programs
- community- and cause-related initiatives

Think Critically

1. Why would a city want to host the Super Bowl?
2. Why is public relations so important for the host city of the Super Bowl?
3. How does a Super Bowl affect the future well-being of a city?
4. Use the Internet to learn more about Houston. What attractions should be highlighted for fans attending the Super Bowl?

SPORTS AND ENTERTAINMENT MARKETING MANAGEMENT TEAM DECISION MAKING

You are chairperson of a committee that is trying to persuade the state athletics association to schedule the high school baseball championships in your city of 200,000 people. Your community has 10,000 hotel rooms available. Twenty new state-of-the-art baseball fields and 15 additional fields in good shape will provide the venue for the games. The regional shopping mall and local university are additional attractions for fans attending the baseball championships.

Devise a strategy to persuade the state athletics association to choose your city for the baseball championships. You must include information about available facilities, demographics for the city, and additional attractions for fans.

Performance Indicators Evaluated

- Understand the meaning of demographics.
- Use demographics as rationale for the proposal.
- Define characteristics needed by a city to host a major sporting event.
- Explain how the characteristics of your city meet the necessary rationale for the event.
- Outline the benefits of having the event in your city.

Go to the DECA web site for more detailed information.

1. What are the most important features to market about your city? Why?
2. Should you talk about competing cities during your presentation? Why or why not?
3. What kind of presentation will be the most effective?
4. Should the reputation (for example, the low crime rate) of your city be emphasized during your presentation? Why or why not?

www.deca.org/publications/HS_Guide/guidetoc.html

CHAPTER 10

Managing Groups and Teams

10.1 UNDERSTANDING GROUP STRUCTURES

10.2 BUILDING SUCCESSFUL TEAMS

10.3 DESIGNING A TEAM-BASED ORGANIZATION

© GETTY IMAGES/PHOTODISC

WINNING Strategies

IF TIGER CAN DO IT, WHY CAN'T I?

Tiger Woods started a revolution in golf several years ago and has become an inspiration for a whole generation of African-American and Asian-American youth. Woods showed that even an individual sport like golf could create a sense of group and team spirit. Woods is a symbol of success and achievement. Everyone wants to be on "his" team. Young African-Americans and Asian-Americans copy his mannerisms and wear his Nike gear. They want to be "just like Tiger."

One of Woods' biggest fans is Michelle Wie. This young golfer from Hawaii became the youngest female ever to win a USGA event at the age of 13. According to Wie, she owes her success to Tiger Woods' influence. Her bedroom is covered with pictures and memorabilia of Woods. Like thousands of other youth, Wie even models her wardrobe after Woods. Just like Tiger, she has her own "power" color—bright red. Woods' dedication to practice and his confidence to try impossible shots inspired Wie to follow in his footsteps. From difficult bunker shots to daring long putts, Wie has mastered the touch necessary to become a golfing sensation.

As for the future, this high-school champion says that she will continue to play golf like Tiger Woods. She hopes that some of his fans will now become hers. What will a teenage female champion mean to women's golf? Apparel manufacturers are betting that Michelle Wie's "red look" will be seen with increasing frequency in athletic wardrobes and on the links. There just might be a new "tiger" in town.

THINK CRITICALLY

1. How did Tiger Woods' success influence Michelle Wie?
2. How could Michelle Wie's success motivate other young female golfers to succeed?

LESSON 10.1

UNDERSTANDING GROUP STRUCTURES

Explain the two basic structures of groups.

Describe factors that influence group behavior.

OPENING ACT

Is surfing a sport or a form of entertainment? More than ever, the answer seems to be that it is both. The renewed interest in surfing has spawned a variety of TV shows, from MTV's *Surf Girls* to WB's™ *Boarding House: North Shore*. Most of the popular shows are reality-based rather than plot-based. The common thread is that the shows display the intimacy of small-group behavior and the desire for thrills. Producers of such shows believe that the surfer lifestyle and expression of freedom is something that most of us secretly would like to follow. Older generations turned to motorcycles for this same expression of freedom. However, for the younger generation, surf's up!

Work with a partner to discuss how the popularity of surfing and surfing entertainment shows might impact small-group behavior and lifestyles.

GROUPS—THE BASIC COMPONENT

Groups are an important component of an organization. They are a critical factor in strategic decision making. To be considered part of a group, people must interact with other group members in such a way that they influence or are influenced by the others. To be effective, groups should be small—usually fewer than ten people.

FORMAL GROUPS

Two basic groups exist within organizations. A **formal work group** is created by management to run the organization and to carry out organizational goals and objectives. This type of group has formal recognition, an identity or title, and a set of goals and purposes. A formal work group can exist for a short period of time or can be extended to a long-term committee or project team.

The formal work group makes many high-level decisions. For example, a sports manager rarely has the time to consider and review scouting reports for possible new team members. The manager assigns this task to a formal work group. This group then reports its findings to the sports manager. Both the manager and the formal work group make decisions based on the data.

INFORMAL GROUPS

An **informal work group** is formed with a different set of criteria than the formal work group. Sports and entertainment managers form informal work groups based on friendship, shared interests, or even proximity, such as sharing office space or sharing a ride with someone. Like formal work groups, informal work groups can be established for varying lengths of time.

Why would a manager trust decision making to such a loosely connected group of people? Think how often you make decisions based on what friends tell you. The sports and entertainment manager also often relies on friends, people who share a common interest, peers from chat rooms, or acquaintances from down the hall to supply information for making decisions. Members of an informal group can also be members of a formal group. For example, an acquaintance with whom you share an interest in running may be a member of a newly created, formal work group.

> **the Global Manager**
>
> Annual revenues of $230 million! Could this be the New York Yankees or the Los Angeles Lakers? No. It is the Manchester United Soccer Club. The $230 million comes from ticket sales, media rights, commercials, and merchandising. Manchester U produces not only great revenues but also outstanding profits—$50.3 million at last count—thanks to its 53 million worldwide fans and some of soccer's most popular players.
>
> Recently, Manchester U sold its greatest superstar, David Beckham, to Real Madrid. Manchester U believes that in order to have continued success, it must shift its focus back to the team and away from stars such as Beckham. Managers are predicting that this decision will ensure the long-term success of the club.
>
> **THINK CRITICALLY**
>
> 1. Why has Manchester U been so successful?
> 2. Would you sell a superstar to ensure your team's success? Explain your answer.

Working in an organization is an interactive, social experience. This experience often causes managers to seek input beyond formal structures. Anytime you ask a more experienced person for advice, you are doing the same thing.

Since informal work groups are not governed in the same way as formal work groups, managers must always be mindful of how decisions are being made. With formal work groups, there is often a record of discussions or at least a process by which decisions are made. In the case of informal work groups, this usually is not true. If the manager makes decisions based on unreliable input, decisions can be flawed. Senior managers are usually aware of this possibility. They encourage managers under them to establish formal groups for critical decision making. Formal groups help to ensure accountability.

There are many classic movies that have not yet been released in DVD format. Turner Classic Movies (TCM) is letting movie fans decide which of 20 classic movies will be released on DVD. By giving movie fans the opportunity to help make this decision, TCM is hoping that fan interest will increase and sales will rise.

Sports and entertainment managers have noticed that informal work groups are growing in number and importance. Some believe that the impact of the Internet as a discussion and communication device is the reason for this change. Others believe that the work environment is responsible. Most organizations are becoming more security conscious. Consequently, friends are considered more reliable than acquaintances or strangers for decision-making purposes.

Consider how you make your own decisions. Do you rely on data sources such as teachers, textbooks, the library, or counselors to make important decisions? Or do you rely more heavily on friends, chat groups, or general entertainment media like magazines or television to provide information critical to decisions such as choosing a college, picking a job, or making a major purchase?

Since decision making usually is the product of several heads rather than just one, management should study the **group dynamic**, or how group members interact and influence one another. Since sports and entertainment managers are aware of the importance of both individual and organizational performance, many are now choosing to spend time understanding just how managers and employees communicate and make decisions. Sports and entertainment organizations must think strategically to be successful. Group thoughts and input, whether from formal or informal work groups, must be organized for the best long-term interests of the organization.

INTERMISSION

What is the difference between an informal work group and a formal work group?

____

____

© BRAND X PICTURES

FACTORS THAT INFLUENCE GROUPS

One of the first decisions that sports and entertainment managers must make as they design their organization is whether group or individual decision making will be the primary means for establishing strategy and policy. The answer to this question is not an easy one.

WHICH FORM OF DECISION MAKING IS BEST?

Views are mixed as to whether individuals or groups make better decisions. Several considerations should be reviewed when determining the role of groups in an organization.

Tasks When decisions are made, what task in the organization is being addressed? In other words, would individuals or groups be better prepared to accomplish this task? Obviously, this depends on the task itself. A sports manager may rely on a group to construct a game plan but may make individual decisions during the game.

Consensus Groups are a way to build consensus, or agreement, in an organization. If employees are part of the decision-making process, they may be more supportive of the solution and more willing to implement it. This is not always the case, but group decision making does have its benefits when it comes to the general acceptance of policies.

Quality of Decisions Some managers believe that as more people are involved, the quality of the decision-making process improves. Others believe the opposite. There is really no right answer to this issue. However, having a variety of creative ideas can help develop a high-quality decision.

Quality of Decision Makers No matter how many people are involved in the decision-making process, the quality of the decision makers is always an issue. Sports and entertainment managers must find the best talent possible. They then must use that talent to increase the likelihood that good, creative decisions will be made.

Group Effectiveness The outcome of a group effort must be achieved easily and efficiently. Group effectiveness often becomes an issue as the size of the group grows. Some members of a large group may not mix well with others. For example, consider all the group members that are involved in picking players during a professional sports draft. Some members of the group may want to use draft picks to rebuild the team with unproven rookie players. Other members may advise trading the team's draft picks and securing proven veterans to further a winning record for the coming season. To be successful, managers must blend the group elements so that they work together and not against one another.

MANAGING GROUP BEHAVIOR EFFECTIVELY

All groups live by rules. These rules may be formal or informal. A formal rule might be that only females can be members of the group. An informal rule might be that no one in the group talks negatively about another group member. Managers must be aware that factors such as group norms, group cohesiveness, and group conformity will have an impact on group effectiveness.

© GETTY IMAGES/PHOTODISC

Group norms are established to regulate informal rules. Once adopted, these norms highly regulate the group and its members. For example, when your group of friends goes to a movie, some group norms might be that everyone must be on time, pay his or her own way, and turn off cell phones during the movie. Continually violating these norms will not sit well with your group.

Group cohesiveness often is a determining factor in whether group norms are followed. Group cohesiveness is what binds groups together. It is the extent to which an individual is attracted to a group. An example of group cohesiveness is when avid fans all wear team colors to a football game. The more cohesive the group is, the more likely individual members are to follow group norms.

Size matters when it comes to group cohesiveness. Larger groups are usually not as cohesive as smaller ones. Therefore, smaller management groups are generally preferred within an organization. These managerial groups often have many other small groups working under their control.

Success breeds group cohesiveness. As groups meet, gather information, plan strategies, make decisions, and then implement those decisions, success builds confidence in the group decision-making process. When first forming groups, managers should make sure that small successes can be achieved quickly. These early successes will give the groups the confidence to attack more difficult and riskier problems. Often a Little League coach works hard with players on baseball fundamentals. Just holding the bat or glove correctly can be a success for some players. As players gain confidence in performing the fundamentals correctly, it is easier for them to face and conquer skills that are more difficult.

Other aspects of work groups that must be considered are the status of being associated with the group, the skills of group members, the types of work to be performed, the opportunity for advancement, and even the risk of failure. As managers consider these issues, they must focus on which of these aspects could build or destroy group cohesiveness.

Group conformity is an indication of how willingly group members adhere to group norms and desire the benefits of group cohesiveness. Most work groups, by necessity, wish to control the efforts and output of their members. The need to conform is a two-edged sword. It is great for unifying the group's opinion, but it can stifle creativity and individuality. Therefore, managers should choose members of important groups carefully. Too many aggressive personalities can be disruptive in small groups. Too many conservative members will bring about little change.

Sports and entertainment organizations must carefully watch the pressures placed on individuals within important decision-making groups. Because of the pressure to conform, many organizations have been damaged by too many "yes people." Since individuals bring information and knowledge to groups, these same individuals are responsible for constructing the group norms. The members who contribute the most to the group are the most likely to have the norms modeled after their own likes and dislikes. When group norms come under fire and group cohesiveness is in question, managers should look to the group's leaders for guidance. To aid group cohesiveness and conformity, managers should

- Make the group smaller
- Seek participation to the point where everyone buys in to developing overall group goals and objectives
- Find other groups with which to compete
- Reward the group as a whole as often as possible
- Find opportunities, such as a retreat, for the group to bond

If an organization is having difficulty with its essential groups, then it should go back to the basics. Managers and executives in the sports and entertainment industries have found that simple solutions to group problems often are the best.

INTERMISSION

What are the differences among group norms, group cohesiveness, and group conformity?

___

___

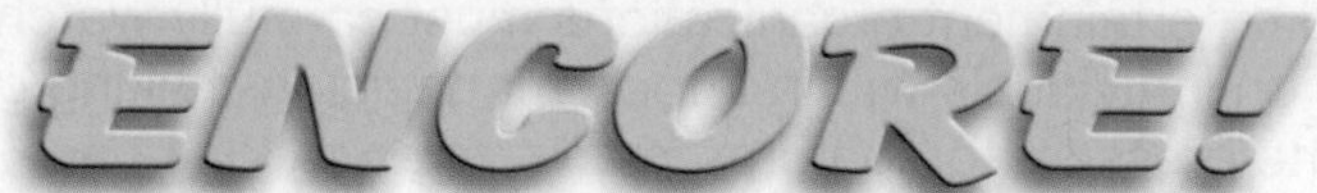

UNDERSTAND MANAGEMENT CONCEPTS

Circle the best answer for each of the following questions.

1. Group norms are established to regulate
- **a.** management
- **b.** informal rules
- **c.** human resource management policies
- **d.** corporate strategies

2. Group cohesiveness is what
- **a.** makes all groups the same
- **b.** makes groups follow the rules
- **c.** makes groups think alike
- **d.** binds groups together

THINK CRITICALLY

Answer the following questions as completely as possible. If necessary, use a separate sheet of paper.

3. Technology Visit the web site for MGM Studios. How many different businesses does MGM run? Comment on the importance of groups for managing these businesses.

____

____

____

4. Communication Form a group of five classmates. Assume that your group will do a term project together over the next few weeks. Since your group must meet and perform a task, write a list of informal rules that your group must follow in order to be successful.

____

____

____

5. Explain the advantages and disadvantages of group conformity. Apply your list to a situation in the sports or entertainment industry.

____

____

____

____

BUILDING SUCCESSFUL TEAMS

Describe the different types of teams used by an organization.

Explain how a manager can build a successful team.

OPENING ACT

Many modern movies emphasize speed, action, and thrills. One sure way to achieve all three is to include plenty of scenes involving fast cars and car chases. Automobile collector Ray Claridge supplies contemporary and antique cars for many of today's action films. Using Claridge-owned cars has become so commonplace that many studios consider him a key member of their production team. Claridge, who owns more than 1,000 automobiles, believes that his cars are just as crucial to any film as the actors who ride in them.

Work with a partner to investigate how expensive props such as cars are provided for movies and television shows. Summarize your findings.

TEAM SHAPES AND SIZES

A team is not just a group of people. A team shares a common purpose, has goals, and is responsible for what it does and does not accomplish. The synergy, or interaction, between team members is often what makes the team approach one of the most valuable tools available to the sports or entertainment manager. Teams often become their own supervisors and are able to complete work tasks with little or no outside direction.

© GETTY IMAGES/PHOTODISC

Are you a video game player? If not, you are in the minority. Many believe that the beginning of the modern action video game began with the violence-based game called *Doom*™. Avid game players focused on the technical breakthroughs of the game, such as animation and 3D graphics, while critics focused on the blatant violence. Social scientists believe that *Doom* provided a wake-up call to society about popular youth entertainment. Today, a more moderate approach in video game entertainment is advocated.

THINK CRITICALLY

1. **Use the Internet to investigate action-oriented video games. Are these games more or less violent today than when they were first introduced?**
2. **What are the drawbacks of violent video games?**

TEAM FORMS

Teams come in many shapes and sizes.

Temporary teams primarily are responsible for offering suggestions on how to solve short-term problems. For example, a temporary team might suggest how to improve productivity or increase revenues. Managers who use temporary teams usually form these teams using other managers and employees who are trusted for their insight and quick thinking. Diversity of thought is encouraged for temporary teams. Temporary teams often do not get much credit for what they accomplish. However, this type of team usually knows that its recommendations are important to upper-level management.

Problem-solving teams are formed by managers to address specific problems that confront the sports or entertainment organization. This type of team looks at short- and long-term problems. The problem-solving team usually has a definite structure and is made up of members from critical divisions within the organization. A good example of this type of team is the **quality circle**, a group that meets regularly and addresses issues that affect the quality of the organization. The Atlanta Braves could use a quality circle to examine fan satisfaction, parking adequacy, revenues versus expenses, and the public image of the team.

Semi-independent teams are given wide-ranging authority to set their own goals and pursue difficult issues that confront the organization. For example, several years ago the NFL and MLB were cited for failure to promote minorities within middle- and top-management ranks. Many of the concerned organizations within the leagues attacked the problem by forming semi-independent teams to examine the charges. The independent nature of these teams gave them the flexibility to overcome barriers and address the problem. Today, most agree that both the NFL and MLB have diversified their management structures.

Autonomous teams can function as independently managed teams. These teams work as cohesive units and address work tasks without management direction. They know their job, and they approach their work in a highly creative manner. Several years ago, an autonomous team was formed to revive interest in the performing arts in Dallas. The team reviewed all previous efforts to revive the arts, generated creative ideas, and attacked the problem beyond the normal confines of tradition and top management direction. The team's solution to the problem was to promote the performing arts programs to blue-collar families. This previously ignored market segment responded well to the customized performing arts programs. The entire community developed a renewed interest in the performing arts.

© GETTY IMAGES/PHOTODISC

New venture development teams examine new ideas, products, and services, and focus on re-growing the organization. New venture development teams helped NASCAR expand its fan base. They reviewed traditional thinking about market segments and expanded promotional efforts to females. Today, NASCAR drivers' images are everywhere from cereal boxes to the cover of *TV Guide*™. New venture development teams for NASCAR opened lines of communication and changed the way problems were addressed.

Managers must remember that solving problems with teams can be as effective as with individual decision makers. Multiple viewpoints, if monitored and controlled, are a plus in any sports or entertainment organization.

INTERMISSION

What types of teams might be used by sports and entertainment managers for decision making?

THE ART OF TEAM BUILDING

Just because you are a member of a team does not mean that you and your team members will be successful in meeting goals and objectives. Developing successful teams is an art to be learned by managers.

TEAMS THAT FAIL

The individuals who can make a team strong also can cause it grief and frustration. There are different views on a team, and those views can be divisive. The team's leadership may be inadequate. There also may be too many leaders on the team, causing members to struggle for power and prestige within the group. Team members can become uncontrollable and

Is gymnastics a team sport or an individual sport? Members of a gymnastics team compete against other teams, but they compete even more vigorously against fellow team members. The gymnasts know that a limited number of them will be selected as team members to participate in competitions. Concerns about achieving or maintaining top rankings plague team members. Because of the pressure of internal competition, do members of a gymnastics team really cheer for and support fellow team members? Maintaining a team spirit on a gymnastics team is a difficult task for any coach.

THINK CRITICALLY

1. Describe the ethical problems that might be present on a gymnastics team.
2. How should a gymnastics coach stimulate true team spirit?

cause the team to lose its focus or purpose. Finally, *groupthink*—too much conformity within the team—can occur.

How does a manager know when a team is not functioning properly? The manager should look for four traditional danger signs.

- Failure to accomplish goals and tasks
- Constant argument among team members
- Sparsely attended meetings
- Lack of effective communication among team members

TEAMS THAT SUCCEED

Observations from managers indicate that successful teams have several characteristics in common. First, members recognize that they are on a team and that team membership carries a certain responsibility. Members take this responsibility seriously. On successful teams, members are on time for meetings and complete their fair share of the work. Team members work on a task until it is completed.

Second, whether it is through a common understanding or a commitment to a company slogan—such as "People are our most important asset"—team members have a sense of purpose. They follow a mission in their team assignment. This mission often gives direction to the team and ties the work tasks of the team to the overall mission of the organization.

Third, successful teams set goals for themselves. Since most teamwork in large sports and entertainment organizations is directed toward specific work tasks, it is important that each project have a beginning and an end. For optimum success of the team, results should be measurable. For example, suppose a work team in a sports organization has the goal of building a better image within the community. The team should document the existing image and determine what is wrong with it, how it needs to be improved, and what actions should be taken for improvement. Once action is taken, some form of feedback is needed to show that the image has changed for the better.

Fourth, successful teams are large enough to accomplish the task at hand and spread the workload of the assignment, but are small enough to ensure effective communication and shared purpose. Team members must be willing to share work responsibilities. Effective teams regularly shift leadership responsibilities so that every member gains leadership experience. This is an effective way for an organization to expand its managerial skill level.

Finally, successful teams share responsibility for success and failure. Teams learn from experience. *Accountability*, or responsibility for actions, ensures that teams carefully consider their decisions.

CHOOSING THE RIGHT TEAM MEMBERS

Successful teams have the ability to select the right members. Selection and development of these team members can be accomplished in many ways.

- Select the most qualified members for a team based on skills and ability.
- Verify that team members can follow operating rules and have demonstrated the knack for personal responsibility.
- Teach team members how to "coach" one another for best results.
- Be willing to change the membership as team and organizational needs change. Long-term membership can isolate the team from other workers, and perspective may be lost.
- Select members from those who either like to work on teams or are willing to work on teams.
- Be willing to continually train members on how to successfully function as a team.

Success in one area may not ensure success in another. For example, teams at Disney succeeded in providing nationally recognized entertainment in Disney theme parks. However, those same teams were not necessarily as successful in developing the first Disney web site. Later teams made significant improvements. Today, Disney's web site is one of the most popular of all youth web sites.

There are many other hints for building successful teams. It is important for each sports and entertainment organization to review its own needs with respect to work teams. It is also helpful to carefully study others who have been successful in team building.

Marketing teams are often willing to spend large sums of company money to advertise their products during prime-time television hours when the ads will be seen by the greatest number of viewers. For example, in 2003, a 30-second spot on the popular television show *Friends* cost advertisers $455,700.

INTERMISSION

List three suggestions for selecting and developing the right team members.

___

___

UNDERSTAND MANAGEMENT CONCEPTS

Circle the best answer for each of the following questions.

1. Quality circles are an example of a

a. temporary team
b. semi-independent team
c. problem-solving team
d. new venture development team

2. All of the following are among the reasons that teams may fail *except*

a. differing views can be divisive
b. groupthink can occur
c. power struggles can happen
d. accountability is present

THINK CRITICALLY

Answer the following questions as completely as possible. If necessary, use a separate sheet of paper.

3. Research Interview a sports or entertainment manager about his or her views toward teams. Ask how teams are used in the organization and what pluses and minuses the manager would identify for using teams to aid in decision making. Report your findings.

____

____

____

4. Technology Use the Internet to contact a news and entertainment organization such as CNN, ABC, CBS, NBC, or FOX. Use the web site's "Contact Us" feature to ask how the organization uses teams to aid in decision-making efforts. If there is no response, select another organization and ask the same question. Summarize your findings.

____

____

____

5. Management Math Assume that you are a manager assembling a team to aid your organization in its decision-making efforts. You estimate that your first work task will take 48 hours to complete. If each team member can contribute three hours per week to the task and the team has eight members, how many weeks will the first work task take to complete?

____

____

DESIGNING A TEAM-BASED ORGANIZATION

OPENING ACT

Some would say that the Boston Red Sox have an old stadium, an old team, and a tradition for losing. The team has not won a World Series since it traded Babe Ruth to the New York Yankees in 1919. However, Red Sox management has a new philosophy to change the past—innovation. The organization has completely changed its approach to managerial responsibility and fan involvement. For Red Sox managers, fans are the key to future team success. One of the first changes was to allow fans to sit atop the fabled "Green Monster" in Fenway Park's left field. At $50 per seat, the idea was an instant revenue producer. Each game day, pre-game activities are moved out to the streets to reach fans. Management is predicting that as fan appreciation and involvement increase so will revenues and the likelihood of winning a World Series.

Work with a partner to investigate how the Boston Red Sox organization is improving fan relationships with innovation. Summarize your findings.

Explain how organizations can be designed to support teams.

Describe a virtual team and its function.

IS TEAM STRUCTURE THE KEY TO ORGANIZATIONAL SUCCESS?

Why are teams so important to sports and entertainment organizations? Research has shown that team-based organizations generally perform better than those that fail to fully implement team concepts.

Why doesn't every organization employ the team-based management style? First, because of their small, independent beginnings, many organizations prefer the individual approach to decision making. Second, many organizations simply do not know how to create or use teams effectively. Finally, creating a team-based organization often is a difficult task.

A **team-based organization** is one where the basic work unit is teams rather than individuals or some other organizational structure. In the team-based organization, all planning, decision making, and implementation of decisions is accomplished by team-oriented work groups. This structure presents a unique set of management challenges. Managers must be able to motivate and control groups. Since most managers are trained to work with individuals, forming and guiding teams is often a difficult task.

In 1803 Thomas Jefferson doubled the size of the United States by purchasing a vast land space from France, now known as Louisiana. In 2003, Louisiana celebrated the bicentennial of the "Louisiana Purchase." Teams of planners marked this historic anniversary with food, song, and hundreds of special events.

TEAM-BASED ORGANIZATIONS REQUIRE SPECIAL PLANNING

Designing an organization that will foster and support the team-based approach to management often requires special planning efforts. To promote productive teams, managers must be aware that teams require special support resources that are sometimes different from those required to support individual decision making.

Organizational Purpose The first resource area that must be in place is **organizational purpose**. Managers must think, "What is my philosophy on how to organize and run this organization?" The answer to this question sets the stage for a team-based approach. Managers must believe that teams are beneficial and that the team-based approach is the most efficient form of decision making.

Communication Managers must design the organization so that communication processes support teams. An organization that has many levels throws up barriers to teams. Flattened organizations—those without many levels—seem to support teams better. This type of organization also supports the team-based concept that work tasks should be spread among all employees.

Managerial Systems The organization's managerial systems must allow teams to flourish and grow. Team growth is often accomplished by creating information systems that tie employees into sensitive data. Management must work hard to erase territorial boundaries that prevent teams from using information provided by all parts of the organization in decision-making efforts and projects.

Team Members The heart of any team is its team members. Sports and entertainment managers must pick the right members to be part of a team. Managers must constantly train all employees to be good team members. This task is not as easy as it sounds. Many employees prefer to work alone.

Team Concept Team-based organizations are characterized by their emphasis on practicing the team concept. If the team concept is to work, all team members must learn how to be innovators, followers, and leaders.

The future of the team-based organization depends on having a managerial staff that embraces the application of these support resources. Building successful teams requires hard work. Ask any championship team manager.

INTERMISSION

Describe a team-based organization.

____

____

VIRTUAL TEAMS

The power of the Internet and sophisticated communication devices allow sports and entertainment managers to experiment with a new form of team—the virtual team. A **virtual team** is a team that does not have physical contact among its members and operates in a non-traditional environment. Team members can be from anywhere in the world. Team meetings are conducted in cyberspace or by teleconferencing.

The virtual team was initiated by managers in the communication industry to solve problems of location and distance among members. Sports and entertainment managers quickly embraced the concept. Virtual teams are popular with organizations involved in global strategies and partnerships. Team members can meet regularly without leaving their individual offices.

The Internet gives managers the opportunity to put a new spin on the virtual team concept. Whether by using sophisticated *intranets* (communication systems within the company) or *extranets* (communication systems outside the company), managers today are only a mouse click away from sharing ideas and receiving input to help solve difficult decisions. Distant team members can be brought even closer together with collaborative software products that aid in specific areas such as strategic planning, inventory control, purchasing processes, and marketing management. Information technology is aiding modern managers in their attempt to produce high-caliber teams. Virtual teams are thought by many to be the future of management in the twenty-first century.

Jazz singer Lea Chase is an African-American woman with a passion. She believes that music is a way to bond the diverse elements in the United States. Whether inspiring thoughts through lyrics or encouraging fans to tap their feet to the rhythm of the musical beat, Chase sees hope for us all if we will just try to make music in all that we do. Will her approach work?

THINK CRITICALLY

1. **How could music bring diverse elements of our society together?**
2. **Music is often called the international language. What does this mean?**

INTERMISSION

What are the advantages of a virtual team?

____

____

© GETTY IMAGES/PHOTODISC

Lead the Way

BARBARA MARCUS

Barbara Marcus is the president of Scholastic, Inc.'s™ children's book publishing division. If you have ever read a Harry Potter book, you might want to thank her for bringing the Potter books to the United States. Marcus is one of the highest-ranking women in the United States in publishing and entertainment. She personally oversees a company that distributes more than 320 million books per year. In addition to the Harry Potter books, Scholastic, Inc. distributes R.L. Stine's *Goosebumps, Clifford—The Big Red Dog,* and The *Babysitter's Club*, just to name a few.

After reading a popular children's book, many adults say, "I could write a book like this." Actually, writing a children's book is quite difficult. It takes a team effort to create a successful product. Distributors like Barbara Marcus surround an author with artists, editors, copywriters, publicists, advertisers, and idea experts. When all these creative people get together, something good usually happens.

When Marcus first became aware of the talent of J. K. Rowling, she immediately bid for the right to bring her now-famous Harry Potter character to the U.S. market. The fifth book in the Potter series, *Harry Potter and the Order of the Phoenix*, will go down in history as one of the most heavily ordered books. A great part of this success is due to Barbara Marcus and her creative team at Scholastic, Inc.

THINK CRITICALLY

1. What has led to Barbara Marcus's success?
2. How does Barbara Marcus use teams to further the goals of Scholastic, Inc.?

UNDERSTANDING MANAGEMENT CONCEPTS

Circle the best answer for each of the following questions.

1. A flattened organization is one
 a. without many levels
 b. without managerial talent
 c. without teams
 d. with numerous managerial levels

2. A virtual team
 a. only meets in the corporate board room
 b. does not have physical contact among its members
 c. must have at least ten hours per week of member contact time
 d. has proven to be a failure as a team-building concept

THINK CRITICALLY

Answer the following questions as completely as possible. If necessary, use a separate sheet of paper.

3. Select a sports or entertainment organization known for its use of team-based management. Describe how the organization uses teams and why it is successful.

____

____

____

4. Technology Use the Internet to find information on virtual teams. Summarize your findings in a one-page report.

____

____

____

5. Assume that you are the newly assigned editor-in-chief of your school's newspaper. Explain how you would use teams to make your newspaper a success. Of the team resources you described, which one do you think would be the most important? Explain and justify your choice.

____

____

____

REVIEW

REVIEW MANAGEMENT CONCEPTS

Write the letter of the term that matches each definition. Some terms will not be used.

a. formal work group
b. group dynamic
c. informal work group
d. organizational purpose
e. quality circle
f. team-based organization
g. virtual team

____ **1.** A group created by management to run the organization and to carry out organizational goals and objectives

____ **2.** How group members interact and influence one another

____ **3.** A team that does not have physical contact among its members and operates in a non-traditional environment

____ **4.** A group formed based on friendship, shared interests, or proximity

____ **5.** An organizational structure where the basic work unit is teams rather than individuals or some other organizational structure

____ **6.** A philosophy on how to organize and run an organization

Circle the best answer.

7. To solve short-term problems, organizations often use
- **a.** temporary teams
- **b.** autonomous teams
- **c.** quality circles
- **d.** none of the above

8. Groupthink occurs because of too much
- **a.** arguing within the team
- **b.** conformity within the team
- **c.** disagreement with group norms
- **d.** all of the above

9. Group conformity is an indication of
- **a.** how willingly group members adhere to group norms
- **b.** how much group members argue within the group
- **c.** how much group members desire group cohesiveness
- **d.** both a and c

10. Autonomous teams
- **a.** function as cohesive units
- **b.** work independently
- **c.** require little or no management direction
- **d.** all of the above

THINK CRITICALLY

11. Discuss with a classmate the nature of formal work groups in a sports or entertainment organization. Cite one example of a formal work group.

12. You have learned that teams are important to sports and entertainment organizations. If you want to work in one of these organizations, how could you demonstrate that you have the ability to work successfully on a team?

13. List the different considerations that should be reviewed to determine the role of groups in a sports or entertainment organization.

14. What actions can a manager take to aid group cohesiveness and group conformity?

15. Create an example where a virtual team might be useful to a sports or entertainment organization. Be specific with your example, and indicate how your virtual team might work.

MAKE CONNECTIONS

16. Management Math You plan to create a team that will help a local theater raise funds for its next season, which begins in three months. If the goal is to raise $200,000, what would be the maximum number of team members that you would want to have to accomplish this goal? Consider how much each team member might have to raise. Remember what you have learned about optimum team size. Justify your team's size by explaining your thought process in this decision.

17. Technology Use the Internet to find an article on teams or groups in organizations. Summarize the article and apply what you learned by commenting on how the article might relate to sports or entertainment management.

18. Communication Most teams have communication rules. Compose a brief memo that outlines how virtual team members should communicate with one another.

19. Human Resources Management You are in charge of interviewing potential employees for a new sports franchise in your city. Franchise management wants all employees to be effective team members. What questions could you ask potential employees to determine if they have what it takes to be an effective member of a team?

20. Management Responsibilities You are a manager who has recently learned that one of your significant management teams has begun to show signs of groupthink. What should you do about this situation?

21. Communication You are the marketing director for a local dirt bike track that has a problem. Concerned parents are threatening to have your track shut down because they think that it is dangerous and invites gang activities. Devise a plan for using teams to communicate the true nature of your track and turn the negative image into a positive one.

22. History Action groups, which have members with a similar interest who want to accomplish a collective goal, have long been a part of local community governments. These action groups are often most visible in a community's parks and recreation planning. Examine the history of your local community's parks and recreation department. Indicate what types of sports and entertainment programs are available and how action groups have affected these services. How would you get involved in such an action group?

23. Marketing Management Your city's local government has decided to sponsor a soap box derby event. Winners will go on to national competition. Devise a marketing plan to attract participants as well as sponsors that will help participants with the costs of their derby cars. Present your plan to the class for discussion.

CASE STUDY

DECA PREP

THE ARMED FORCES AND NASCAR

Marketing is about creating relationships that are beneficial to all parties involved. The armed forces hope to gain the benefits that organizations such as Kellogg™, Home Depot, and Pfizer™ have received from being long-standing sponsors of NASCAR.

NASCAR opened its 2003 season in Daytona Beach with five branches of the U.S. armed forces—the Army, Navy, Air Force, Marines, and National Guard—as team sponsors. The armed forces collectively spent about $28 million on NASCAR sponsorship and related activities in this first year.

The top goals of the sponsorship include raising awareness of the armed forces, generating recruiting leads, and retaining individuals already in the military. Resources used to achieve these goals are substantial, with nearly $600 million spent on advertising in the first year of the sponsorship. Much of the advertising airs during network sporting events and other programming that draws young male viewers.

The Army intends to use NASCAR to attract its primary target market of 17- to 24-year-old males who watch sports and follow NASCAR. The Army believes that it can generate 80,000 recruiting leads from the sponsorship program per year and expects to turn about 1,200 of these recruits into soldiers annually. This is a much better response than the Army gets from most of its marketing campaigns. Currently, the Army must contact 120 leads before landing one soldier. The Army's role in NASCAR includes a league sponsorship, a touring interactive area, and a blitz of television support.

The Army logo is displayed on the hood of car No. 01 on the Winston Cup circuit. This number ties in with the "Army of One" theme. The Army purchased in-car cameras to make sure that the car gets prime television exposure. The Army also purchases commercial time during the Winston Cup broadcasts and flashes a toll-free number for those who might want to learn more about joining.

Army recruiters are visible at NASCAR events in interactive areas that include a short video, race car simulators and games, and a pit stop challenge to generate the interest of prospective military recruits.

The Air Force will invest about $2.25 million per year into an associate sponsorship with the Winston Cup team. The Air Force logo is displayed on the rear corners of a car driven by popular veteran Ricky Rudd. The Marine Corps will spend about $2.25 million per year as the primary sponsor of a team in the Busch Series, a proven military recruiting ground. The Navy will spend about $1.5 million per year as the primary sponsor of a Roush Racing team in NASCAR's Craftsman Truck series. The National Guard sponsors a Winston Cup entry, putting its colors on a car driven by Todd Bodine.

Recruiters will use show cars and racing simulators to gain access to high schools and trade programs. A NASCAR show car in a high-school parking lot catches a lot of attention. Each of the military branches will show cars at schools from the West Coast to the East Coast.

Think Critically

1. Why is the relationship between the armed forces and NASCAR a good one?
2. Does the military's NASCAR sponsorship reach its intended target market? Why or why not?
3. Why does the armed forces need to use more visible tactics to recruit young people?

SPORTS AND ENTERTAINMENT MARKETING MANAGEMENT TEAM DECISION MAKING

The Association of Black Coaches has hired you to establish a sponsorship for televised NCAA football and basketball events. The focus of this sponsorship is to recruit more African-American youth into the teaching and coaching professions. The ultimate goal is to eventually increase the number of African-American coaches at universities and colleges throughout the United States.

You must develop a marketing strategy for this sponsorship. The strategy must include commercials, visibility at televised games, catchy slogans, testimonials, and visible products that indicate sponsorship.

Performance Indicators Evaluated

- Understand the goal of recruiting more African-American youth to become teachers and coaches.
- List prospective sponsors and describe the strategies you will use to get their commitment.
- Describe promotional strategies, commercials, slogans, and products that will indicate sponsorship.
- Explain the use of effective testimonials for the sponsorship.

Go to the DECA web site for more detailed information.

1. What will be the theme of the sponsorship's commercials?
2. Will you sponsor the half-time report or instant replay? Why or why not?
3. How will sponsors be visible at televised sporting events?
4. Outline your marketing strategy.

www.deca.org/publications/HS_Guide/guidetoc.html

CHAPTER 11

Managing Operations

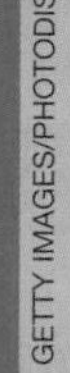

11.1 OPERATIONS MANAGEMENT
11.2 CONTROL THROUGH EVALUATION

© GETTY IMAGES/PHOTODISC

© GETTY IMAGES/PHOTODISC

© GETTY IMAGES/PHOTODISC

WINNING Strategies

RIVER RATS

What has more speed than river rafting, more thrills than surfing, and the need for more control than kayaking? The answer is riverboarding. Riverboarding originated in 1975 when Bob Carlson dropped out of college to pursue his dream of starting a rafting gear company. He soon invented a more exhilarating sport and named it riverboarding.

Carlson adapted boogie boards, which are used to train white water rafters, to meet the needs of people who wanted to really "get down" with a river. The riverboard is bigger, easier to hold, and more flexible than the traditional boogie board. Once he perfected the design, Carlson began selling the riverboards to rafting enthusiasts who were looking for more excitement.

Unlike those who participate in white water rafting or kayaking, the riverboarder does not get pitched into the river. The riverboarder is already there! The sport takes arm strength and an ability to read the water and currents. Some experts even attempt surfing moves and stances in particularly fast or swirling sections of the river. With all the required safety equipment, riverboarders look like something out of an action/adventure movie. The gear, including helmets, goggles, and life vests, is necessary to prevent serious accidents.

Riverboarding is all about control. A riverboarder's control ensures safety and success. Lack of control can lead to disaster. If you think about it, the same is true for any sports or entertainment organization.

THINK CRITICALLY

1. Why do you think riverboarding has caught on with daring sports enthusiasts?
2. Why is control important in riverboarding and in sports and entertainment organizations?

OPERATIONS MANAGEMENT

Describe the operations management function.

Discuss competition as it relates to operations planning.

OPENING ACT

A torn anterior cruciate ligament (ACL) is one of the most painful sports injuries. Women's knees are especially vulnerable to this injury. In fact, female athletes sustain far more career-ending ACL injuries than their male counterparts. To offset this problem, trainers are using quality control processes similar to those used in manufacturing operations to plan training schedules for female athletes. These programs seek to enhance balance, body/joint awareness, movement technique, and muscle strength. Employing quality control processes has significantly reduced ACL injuries.

Discuss with a partner how injuries to athletes are similar to defects on an assembly line. How can studying quality control procedures help to reduce injuries?

THE OPERATIONS MANAGEMENT FUNCTION

The process of managing resources that are needed to produce an organization's goods and services is called **operations management**. Operations managers design the systems that run an organization. They produce the products and services that are basic to the business. Factors that the operations manager must control are quality, timing, cost, and efficient use of employees.

An operations manager takes **inputs**, such as materials, labor, machines, management, and money, and transforms them into **outputs**, or goods and services. This transformation process is the beginning of an organization's value chain. A **value chain** extends from supplier to consumer and includes all of the activities that bring value to the customer.

OPERATIONS RESPONSIBILITIES

Operations managers typically are responsible for selecting production processes, locating facilities where the work will be completed, assessing the quality of work, and managing inventory. Operations managers also organize work, design jobs, and schedule tasks.

Operations are directly linked to the finance and selling functions. These functions secure the resources necessary for the operations to be performed and sell the end result of the operations process.

THE HISTORY OF OPERATIONS MANAGEMENT

Beginning with the Industrial Revolution in the late 1700s, managers began to see the need to organize work and production tasks. Industrialists such as James Watt, who invented the steam engine, and Eli Whitney, who developed the concept of interchangeable parts, were early proponents of an organized operations system. In the early 1900s, managers began to look to science to solve problems in manufacturing and labor use. During this period, Fredrick W. Taylor, the father of scientific management, and Henry Ford, creator of the moving assembly line, were among the notables who embraced a new way of approaching operations management.

The field made steady progress throughout the twentieth century with developments in human relations, statistical analysis of processes, and globalization of manufacturing. A quality revolution ensued, and information was used to make better decisions. Sports and entertainment organizations participated in this process by embracing developments such as organized labor, database information management, and the movement of sports and entertainment events abroad.

Today, women hold about 16 percent of top management positions in the 500 largest U.S. companies. Many of these positions are in operations management.

INTERMISSION

What are the responsibilities of an operations manager?

____

____

EFFICIENT OPERATIONS INCREASE COMPETITIVENESS

The extent to which an organization can produce goods and services better than other organizations in the same industry is known as **competitiveness**. The New York Yankees, the Oakland Raiders, the Los Angeles Lakers, the Detroit Red Wings, and the Disney Company have a rich history of competitiveness. One of the keys to any organization's long-term success and competitiveness is productivity.

Productivity is the ratio of outputs to inputs. For example, if a dance and theater company is able to generate \$1 million in revenues from \$250,000 in costs, then its ratio indicates that it is being productive. This ratio must be put into perspective with other industry competitors. If another dance and theater company is able to generate \$1 million in revenues with only \$100,000 in costs, then the second company is more productive than the first one.

© GETTY IMAGES/PHOTODISC

It's January 6, 1994, 2:35 P.M. in Detroit. Ice skater Tonya Harding's husband and three of his friends perform the unthinkable act. They club Harding's rival, Nancy Kerrigan, on the knee as she leaves the Olympic Trials. Fifty days later, Kerrigan wins a silver medal at the Olympic Games. Harding finishes eighth and is eventually banned from the U.S. Figure Skating Association for life. The attack, in a bizarre way, helped the sport of figure skating. People who had previously ignored figure skating were drawn to the Harding–Kerrigan spectacle, and many remained hooked on the sport.

THINK CRITICALLY

1. Why do controversies sometimes generate positive publicity for sports?
2. Do you think the media are partially responsible for creating a frenzy surrounding a controversial event, or are the media just doing their job? Explain your answer.

COMPETITION WITHIN INDUSTRIES

History has shown that there is more competition within industries where there is equality among organizations. The number of leading companies within the industry, the market share of the leaders, the leaders' profitability, and the industry's ability to innovate and attract new resources can measure industry competitiveness. To prevent competition from the outside, an industry may erect **barriers to entry**. These barriers make it difficult for new firms to enter the industry. Barriers to entry sometimes can create problems. For example, when the federal government heavily regulated the broadcast media, the industry often failed in quality, productivity, and innovation. Once the barriers were removed, cable television and the Internet changed the way we receive information and entertainment.

Barriers to entry take several forms.

- **Investment** To be a primary competitor in most professional sports requires an investment of more than $100 million.
- **Economies of Scale** Primary competitors gain efficiencies in the services they provide because the costs of producing the services decrease as more are produced.
- **Access to Supplies and Distribution** Larger competitors have more options for conducting their business operations than do smaller businesses.
- **Attraction of Better Management Talent** Large organizations are able to bid for the services of highly trained and successful managers.

GAINING THE COMPETITIVE EDGE WITH OPERATIONS

How do successful sports and entertainment organizations use operations to gain a competitive edge? According to analysis, organizations that fail to innovate doom themselves to second-rate performance. A competitive firm must perform at least as well as its rivals. However, performance level can be deceptive. Problems change on a daily basis. Operations managers are constantly looking for new and creative ways to solve problems. **Best practices** are management and work processes that lead to superior performance.

Best Practices in Operations Management

- **Keep competition intense.** Any coach would rather play a good team than a poor one.
- **Develop a strategy.** All championships are won with superior strategies. Produce a product or service that is loved by consumers.
- **Provide more services at a lower cost than rivals.** Consumers appreciate valuable services.
- **Emphasize quality.** Then emphasize it again.
- **Be adaptable and flexible.** Respond to problems and challenges from competitors and the market.
- **Use technology.** Assist management with the latest technology whenever possible.
- **Empower workers to solve problems.** Help operations processes to work the way they should.
- **Keep ethics in the forefront.** Ethics should command all that you do.
- **Practice, practice, practice.** Practice makes perfect.

COMPLETING THE LOOP

Operations management is not just about machines, assembly lines, or looking over employees' shoulders. It is about assuring quality. It is about designing work tasks as they should be designed. As a manager, pretend that you will have to do the job yourself when selecting production processes. Operations management also involves relationships with those outside the organization—the supply chain. Finally, operations management initiates the strategies designed by top management. It also provides the checks and balances by which the strategies can be judged.

INTERMISSION

List three "best practices" that can give an organization's operations a competitive edge.

____

____

UNDERSTAND MANAGEMENT CONCEPTS

Circle the best answer for each of the following questions.

1. The process of managing resources that are needed to produce an organization's goods and services is known as
a. the value chain
b. economies of scale
c. operations management
d. competitiveness

2. The ratio of outputs to inputs is called
a. barriers to entry
b. economies of scale
c. the value chain
d. productivity

THINK CRITICALLY

Answer the following questions as completely as possible. If necessary, use a separate sheet of paper.

3. You are a consultant hired to review the operations of a movie theater in your city. List all the operations that might be necessary for a movie theater to bring a film showing to an audience. Which of these operations is the most critical? Explain your answer.

____

____

____

4. After examining the best practices in operations management, choose three that you believe would be most important to improving the operations of your school's athletics program. Why did you pick these three? How could benefits be derived from these best practices?

____

____

____

____

5. **Communication** Write a job description for an operations manager at a local television or radio station.

____

____

____

CONTROL THROUGH EVALUATION

OPENING ACT

When broadcast entertainment and sports meet one another head on, who is in control? In the past, sports teams and leagues seemed to have the upper hand. Without the sports talent, there was no "show." Today, sports entertainment networks are trying to reduce their dependency on sports. In 2003, ESPN began producing original shows and made-for-TV movies. Some of ESPN's new shows are reality-based. For example, *Dream Job* is an *American Idols*-style show for aspiring *SportsCenter* anchors. Producers are now busy designing more original programs and movies. ESPN believes that viewers are ready for a change. ESPN is prepared to build on its early programming successes with even more dramatic experiments in the future.

Discuss with a partner why ESPN would make a move into the reality-based television and made-for-TV movie businesses. How could such a move give ESPN more control of its products and its viewing audience?

Explain why management control is important.

Describe how organizations control their operations.

WHY IS CONTROL IMPORTANT?

The process that ensures all of the organization's activities and tasks are going according to the established plan is called **control**. Control is accomplished by comparing the day-to-day performance of the organization to some predetermined standard or objective. If the standard or objective is not met, **deviation** occurs and corrective action must be taken.

Most managers view control in the same way that they view planning. Many of the same questions must be asked to effectively plan or to effectively control. One major difference exists between planning and controlling. In controlling, an action already has been taken. Control reminds managers about past successes and failures and helps them stay focused on plans and objectives. Control helps managers avoid future mistakes.

THE POWER OF CONTROL

An operations manager receives certain benefits from implementing a control system.

- Control prevents crises because the manager knows what is going on at all times within the organization. Small problems can be corrected before they become bigger issues.

- Whether the sports or entertainment organization is offering a product or a service, control helps the business produce a standardized output with respect to quality and quantity.
- Control is the primary mechanism for reviewing and assessing employee performance. Based on assessment, the manager may adjust employee goals and objectives.
- Control is used to evaluate plans. All plans eventually need to be changed, modified, or even cancelled based on changes in the organization's environment.
- Control is the guardian of company assets. The control system, if used correctly, protects against inefficiency, waste, and theft.

Nancy Lopez started playing golf at the age of eight under her father's guidance. In 1978, her rookie year in the LPGA, Lopez won nine tournaments, including a record-setting five in a row. She was inducted into the LPGA's Hall of Fame in 1987 as its eleventh member. Lopez completed her final full season on the LPGA tour in 2002. Like many other athletes, Lopez uses the Internet to market customized products that she endorses. Nancy Lopez Golf offers leading products that "enhance the complete golf experience for women."

THINK CRITICALLY

1. **Why do athletes introduce their own customized products?**
2. **Is the Internet the best place to market these products? Explain your answer.**

One of the chief tools used by the operations manager to establish a system of control is feedback. **Feedback** is information about an organization's performance. Through feedback, the organization is able to see what does and does not work. All employees are part of the feedback system, which often includes a manager who regulates the feedback. The system also includes a **sensor** who determines if the feedback exposes a deviation from a standard and a **controller** who brings the organization back to where it should be.

Assume that a women's sports team wants to know if it is achieving its financial goals for the current season. Financial information, such as ticket sales, is reviewed weekly. This information is compared to projected goals or standards that should be met if the team is to be profitable. If revenue marks are missed, the sensor alerts management. Management then attempts to determine the cause, which could be anything from poor weather to poor team performance. The cause also could be due to waste or inefficiency. Once the cause is known, the controller then tries to remedy the problem. The controller can allow for poor weather, but the controller cannot change poor team performance. However, the controller could turn to some other form of revenue generation to offset the shortfall in ticket sales. If the loss in revenue is due to waste or theft, the controller becomes more of an investigator than a strategist. The controller should be a person who is able to fulfill a variety of management tasks.

Sometimes control can be an illusion. A manager may perceive that all is well and that control is working as it should be. In many organizations, this is not the case. To effectively control, the manager must first establish an *attitude* of control. Employees must embrace the idea of meeting standards and correcting deviations. If employees have the proper attitude of control, even the lowest-level employee will feel comfortable to make suggestions and corrections that will prevent problems.

INTERMISSION

What are the benefits of a control system in an organization?

____

____

HOW DO MANAGERS CONTROL?

To control an organization's operations, a manager must understand the requirements of a control system. The manager then must ensure that all controls match these basic requirements.

MANAGEMENT RESPONSIBILITIES

Standards of Performance The first requirement of a control system is to construct standards of performance. A standard is a reference point. A standard might be winning a certain number of games or achieving a certain number of viewers. In specific terms, the standard might be expressed in revenues gained, costs controlled, or profits earned. For example, if concession sales at a ballpark are expected to be $20,000 per game, then $20,000 is the standard. The standard is what is expected of the organization or individual.

Standards can be unrealistic. If a baseball manager expects that all players will get a hit every time they bat, the standard is not realistic. It probably will never be met. Control must come from realistic objectives.

Monitoring System The second requirement of a control system is to establish a monitoring system for evaluating whether standards are being met. A control system is no better than its monitoring function. Because the monitoring system regularly collects data, it is able to detect problems. For example, if a .333 batting average standard is set, the team's manager will continuously need to monitor the number of at-bats to know if players are meeting the standard. If the manager only checks batting averages at the end of the season, there will be no possibility for correction or improvement until the next season.

© GETTY IMAGES/PHOTODISC

When was the last time you watched an NFL football game in Europe? Probably never, right? Most Europeans would say the same thing. For the last few years, the NFL has been funneling talent to NFL Europe in an effort to find an audience among the continent's soccer-crazed fans. To date, it has had few successes. The league and players' union have been donating about $40 million annually to get the new league off the ground. The Europeans appreciate the money, but they do not seem to appreciate the game. What has the NFL learned from this experiment? Fans around the world are diverse when it comes to sports. Many do not appreciate U.S.-style football.

THINK CRITICALLY

1. Do you think NFL Europe was a good experiment or a bad experiment? Explain your answer.
2. What are the reasons that the NFL might want to bring its game to Europe?

Performance monitoring must be an ongoing action. Television shows constantly monitor ratings. Athletes and their managers frequently check performance against standards. Timing is extremely important if faulty performance is to be corrected.

Correction The third requirement of a control system is to develop a process for correcting deviations. Just knowing about deviations is not enough. Correction must take place. Too often, managers do nothing with the results of performance monitoring. For example, many TV shows run well past their prime before they are cancelled. Poor reviews and ratings should be an immediate wake-up call to producers.

As managers design effective correction systems, they should be familiar with tools that will eliminate the root causes of the problems. Also important are tools to correct defects and tools to improve individual performance. Good managers know how to create a superior corrections tool bag.

A CONTROL SYSTEM FOR EVERY ORGANIZATION

Over time, managers have simplified the control process into three distinct forms. These forms are diagnostic controls, boundary controls, and interactive controls.

Diagnostic controls ensure that standards are met. They also ensure that any deviations from established standards are dealt with effectively. Examples of diagnostic controls are budgets, income statements, balance sheets, and operations and financial analyses. Diagnostic controls free managers from constantly monitoring all that is happening in the organization. The managers' primary responsibility is to establish the standard and then empower employees to monitor performance against the standard. It is important to train employees to deal with deviations. If managers and employees use diagnostic controls correctly, it will soon become evident where profit and revenue are generated within the organization.

Boundary controls are usually expressed as codes of conduct. These rules indicate to employees what can and cannot be done in an organization. Boundaries often are expressed as ethical rules that employees and managers are expected to follow. Obviously, these boundaries are of no value unless everyone agrees that they serve a purpose and that exceeding the boundaries is not in the best interest of the organization. In the entertainment and broadcast industries, governmental controls often mandate what constitutes proper behavior. Boundary controls are especially important for organizations that embrace trust and honesty as part of their core values.

As ex-player/manager Pete Rose learned, betting on baseball games is not tolerated. He exceeded a boundary control of his profession and his team.

Interactive controls are gaining popularity. Ask small business owners how they control their organizations and the common reply will probably be "by keeping my hands on what is happening." Small business owners are able to talk to employees on a daily basis. This frequent contact is interactivity in its basic form. For larger businesses, which characterize most sports and entertainment organizations, interactive control can mean weekly strategic meetings among top managers and staff. Or it may mean online data collection that is processed and analyzed for content and then relayed to the appropriate managers.

Regardless of the data received via information systems, personal contact is necessary in order for interactive controls to work. When managers meet, they are able to review the competition, evaluate recent strategic moves, and examine market trends. They also can track changes in revenue flows or performance of operational areas such as concessions or consumer wearables. During these meetings, managers can decide whether recent increases or decreases in revenues and profits are acceptable. Managers then will take corrective action based on what the interactive controls have monitored.

the Global Manager

It often has been said that the United States exports too much of its culture to foreign countries. Regardless of whether this is true, one industry that thrives on exporting the "American way" is Hollywood. Despite the problems created by global terrorism, the Middle East is still hot for Hollywood. Although the lifestyles portrayed in U.S. films are often criticized in the Middle East, the passion for these films does not seem to be wavering. Most theater managers in the Middle East show films that will earn high advertising revenues. At present, showing films from Hollywood secures the most revenues. This trend will likely continue until other forms of entertainment match the creativity of the U.S. industry.

THINK CRITICALLY

1. What are the dangers of exporting too much U.S. culture to foreign countries?
2. Are U.S. films and television shows good or bad for the Middle Eastern culture? Explain your answer.

© DIGITAL VISION

There are two primary problems with interactive control systems. First, many managers do not like to share, especially when it comes to information. Sharing information often points out weaknesses or poor decision making. Cover-up is more common than most managers would like to admit. Second, interactivity means that managers must be willing to work as a team to solve problems. Even in team-based sports, this is not an easy task.

Without control, organizations will fail to meet objectives. With control and proper evaluation of deviations, organizations have a much better chance of meeting the challenges of the modern-day competitive environment. The old adage "be in control or be controlled" is still true today in the sports and entertainment fields.

INTERMISSION

List the three types of control systems and briefly define each.

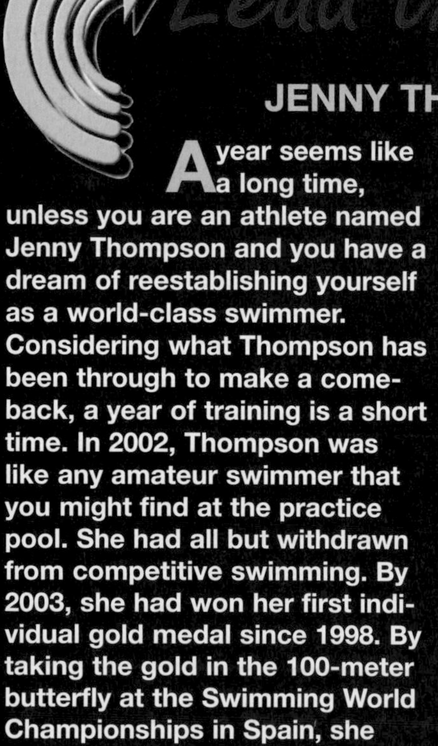

Lead the Way

JENNY THOMPSON

A year seems like a long time, unless you are an athlete named Jenny Thompson and you have a dream of reestablishing yourself as a world-class swimmer. Considering what Thompson has been through to make a comeback, a year of training is a short time. In 2002, Thompson was like any amateur swimmer that you might find at the practice pool. She had all but withdrawn from competitive swimming. By 2003, she had won her first individual gold medal since 1998. By taking the gold in the 100-meter butterfly at the Swimming World Championships in Spain, she rebounded to win her eleventh medal in world competition. Thompson's strategy for reestablishing herself in the world of competitive swimming was to reexamine her style, her discipline, and her desire. Controlling one's self is always a difficult challenge. Most experts would say that Thompson has mastered control and is back in the race toward a world championship in her sport.

THINK CRITICALLY

1. **What does control have to do with winning?**
2. **Describe another example where control has led to success in the sports or entertainment field.**

UNDERSTAND MANAGEMENT CONCEPTS

Circle the best answer for each of the following questions.

1. Rules that indicate to employees what can and cannot be done in an organization are
- **a.** diagnostic controls
- **b.** boundary controls
- **c.** interactive controls
- **d.** virtual controls

2. Which of the following is not a basic requirement of a control system?
- **a.** a monitoring system
- **b.** correction
- **c.** standards of performance
- **d.** a sensor

THINK CRITICALLY

Answer the following questions as completely as possible. If necessary, use a separate sheet of paper.

3. Why is control so important to the management of an efficient sports or entertainment organization?

____

____

____

____

4. How does a feedback system work? Give an example.

____

____

____

____

5. Explain what interactive controls are and how they are used in a sports or entertainment organization.

____

____

____

____

____

CHAPTER 11 REVIEW

REVIEW MANAGEMENT CONCEPTS

Write the letter of the term that matches each definition. Some terms will not be used.

____ **1.** Extends from supplier to consumer and includes all of the activities that bring value to the customer

____ **2.** The ratio of outputs to inputs

____ **3.** Materials, labor, machines, management, and money

____ **4.** Make it difficult for new firms to enter an industry

____ **5.** Occurs when a standard or objective is not met

____ **6.** Determines if feedback exposes a deviation from a standard

____ **7.** Brings the organization back to where it should be

____ **8.** Goods and services

____ **9.** The extent to which an organization can produce goods and services better than other organizations in the same industry

____ **10.** Information about an organization's performance

a. barriers to entry
b. best practices
c. competitiveness
d. control
e. controller
f. deviation
g. feedback
h. inputs
i. operations management
j. outputs
k. productivity
l. sensor
m. value chain

Circle the best answer.

11. Which manager takes inputs and transforms them into outputs?
a. accounting manager
b. operations manager
c. economics manager
d. asset manager

12. Best practices
a. are rare in the sports and entertainment industries due to regulation
b. transfer power to owners in sports and entertainment industries
c. are management and work processes that lead to superior performance
d. are none of the above

13. Which of the following industrialists was a pioneer in the operations management field?
a. Eli Whitney
b. James Watt
c. Henry Ford
d. all of the above

14. One of the chief tools used by an operations manager to establish a system of control is
a. standards
b. feedback
c. productivity
d. deviation

THINK CRITICALLY

15. Briefly discuss the history of operations management in the United States.

16. Contact an operations manager for a sports or entertainment organization. Interview the person about his or her job responsibilities. What is the operations manager's greatest challenge? Report your findings to the class.

17. Describe the importance of best practices in operations management.

18. Identify a sports or entertainment organization that you believe "does it right" with respect to its operations management techniques. Describe and explain the techniques used.

19. You have just been assigned the task of devising a control system for a sports or entertainment activity at your school. Outline the actions you will take to establish this control system.

MAKE CONNECTIONS

20. Management Math Operations managers measure productivity by the ratio of outputs to inputs. If revenues at a local theme park are $30,000 a day for two weeks and total costs for the two-week period are $300,000, is the theme park being productive? Explain your answer.

21. Technology Use the Internet to locate three articles on operations management. How does operations management apply to the sports and entertainment industries? Report your findings to the class.

22. Communication To illustrate a boundary controls process, write a code of conduct for taking a major test in your class. Explain how your teacher could use this control mechanism to ensure test-taking honesty.

23. Technology Search the Internet to locate information about jobs in the sports and entertainment industries that relate to operations management. Report your findings to the class.

24. Human Resources Management You are the human resources manager for a large entertainment organization. Write a job description for a new operations manager that you would like to add to your staff. Be specific about the work tasks to be performed and the skills that the candidate will need.

25. Management Responsibilities You have information from diagnostic controls that your organization has a problem with employee theft. The difficulty lies in knowing how and by whom the theft is occurring. Considering what you have learned about control, write a memo to your employees that will help to resolve the problem in a fair manner.

26. Communication As an operations manager, you would like to try the interactive controls approach in your organization. How can you use the Internet to establish such a system? What elements will make up your new control system? Choose a sports or entertainment business and apply your plan to that organization. Explain how you will use interactive controls and what you expect your results to be.

27. Human Resources Management You are the human resources manager of a major entertainment organization. You have been asked to speak to a group of high school students about the control process and how it is used by organizations to increase effectiveness and efficiency. You realize that your subject may be boring to many in your audience. Find an example to make the subject interesting and challenging to the students. Outline what you will say and what your example will be.

WHO WANTS TO PLAY FULL-CONTACT WOMEN'S FOOTBALL?

In 1999, the Women's Professional Football League (WPFL) began soliciting players by contacting coaches from rugby, track and field, and flag football to play in an exhibition tour. The tour was designed to test the marketability and demographics of women playing full-contact American football.

The 1999 "No Limits" Barnstorming Tour played exciting games in front of enthusiastic crowds in St. Paul, Green Bay, Chicago, New York, and Miami. The successful tour proved that the WPFL was a viable idea and a marketable product.

The WPFL has grown from two teams to 19 teams, with two dominant rival leagues. The three-time champion Houston Reliant Energy team holds the formula for full-contact women's football.

Tryouts in Pearland help to explain Houston's 30—2 record since 1999. Nearly 100 women, ranging in age from 18 to 44, tried out for the team in 2003. Women making the team ranged in size from 5' 11" 305-pound offensive lineman "Big Sue" Roberts, a Wal-Mart cashier, to 5' 1" 120-pound wide receiver Angela Price-Hardemon, a pharmacy office manager.

The Energy's roster is an example in diverse backgrounds. Jocelyn Garriga has been a firefighter with the Houston Fire Department for ten years. Offensive lineman Christina-Melissa Tamez is a motivational speaker. Sisters Sheila and Alicia Nava and Daphne and Tabitha Polk play for the Energy. Wide receiver Karen Mones is a personal trainer and owns a strength and conditioning company. Nakia Henry is the first deaf player to earn a spot on the team.

It costs money to play women's professional football in Houston. A flyer passed out at tryouts itemizes the cost of joining the team. Players pay more than $500 for their own uniforms since the Houston Energy draws barely 1,000 fans per game.

Owner Robin Howington, an oil-industry executive and player for the team, has invested more than $140,000 in the Houston Energy. Each player received a check for $12 for 12 games after the Energy won the WPFL title in 2002. Despite the lack of pay, little glory, and nasty injuries, most of the players from the previous season return for tryouts.

All of the players, from highly paid professionals such as psychologists and neurosurgeons to stay-at-home moms, sacrifice their autumns practicing twice a week for "an opportunity of a lifetime." Four-hour workouts leave participants tired, sore, and sunburned, but not turned off.

Most women are drawn to full-contact football for the opportunity to be as aggressive as men are. WPFL players spend more than three hours per game wrestling with their opponents. Most women who try out for the WPFL have finally found their league and are not discouraged by the lack of funds.

Unfortunately, the WPFL has not gained popularity with fans, with fewer than 1,000 people attending per game. WPFL teams are finding it difficult to land corporate sponsors. The WPFL wants to send a message to young girls that they can be champions on the football field.

Think Critically

1. Why do women try out for the WPFL?
2. Is the WPFL truly open to all women? Explain your answer.
3. Why doesn't the WPFL disband since there is a lack of funds and fans?

SPORTS AND ENTERTAINMENT MARKETING MANAGEMENT TEAM DECISION MAKING

The WPFL's Houston Reliant Energy has had a 30-2 record since 1999. Success can be attributed to women who take the sport seriously and put in the time to perform like champions.

You have been hired to develop a promotional strategy to raise the awareness of the WPFL and the Houston Energy. You will design billboards, television advertisements, and special promotions to be carried by area retailers. You also will develop special group nights to attract more fans to games.

It is your job to land several corporate sponsors to pay for advertising and the team's uniforms. Prospective sponsors rely heavily on women for their success. Your biggest challenge is to find a sponsor who wants to buy the team. The owner must be willing to pay respectable salaries to the players.

You will present your promotional strategy and corporate sponsorship proposal to prospective corporations and owners. As you develop your marketing strategies, keep in mind that you want to attract both female and male fans to the WPFL games.

Performance Indicators Evaluated

- Understand the multiple tasks that you must accomplish.
- Explain strategies for more educational awareness of women's football.
- Describe how information will be gathered about prospective fans.
- Describe special promotions designed to attract more fans.
- Discuss strategies to land corporate sponsors.
- Demonstrate teamwork skills.

Go to the DECA web site for more detailed information.

1. How will you increase public awareness and respect for the WPFL?
2. What are the promotional themes that you will use for the WPFL and the Houston Energy?
3. Outline the special promotions you will run to increase attendance at games.
4. What corporations will you approach for sponsorship? Why?

www.deca.org/publications/HS_Guide/guidetoc.html

CHAPTER 12

Managing With Information Technology

12.1 MANAGEMENT INFORMATION SYSTEMS

12.2 IMPLEMENTING STRATEGIES WITH AN MIS

© GETTY IMAGES/PHOTODISC

BROADWAY MEETS THE INTERNET

There was a time when the only place to see a Broadway play was New York City. Today, Broadway plays can be seen in most major cities throughout the United States. A "traveling Broadway" is possible due in part to an e-commerce company called Broadway Across America (BAA). This web-based company is responsible for ticket sales for the majority of on-the-road Broadway plays.

Broadway Across America promotes the plays, secures season-ticket holders for local theaters, and provides information about future performances. It connects culture-starved consumers to a national network of arts and entertainment. The organization also allows consumers to do the majority of their cultural arts shopping online. According to recent statistics, more theater patrons are using BAA than are using traditional box office or ticket broker services.

Once BAA has a prospective customer's e-mail address, it is able to send timely promotions to that consumer. Additionally, and probably of greater value to Broadway, BAA has built a reliable database of consumers who are interested in the arts and entertainment. The list is extremely valuable to anyone seeking this particular target market.

The future for organizations such as Broadway Across America seems bright. Success will be built on the increasing trend of consumers using the Internet to shop online and gather information about products and services. Now, Broadway is as close as your computer screen.

THINK CRITICALLY

1. Why would a local theatrical organization be interested in using a service such as Broadway Across America to increase its business?
2. Visit Broadway Across America's web site. Report five facts that you learn about the organization.

LESSON 12.1

MANAGEMENT INFORMATION SYSTEMS

Explain the evolution of management information systems.

Describe the components of a management information system.

OPENING ACT

One way that young musical artists can take control of their future is to attend the annual Atlantis Music Conference (AMC) in Atlanta, Georgia. The AMC's purpose is to focus the attention of the national and international music industries and related press on southeastern U.S. music and its artists. Small group discussions and panels are major activities of the conference. Young artists can attend panel sessions on everything from "getting your band started" to "securing investments for cutting a CD." Attendees also get the chance to talk to recording-industry professionals who are searching for new talent. The AMC uses the Internet to spread its message. The organization's web site has become an additional venue for young musical artists in their quest for fame and glory.

Work with a partner. Visit the Atlantis Music Conference web site. Discuss how AMC uses the Internet to attract attendees and promote its message to young artists.

MANAGERS IN THE INFORMATION AGE

To effectively plan, organize, implement, and control decisions, managers must have accurate, up-to-date information. Gathering and processing information has always been a challenge for managers in the sports and entertainment fields. Sports championships and entertainment customers are won and lost on the speed and accuracy of information obtained by managers. The Information Age, where computer technology and information systems are joined, has greatly increased a manager's ability to track, analyze, and forecast the needs and wants of target markets.

Since the early 1980s, managers have complained about a lack of relevant information. Although much information existed for managers to gather and process, the cost of obtaining that information was a serious consideration. Managers also found that even when they obtained information, it often was the wrong type or was in the wrong form. Frequently, managers received more information than they needed. **Information overload** occurs when there is a glut of print, sound, and image communication. The solution to these information difficulties arrived with the advent of the personal computer and the Internet.

THE MIS—AN AID TO MANAGERS

A **management information system (MIS)** is an integrated approach to providing interpreted and relevant information to managers. An MIS increases managers' ability to make strategic decisions. **Data** is the raw material of information systems. The main component of data is facts about people, places, and things. **Information** is data that has been interpreted to meet the needs of the managers who acquired it.

HOW THE MIS EVOLVED

The personal computer and the Internet age brought about changes in the data acquisition process. The process first began with **data processing**—capturing, processing, and storing data. The type of data collected was transaction-oriented, such as daily sales receipts. It was short-range in nature and was associated with daily operations. It often was detailed in a narrow sense. Managers needed a better system to solve today's complex problems.

The MIS is different from data processing. The MIS is oriented toward decision making. It contains more summaries and fewer details and is associated with middle- and long-range planning and operations. It is periodic, ongoing, and prediction- and control-oriented.

Today, data processing provides the databases for an MIS. A **database** is a collection of data that is arranged in a logical manner and organized in a form that can be stored and processed by a computer. These databases become the pillars upon which the MIS is built. When management information systems were first used by managers and programmers, there was only one type of MIS. Today, management information systems have been redesigned to meet the specific needs of managers who face problems and decisions in a variety of businesses and industries. The sports and entertainment industries are no exception.

Becoming a Hollywood star may not be an especially realistic career goal for most people. But for Hispanics, it is like an impossible dream. America's Hispanic population is estimated at 37 million, with Hispanic moviegoers accounting for about 15 percent of U.S. film admissions. Yet, Hispanic movie stars are few and far between. For Hispanic actresses, the situation is even shakier. Once you get past Jennifer Lopez, of Puerto Rican parentage, and Mexican-born Salma Hayek, the roster is slim. The most encouraging sign is that more Hispanic-Americans are attempting to produce and direct their own films. Linda Mendoza and Maria Escobedo are rarities among Hollywood film directors in that they are both females and Hispanic-Americans.

THINK CRITICALLY

1. **Why do you think that Hispanics have such a difficult time "making it big" in Hollywood?**
2. **Does Hollywood's general indifference toward Hispanic actresses suggest a lack of management vision at major movie studios? Explain your answer.**

Today, 80 percent of all Hispanic-Americans watch or listen to some form of Spanish-language programming. Fifty percent of Hispanic-Americans also watch or listen to English-language programming. This type of information affects the decisions of many broadcast entertainment managers.

INTERMISSION

What is the difference between data and information?

____

____

COMPONENTS OF AN MIS

The components of an MIS are crucial to its ability to process information. In a simple MIS, five components supply resources to the system. The sports and entertainment manager must learn how to use these five components in order to make decisions and construct strategies.

- **People resources** include systems analysts, programmers, computer operators, and end users of the system. People resources tell the system what to do and benefit from the results of its usage.
- **Hardware resources** consist of machines, such as computers and computer equipment, and media, such as floppy disks. Hardware is often customized for individual systems.
- **Software resources** are comprised of programs to run the system, as well as procedures to keep the system operating effectively.
- **Data resources** match the needs of users to the data gathered or stored by the MIS. For example, customer records are normally maintained by a management information system.
- **Information resources** can be customized and generated from the MIS. Information resources include management reports and business forms.

Many components of the MIS interact simultaneously. Each MIS begins with an input of data. This data can come from internal or external sources. As the data is input by a people resource, information processing is initiated. A database connects through a hardware resource to a software resource to perform a function. As data from the original input is processed, information becomes organized in a useful form. The data resources then can be presented to management as information resources. The end result of the MIS sets the stage for managerial decision making.

MAKING DECISIONS WITH AN MIS

Problem solving with an MIS can be thought of as a series of steps. Assume that the women's softball program at a small university wants to use an MIS to help prepare for an upcoming season in a highly competitive conference. The coach hires an information specialist and a computer operator to help construct the MIS. Once the system is ready, a variety of information is input. This information includes personal and team statistics, competitive information on players and personnel, and other factors that affect game strategy.

The coach decides to focus on building a stronger team for the future. Recruiting has been good in the past, but it can be improved with an MIS. The coach begins to accumulate data on high school and junior college players that fit profiles of excellence or needs of the softball program. By inputting weekly data on performance, injuries, and recruiting efforts, the coach will be able to follow prospective players throughout the season. This usage of the management information system not only impacts decision making but also demonstrates one of the characteristics of an MIS—a long-term orientation. Think of the value for the coach if she were able to follow a prospective player's high school performance for three years.

As additional data is gathered during a recruiting season, the coach can modify and clarify existing data. Suppose the coach learns that an excellent prospect is leaning toward a rival university because the player's sister attends that school. This scenario would probably dramatically reduce the chances of successfully recruiting this player. Coaches have learned that by using an MIS, decision making not only becomes easier but also becomes better.

Now, assume that the coach learns by reading summary scouting reports that a star high school pitcher who was leaning toward a rival has decided to explore other options. The coach can quickly prepare a report to distribute to her scouts that shows average playing time of pitchers and how her program has used freshman pitchers in the past five years. This data can be presented to the prospect at the right time to influence the player's decision.

In today's world of sports, it is assumed that bigger and newer is better. Sports owners often say, "We could play better and win more often if we just had a new stadium." In 2003, however, MLB attendance declined by almost five percent even though there were many new stadiums and more on the way. In the NFL, there is growing disparity between the "haves" and "have nots." Tennessee Titans owner Bud Adams moved his Houston Oilers team in a dispute over a new stadium. After he moved, Houston built a new stadium for its new team, the Houston Texans. The loyal fans ultimately pay the price for the growing controversy about stadiums and their adequacy.

THINK CRITICALLY

1. **How do stadium size and newness affect the success of a sports franchise?**
2. **Should fans pay the price for new stadiums? Explain your answer.**

GAINING THE COMPETITIVE EDGE WITH INFORMATION

An MIS can make decision makers more efficient. Information is organized and at the decision maker's fingertips. Information can be accessed at critical stages in the decision-making process.

An MIS does not have to be accompanied by elaborate databases, rooms of equipment, and many employees. An individual's personal digital assistant (PDA) can organize data to build a simple MIS.

the Global Manager

According to industry publicity, iSight from Apple Computers captures a quality picture and clear sound. The Apple camera sits atop the computer screen and allows the user to see and talk to the person on the other end of the computer "phone call." iSight follows a string of Apple introductions into the highly competitive computer entertainment market. New applications are arriving quickly. Global conferencing allows an entire conference to immediately become part of the organization's MIS for all decision makers to see. The ability to video chat almost anywhere lets scouts report from a sporting event, complete with live pictures. If Apple has its way, scouts traveling the world searching for talent may look more like computer geeks than coaches.

THINK CRITICALLY

1. Using the Internet, locate three other innovative tools for acquiring data for the MIS in a sports organization.
2. Discuss how entertainment organizations might use the technology described above to improve competitiveness.

Organizations now use management information systems to gain a competitive edge. A competitive edge allows the manager to position the company to take advantage of opportunities as they arise. It also allows the manager to meet threats before they become major obstacles.

The primary drawbacks of an MIS are that it can be expensive to set up and maintain, and it is run by people. The old saying "garbage in, garbage out" is appropriate with respect to an MIS. The system is only as good as those who construct and maintain it. Managers must be aware of the type of data needed for decision making and must ensure that the data is collected properly. If data is falsified or incomplete, then decisions made using that data will suffer.

An organization should start slowly when building a management information system. It can expand as more resources are gathered. Some experts believe that the MIS not only pays for itself but also becomes a source of profit for the organization. Whether this is true or not for the average sports or entertainment organization is debatable. However, history has shown that without information and a system to acquire and process it, an organization cannot successfully compete in today's marketplace.

SUCCESS IS IN THE SOLUTION

Success in management and business comes not from having a management information system but from having a system that aids managers in their decision-making abilities. The ultimate test of an effective MIS is whether optimal decisions are made and whether those decisions are implemented correctly.

INTERMISSION

How can a sports or entertainment organization gain a competitive edge by utilizing an MIS?

____

____

UNDERSTAND MANAGEMENT CONCEPTS

Circle the best answer for each of the following questions.

1. Data that has been interpreted to meet the needs of the managers who acquired it is
   a. information **c.** a statistic
   b. evidence **d.** a database
2. Which of the following is not a component of an MIS?
   a. data resources **c.** competitive resources
   b. hardware resources **d.** people resources

THINK CRITICALLY

Answer the following questions as completely as possible. If necessary, use a separate sheet of paper.

3. **Technology** You have been hired as a consultant to design a management information system for a local band that you believe will make it big. The band has secured $30,000 to develop and initiate the MIS. Describe the MIS you would design and what it would do for the band in the long run.

   ____

   ____

   ____

   ____

4. Assume that your high school football team has a fully functioning MIS. How could the MIS be used to gain a competitive edge in the team's operations and decision making?

   ____

   ____

   ____

5. **Communication** Write a job description for an MIS specialist for one of the four major television networks (ABC, CBS, NBC, or FOX). Identify what you perceive to be the primary qualities and skills necessary to land this job.

   ____

   ____

   ____

LESSON 12.2

IMPLEMENTING STRATEGIES WITH AN MIS

Discuss the implementation of strategies using an MIS.

Describe how decision support systems can be used by management.

OPENING ACT

Robo Wars are challenges between man-made robots that would have been unimagined only a few years ago. Robo Wars are held around the country on college and high school campuses. They are featured events on several cable TV technology channels. One of the major sponsors of these high-tech events is Sony™. Several years ago, Sony produced Aibo, a fully functioning robo pet that behaves in many ways like "man's best friend." Aibo gave Sony a reason to pursue a lifelong corporate dream—robotics for consumers. Each year, Sony donates several Aibos for the Robo Cup American Open held at Carnegie Mellon University. Student teams attempt to play soccer with these small, robotic creatures. Participants learn about robotics, applications of computer science, and team strategies.

Work with a partner. Discuss why Sony would sponsor an event such as the Robo Cup American Open. What do you believe will be the future of this type of entertainment event? Will it ever be considered a real sport? Explain your answers.

THE REAL KEY TO SUCCESS—IMPLEMENTATION

Great strategies and creative plans are meaningless if they are not properly implemented. More often than not, implementation problems are human-related rather than technical-related. To succeed, any functioning MIS department must have the full support of the people it serves. Cooperation must be secured from a variety of diverse groups. Executives, mid-managers, supervisors, and line employees, in addition to the MIS department, must all "buy into" using management information systems to plan and carry out the strategies of the organization.

Most managers today understand that management information systems are changing the workplace. Decisions can be made faster, with more information, and have a better chance of being correct than ever before. These same decisions also can be implemented almost as soon as they are made. Speed of implementation often becomes the competitive edge that the organization needs in order to stay on top.

OVERCOMING IMPLEMENTATION PROBLEMS

Managers have found that several strategies help to overcome difficulties with implementing MIS-based decisions.

Executive Involvement Nothing of any significance will happen without top management's involvement. Top management must understand strategies and organizational difficulties if problems are to be solved. Additionally, budgets for implementation are usually the responsibility of top managers.

Necessity Managers must determine if the MIS is necessary. Implementation begins with problems. For implementation to succeed, it must be tied to a problem that is worth solving. Information collected through the MIS to solve the problem then becomes justified.

Endorsement Employees must endorse a solution for it to work. Players on a team will not carry out a coach's strategy unless they believe in it. The same principle applies to employees' support of a manager's strategy.

Training Support for implementation can be gained with training and education. Many MIS applications used to implement strategies are foreign to the average person. Explanations often are needed.

Rewards There should be rewards for successful strategy implementation using an MIS. If employees use the MIS properly, they should see immediate benefits and gains in productivity. If not, employees will often abandon the newer methods of implementation and return to older, more familiar methods.

Feedback The MIS needs feedback from end users to determine if plans are working well. Users should let managers know if decision making has been aided, if implementation has improved, or if changes are still needed to make things right.

Organizations that follow these strategies generally are able to improve decision making and implementation using an MIS. Organizations that fail to improve generally find that support is lacking in some critical component of the system. For example, assume that a local sports franchise wants to move its ticket sales division to the Web. This move will mean that instead of selling tickets through sales calls and telemarketing, the sales force will need to learn e-marketing techniques in order to reach a larger market base.

In this case, change will not come easily. Old-style sales forces are verbal rather than visual and relate more to individuals and small groups through personal contact rather than to larger groups through cyberspace. Technology also might be a threat to these old-style sales people. The sales force may hesitate to learn the new sales tools. They may find reasons to suggest that the Internet move was a bad one. They might even leave the organization in protest.

Change almost always is difficult. The sales force will probably fail to see that the move to the Internet could improve their commissions by increasing their sales. Instead of appealing only to local markets, the sales force will now be able to sell nationally or even internationally.

It is the responsibility of the MIS department to thoroughly educate the sales force before attempting a move into cyberspace. Today, an increasing number of sports organizations have embraced online sales. Increased ticket sales and fan support have justified their move.

INTERMISSION

What are the strategies for overcoming implementation problems?

____

____

USING DECISION SUPPORT SYSTEMS IN IMPLEMENTATION

Recent advances in MIS have provided management with a variety of decision support systems. A **decision support system (DSS)** is a complex set of computer hardware and software that supports a single manager or a small group of managers who work as a problem-solving team. A DSS allows managers to access and process specific information from a larger MIS. A DSS is often used to isolate problems that need special attention or that require a longer solution period. Examples of sports and entertainment problems that should receive DSS attention are the location and construction of a new stadium, the acquisition of off-site operations, mergers or joint ventures with other organizations, and the development of a new entertainment venue.

© BRAND X PICTURES

Unlike an MIS, which is a more general management aid, a DSS can focus on specific problems and make recommendations. Many sports and entertainment organizations are adopting decision support systems as managers become familiar with their potential as a powerful decision-making tool.

GROUP DECISION SUPPORT SYSTEMS

A **group decision support system (GDSS)** is used to facilitate solutions in group meetings. The basic purpose of the GDSS is to remove communication barriers that often delay group decision making. A GDSS is especially helpful if group members have diverse backgrounds or conflicting agendas.

As sports and entertainment organizations continue to diversify and expand operations globally, the need for group decisions will naturally increase. For example, if a movie studio expands its operations into a foreign market, a team of managers from the new market could provide valuable insight into local standards, market needs, cultural taboos, and government regulations. A GDSS can organize this input so that it can be shared with the studio's managers.

EXECUTIVE INFORMATION SYSTEMS

An **executive information system (EIS)** is a highly interactive system that provides top management with flexible access to other information systems. This access allows for better monitoring and information gathering. An EIS is a natural outgrowth of other MIS operations. Information supplied by an EIS is gathered for a select few and is often highly customized.

To be effective, the EIS must be quick, user-friendly, and non-technical in nature. It must be able to anticipate information that executives might want or need. It should be able to extract as well as create information, retrieve internal and external data without the assistance of others, and be accessible anywhere and anytime. If these requirements are not met, the EIS will hamper rather than help decision making.

TRANSACTION PROCESSING SYSTEMS

A **transaction processing system (TPS)** assists functional areas such as sales and marketing, finance, accounting, and human resources. The TPS accumulates information specific to functional and operational problems.

With a TPS, an organization can track orders and order processing systems and manage accounting functions. A TPS also can supply information for the human resources department regarding compensation, training and development, and critical record keeping. Consider the difficulties that sports franchises have with players and their complex contracts. Athletes often are part-owners of their franchises and receive a percentage of profits. A TPS helps to track organizational operations so that all parties spend more time making money rather than fighting about contracts and obligations in court.

Part of the fun of using the Internet for entertainment purposes is the ability to customize products and information. In the past, people had to accept programming and information that was relevant to the masses rather than to the individual. The Web user is now able to find answers to questions, link to individually oriented entertainment, and even customize products, from tennis shoes to wedding rings, in ways that were not possible a few years ago.

THINK CRITICALLY

1. **Find a web site where you can customize a product. Pick a product and go through the customization process. Critique your experience.**
2. **Create an example that illustrates a person's ability to customize information for entertainment decision-making purposes using the Internet.**

EXPERT SYSTEMS

Not every organization has the luxury of being able to hire consultants, or experts, to handle specialized or difficult problems. Outsourcing is a valuable tool, but most organizations prefer to handle their own challenges and problems.

An **expert system (ES)** enables an organization's computer system to make decisions that typically are made by consultants. The ES is different from the DSS in that the ES reflects how an expert would solve the problem rather than how the organizational manager would solve the problem. All that is necessary to get "expert" advice is to utilize the ES.

The ES can explain how a decision was reached. Consequently, if an error is made, it will not be repeated as a normal process of decision making. The ES often gives managers the ability to extend their own intelligence. Although experts usually design it, once the ES is created, the organization can often wean itself from expensive consultants.

INTERMISSION

What is the difference between an MIS and a DSS?

____

____

IBM AND THE NFL

The NFL has brought about many broadcasting innovations in an effort to enhance the viewing and entertainment functions of professional football. In 2003, the NFL made another move that caught rivals off guard. The league signed IBM to a multi-year contract to serve as the NFL's "official information technology partner." For this privilege, IBM will pay $6 million a year and provide $25 million in advertising spending.

Most observers believe that IBM is positioning itself to pull large sports leagues into the twenty-first century with respect to management information systems. By assisting with the advent of the NFL's management information system, IBM will be able not only to sell its current MIS products but also to create new products that will be of interest to other sports leagues.

THINK CRITICALLY

1. What will IBM gain from this new partnership?
2. What will the NFL gain from this new partnership?

UNDERSTAND MANAGEMENT CONCEPTS

Circle the best answer for each of the following questions.

1. Which of the following is a complex set of computer hardware and software that supports a single manager or a small group of managers who work as a problem-solving team?
a. expert system (ES)
b. transaction processing system (TPS)
c. decision support system (DSS)
d. executive information system (EIS)

2. Which of the following attempts to eliminate an organization's dependency on consultants?
a. expert system (ES)
b. transaction processing system (TPS)
c. decision support system (DSS)
d. executive information system (EIS)

THINK CRITICALLY

Answer the following questions as completely as possible. If necessary, use a separate sheet of paper.

3. What is the general purpose of a decision support system (DSS)?

____

____

____

____

4. How does a group decision support system (GDSS) work?

____

____

____

____

5. What would be the advantages of developing an expert system (ES)?

____

____

____

____

REVIEW

REVIEW MANAGEMENT CONCEPTS

Write the letter of the term that matches each definition. Some terms will not be used.

____ **1.** The raw material of information systems
____ **2.** Capturing, processing, and storing data
____ **3.** Data that has been interpreted to meet the needs of the managers who acquired it
____ **4.** A collection of data that is arranged in a logical manner and organized in a form that can be stored and processed by a computer
____ **5.** A system that assists functional areas such as sales and marketing, finance, accounting, and human resources
____ **6.** A system used to facilitate solutions in group meetings
____ **7.** A glut of print, sound, and image communication
____ **8.** An integrated approach to providing interpreted and relevant information to managers

a. data
b. data processing
c. database
d. decision support system (DSS)
e. executive information system (EIS)
f. expert system (ES)
g. group decision support system (GDSS)
h. information
i. information overload
j. management information system (MIS)
k. transaction processing system (TPS)

Circle the best answer.

9. What type of resources includes systems analysts, programmers, computer operators, and end users of the MIS?
a. hardware resources
b. information resources
c. data resources
d. people resources

10. All of the following are strategies that help to overcome difficulties with implementing MIS-based decisions except
a. endorsement
b. rewards
c. feedback
d. software resources

11. Which of the following systems would be used if an organization wants its top managers to monitor the operations of the business?
a. executive information system
b. transaction processing system
c. expert system
d. group decision support system

THINK CRITICALLY

12. Briefly explain how management information systems evolved.

13. Contact an information systems manager for a sports or entertainment organization. Interview the person about his or her job responsibilities. What is the manager's greatest challenge? Report your findings to the class.

14. Compile a list of advantages for using an MIS in a sports or entertainment organization.

15. Compile a list of disadvantages for using an MIS in a sports or entertainment organization. How can these disadvantages be overcome?

16. You have been assigned the task of designing an MIS for a sports or entertainment event at your school. Outline what you will do to establish the management information system.

MAKE CONNECTIONS

17. Management Math Last year, your organization spent $200,000 on consultant services. This year, a consultant is willing to design an expert system for your organization for $180,000, which includes the designer's salary. Considering these figures, how would you justify your organization's implementation of an expert system that may be out of date in two years? Support your reasons with figures.

18. Technology Use the Internet to locate two articles about decision support systems. Explain how these systems can be used in sports and entertainment organizations. Report your findings to the class.

19. Communication Create an illustration that demonstrates how a group decision support system (GDSS) could be used to solve a problem at your school. Be sure to include all those who will be part of the group and what information they might contribute or need.

20. Technology Search the Internet to locate three jobs in sports and entertainment organizations that are related to management information systems. What qualifications are required for the positions? Report your findings to the class.

21. Human Resources Management Assume that you are the human resources manager for a large sports or entertainment organization. What job skills would you like to see in an MIS director? Separate the necessary software, hardware, and people skills of this director.

22. Management Responsibilities You are faced with a managerial dilemma. You have some employees in your department who are capable of switching to an MIS for the purpose of making better decisions, and you have other employees who are not. What will you do with the employees who seem to be incapable of switching to an MIS? Write a memo to the department head that outlines your thoughts.

23. Communication As an MIS manager, you would like executives to make better use of the MIS that was established by the top managers themselves. However, many top managers do not use the system. Outline a strategy to remedy this problem. Given the nature of the problem, what would be the best way to communicate your recommendations to top management?

24. Human Resources Management As the human resources manager of a major sports organization, you have been asked to speak to a group of high school students about the job opportunities in MIS with your organization. You realize that many in the audience do not trust large organizations and do not wish to work for them. What information will you use to capture your audience's attention? How will you interest skeptics in MIS job opportunities with your organization?

DELTA—PLAYING THE CUSTOMER'S SONG

Delta Air Lines plans to gain a piece of the profitable discount airline market with the April 15, 2003 launch of its new airline called Song. Song's president John Selvaggio, says that Song is all about making flying fun.

Song actively competes with the young JetBlue, a leading airline that flies between New York and Florida. Song plans to upstage JetBlue with its state-of-the-art entertainment system, leather seats, additional legroom, and branded beverage and food choices. Song offers 24 channels of free seatback satellite television and multi-player interactive games. Additionally, Song outdoes JetBlue by offering on-demand audio and movies.

Customer Feedback

Song regularly updates its services and amenities based on customer feedback. Customers have the ability to vote on products and services via the Song web site. Additional services to be offered in the future include in-flight shopping and online product purchase capabilities.

Song's flight attendants wear designer uniforms while selling trendy sandwiches and entrees. Thai noodle salads and veggie soft tacos are examples of the unique fare that is available. Flight attendants make comical announcements, whoop it up, and entertain their passengers.

Song offers simplified pricing. Fares are one-way and do not require a Saturday-night stay. The earlier you purchase a ticket, the less you will pay.

Song's initial route included 144 daily flights between the Northeast and key Florida leisure destinations, Atlanta, and Las Vegas. Song plans to grow slowly. Los Angeles and San Juan, Puerto Rico are two of Song's newest destinations.

May Serve as Model

If Song succeeds, it may serve as a model for other major airlines seeking a profitable formula to compete against Southwest, JetBlue, AirTran, and other discount airlines. Continental, United, and US Airways all have unsuccessfully tried low-fare brands in the past.

Delta previously operated Delta Express, a low-fare airline that also flew between the Northeast and Florida. Delta Express made money for three years and then began experiencing losses in 2000. The airline eventually went out of business in 2003. Song promises not only lower fares but also lower operating costs, giving it a better chance at success than previous attempts by other major airlines.

Song's 36 Boeing 757s will have 37 more seats to fill than JetBlue's Airbus I-320s. Additional challenges facing the new airline include consumers distracted by overseas military operations, international unrest, and a lagging economy.

JetBlue is not worried about the competition from Song. A JetBlue spokesperson compared the new airline to an over-the-hill product trying to retain its youth with paint and window dressing.

Think Critically

1. **Why are major airlines paying attention to strategies used by JetBlue and other discount airlines?**
2. **What are Song's chances for success?**
3. **What services do you think airline passengers really want?**

SPORTS AND ENTERTAINMENT MARKETING MANAGEMENT TEAM DECISION MAKING

Song Airlines wants to be the official carrier for the New York Giants, Jets, Yankees, and Mets. Fans can count on great rates to attend their favorite football and baseball games on the East coast.

You have been hired as a consultant to help Song achieve its goal. You must devise a marketing strategy to gain the loyalty of these professional sports teams and their fans. Key elements to stress in your promotions are Song's low fares, policy of no Saturday-night stay required, fun attendants, great food, and an overall enjoyable flying experience.

You should be aware that Southwest Airlines and JetBlue already have a hold on some of the target market you plan to capture. You must overcome this competition by describing how Song gives customers more value for their dollar.

Performance Indicators Evaluated

- Describe factors that set Song apart from the competition.
- Emphasize value received by Song's customers.
- Understand the importance of Song's marketing relationship with the professional sports teams.
- Explain promotional strategies designed to hook professional sports teams on Song Airlines.

Go to the DECA web site for more detailed information.

1. What methods of promotion do you plan to use for this campaign? Why did you choose these methods?
2. What three things do you want to highlight most for prospective customers? Explain your choices.
3. Describe a television commercial that you will make for Song. Who will be in the commercial? Why?
4. Outline your complete marketing strategy for Song Airlines.

www.deca.org/publications/HS_Guide/guidetoc.html

INDEX

A

ABC, 41
ACL. *See* Anterior cruciate ligament
Action Performance Company, 48
Action phase, 171
Adams, Bud, 291
Advanced computer technologies, 197
Advertising
  Minnesota Twins, 76–77
  prime-time television, 253
  recruiting applicants, 192
  recruiting U.S. armed forces, 264
  rotational signs, 12
African-American population, 175
Agent, 64, 82
  characteristics of, 66–67
  conflicts of interest, 69
  fees and competition, 67–69
  and leadership, 65
  See also General manager; Owner
Aibo, 294
Air Force, 264
Air Jamaica, 130
AirTran, 304
Air Transport Association, 130
Alabama Renegades, 107
Alexander, Leslie, 70
All in the Family, 186
Amateur sports
  business of, 41–42
  function of management for, 35
  growth of, 34–36
  managing, 34–38
  managing diversity in, 40
  marketing managers of, 36
  percentage of family budgets for, 42
AMC. *See* Atlantis Music Conference
American Idol, 150
America Online, Inc., 134, 230
Anderson, Kristen, 223
Annual Kodak Albuquerque International Balloon Fiesta, 121
Anterior cruciate ligament (ACL), 268
AOL Music, 230
AOL Time Warner, 134
Apple Computers, 292
Arena Football League, 3
Arizona Diamondbacks, 172
Army, 264
Athlete, paying, 40–41
Athletic director, 28–29, 39, 204
Atlanta Braves, 250
Atlantis Music Conference (AMC), 288
AT&T Rose Bowl, 11
Authority, 8, 119
Autocratic-decision making, 136
Autocratic leader, 222–223
Automobile. See Car buying
Autonomous teams, 251
Avon, 57

B

BAA. *See* Broadway Across America
Babby, Lon, 67
Babysitter's Club, 258
Balloon Fiesta, 121
Baltimore Orioles, 225
Barriers to entry, 270
Baseball agents, 69
Bauer, Frank, 65
BCS. *See* Bowl Championship Series
Bechler, Steve, 225
Beckham, David, 143, 243
Belief, entertainment and, 210
Benchmarking, 177
Ben & Jerry's Ice Cream, 167
Best practices, 271
Bieniemy, Eric, 204
Big league sports. *See* Sports, professional
Big Red Dog, The, 258
Big Twelve Conference, 29
Billboard, 213
Billy Bob's of Texas, 133
Black, Shirley Temple, 79
Boarding House: North Shore, 241
Bob Devaney Sports Center, 13
Boogie board, 267
Boston Marathon, 80
Boston Red Sox, 114, 162, 255
Boundary controls, 277
Bowl Championship Series (BCS), 11, 41
Brainstorming, 144
Brainwriting, 145
Brand marketing, 98
Brazil, 97
Broadway, 287
Broadway Across America (BAA), 287
Brooks, Michael, 68
Budget
  for college athletics, 39
  percentage of family, for sports, 42
  setting, for local events, 81–82
Burn, Dallas, 142
Business culture, 196–197
Business information management, 7–8, 30
Business management principles, 6–8
Business organization, 96
Business plan
  for local events, 80
  measuring success of, 61–62
Business strategy, 162, 171
Business trends, 197–198

C

Calder Cup, 168
California Angels, 172
Capital goods, 88
Capitalism, 88
Car buying, war effects on, 130
Career
  counseling for, 201
  management, 201–205
  path, 201
  plan, 201, 203–204
  qualifications for, 203–204
  starting, 202
Career-level job, 202
Carlson, Bob, 267
Carnegie Mellon University, 294
Carnival, 17
Carr, David, 65
Case study, From "Know 'Em to See 'Em," 76–77
CBS, 41, 161
CBS SportsLine.com, 87
Census (2000), 156
Centralized organization, 96
Cereal company, 175
Chambers, Buford, 37
ChampionChip, 80
Change
  agents of, 227–231
  leadership necessary for, 231–232
  signs of, 228
  steps for, 229–230
Charlotte Sting, 62
Chase, Lea, 257
Chat room, public, 149
Cheers, 186
Children's entertainment market, 161
Chinese Academy of Social Services, 204
Cincinnati Bengals, 204
Clifford, 258
Coca-Cola, 87
College and amateur sports, 26–49
  economic impact, 39–43
  fan misbehavior, 31
  managing amateur sports, 34–38
  managing college athletics, 28–32
  success of sports camps, 27
College athletic director, 28–29, 39
College athletics
  agents giving money to student athletes, 68–69
  budgets for, 38–41
  financial impact of, 39–41
  management functions, 28–30
  managing, 28–34
  nature of management, 31
  role of NCAA in, 30
College championship, management of, 11
College coach, 204
College events, managing, 86–90
  economic environment in, 86–87
  factors of production in, 88–89
  Texas A&M, 86
  utility, 87
Colona, Andre, 65
Comedy clubs, 17
Commission on Opportunity in Athletics, 40
Communication, 54, 117, 121
  between managers and employees, 218
  skills in, for employees, 199
  to support teams, 256
  See also Downward communication; Upward communication
Communism, 89
Communities, knowledge, 149–150
Community entertainment events, 16–17
Community involvement, 92–93
Competition, 88
  fees and, 67–69
  within industries, 270
  using information, 291–292
Competitiveness, 269–271
Competitive trends, 175
Comstock, Nebraska, 24
Comstock Rock, 24
Comstock Windmill Festival, 24–25
Conditions, for decision making, 137–139
Conflict of interest, 68

Consistency, 224–225
Consultative-decision making, 136
Consumer behavior, 130
Continental, 304
Control
defined, 273
power of, 273–275
why managers should practice, 122–123
Controller, 274
Controlling
defined, 5
professional sports and, 54–55
Control system, 275–278
Coordinating, 193
Corbi, Lana, 114
Corporate strategy, 161, 171
Correction, 276
Cosby Show, The, 186
Cost leadership, 162
Cost standards, 55
Country Stampede, 16
Cover letter, 192
Creative decision making. *See* Nonprogrammed decision
Critical-thinking skills, 199
Cultural and lifestyle trends, 175
Culture, business, 196–197
Customer departmentalization, 118
Customer satisfaction, 32
Cyber management
event information, 16
information about sporting venues, 54
sports camps, 37
Cyber Management features, 16, 37, 54, 87, 123, 145, 161, 202, 230, 250, 274, 297

D

Dallas Cowboys, 70, 162
Data, 289–290
Database, 289–290
Data processing, 289
Data resources, 290
Davis, Al, 93, 111
DeBartolo, Edward J., 194
DeBartolo Corporation, 194
DeBartolo York, Denise, 194
DECA. *See* Distributive Education Clubs of America
DECA Prep case studies
Creating a Successful Sitcom, 186
Delta—Playing the Customer's Song, 304
Few Can Afford Membership in Private Golf Clubs, 156
From "Know 'Em" to "See 'Em", 76
From Windmill Festival to Rock Festival, 24
Hosting the Big Event, 238
NASCAR and Armed Forces, 264
NASCAR's Image and Teenagers, 48
Upselling Strategy, The, 104
War Anxiety Puts Life on Hold, 130
When Beliefs Conflict with Entertainment, 210
Who Wants to Play Full-Contact Women's Football?, 284
DECA Prep events (Sports and Entertainment Marketing Management Team Decision Making), 25, 49, 77, 105, 131, 157, 187, 211, 239, 265, 285, 305
Decentralization, 117
Decentralized organization, 96
Decision making, 132–157
advantages and disadvantages of, 142–143
conditions for, 137–140
environment for, 137
five-step process for, 8
group, 141–146
managers and, 134–140
knowledge management and, 147–152
skills for, 199
styles of, 136
tools for, 144–145
Decision support system (DSS)
defined, 296
using, in implementation, 296–298
Defensive strategies, 161
Degrees of certainty, 138
Delegate, 53, 119, 196–197
Delphi technique, 145
Delta Air Lines, 304
Delta Express, 304
Demand, 86
Deming, Dr. W. Edward, 32
Democratic leader, 223
Demographics, 18, 198
Demographic trends, 175
Dempster House, The, 24
Dempster Manufacturing, 24
Denver Broncos, 3
Departmentalization, 118
Departmental structure, 118
Descriptive plan, 110–111
Designing Women, 186
Detroit Pistons, 67
Detroit Red Wings, 269
Development phase
completing, 170
environmental analysis, 169–170
policies, procedures, and rules, 168
of strategic management, 167–170
Deviation, 273
Diagnostic controls, 276
Dick Van Dyke Show, The, 186
Differentiation, 162
Digital Economy, The, 228
DirectTV, 161
Disney, 161, 253, 269
Disney Theme Parks, 131
Disney World, 17
Distributive Education Clubs of America (DECA), 203
Diversity, 198
Dominos Pizza, 48
Doom™, 250
Downsizing, 230
Downward communication, 114
Dream Job, 273
Drugs, over-the-counter, 225
DSS. See Decision support system
Dunkin' Donuts, 98
DVD, 244

E

Economic environment, 86–87
Economic system, 88–89
Economic trends, 175
Economy, war effects on, 130
EIS. *See* Executive information system
Employee, 191–192, 224–225
communication between manager and, 218
empowerment of, 8, 232
how manager beliefs influence performance, 221–222
motivation of, 32, 121
performance of, 193–195
what's important to, 191
See also Work teams
Employee relations, 193
Employee rewards, 224–225
Employment, 191–192
Empowerment, 232
Endorsement, 295
Enforcement, military and law, 178
Enlightened leadership, 231–232
Entertainment
beliefs and, 210
Internet for, 297. *See also* Events
Entertainment management
college events, 86-90
comedy clubs, 17
community events, 16–17
defined, 4–6
human resources, 15
local events, 80-85,
managing diversity, 18
professional sports, 91-94
responsibilities, 7-8
special events, 95-99
state fairs, 17–18
Entrepreneurship, 88
Entry, barriers to, 270
Entry-level occupation, 202
Environment, 117
for decision making, 137
leaders in changing, 212–239
Environmental analysis, 169–170
Environmental scanning, 175–176
Epcot, 130
Ephedrine, 225
ES. *See* Expert system
Escobedo, Maria, 289
ESPN, 273
Estefan, Emilio, 213
Estefan, Gloria, 213
Ethics in Action features, 5, 31, 65, 88, 115, 138, 175, 193, 225, 252, 270, 291
Evaluation, control through, 273–279
Events
creating special, 98
managing, 95–99
marketing and sales, 98
organizational structure, 95–96
producing, 81–83
See also College events; Major events; Professional sports, managing
Everybody Loves Raymond, 186
Executive, 31, 202
Executive information system (EIS), 297
Executive involvement, 295
Expert power, 216
Expert system (ES), 298
External environment, 169, 175
Extranet, 257

F

Facilities, 12–13
Factors of production, 88–89

Fan misbehavior, 31
Fans, catering to young, 92
FBLA. *See* Future Business Leaders of America
FedEx Orange Bowl, 11
Feedback, 274, 295
Feedback system, 123
Fees, 67–69
Figure skating, 160
Filene Shouse, Catherine, 217
Final Four Championship, 11, 41, 89
Financial management, 12, 35, 55
  college athletic directors in charge of, 29
  of college athletics, 39–41
  defined, 7
  planning big league sports events, 52–53
Financial managers, role of, 124
Financial plan, 80
Financial security, 191
Finch, Dènnie, 161
5K run, 92
Flattened organization, 96
Fleming County Covered Bridge Festival, 83
Flexible viewpoint, 222
Flores, Tom, 93
Florida State, 68
Focal point teams, 199
Focus, 162
Ford, 130
Ford, Henry, 269
Formal plan, 109
Formal rule, 245
Formal work groups, 242–243
Form utility, 87
Fox Network, 48, 150
Friends, 186, 253
Fringe benefits, 191
From "Know 'Em to See 'Em" case study, 76–77
Ft. Worth, Texas, 133
Function, operations management, 268–269
Functional departmentalization, 118
Functional strategies, 162
Funding college athletics. *See* Financial management
Future Business Leaders of America (FBLA), 203

G

Gamecocks, 210
Garrell, Timothy, 36
Garriga, Jocelyn, 284
Gatorade, 95, 98
GDSS. See Group decision support system
Gender-equity law. *See* Title IX
General manager, 70. *See also* Agent; Owner
General Motors, 87, 130
Geographic departmentalization, 118
"Get To Know 'Em" campaign, 76–77
Gilson, Carol "Gil," 189
Globalization, 197
Global Manager features, 12, 36, 56, 84, 114, 143, 163, 204, 217, 243, 277, 292
Golden Girls, The, 186
Golf club, 156
Gonzalez, Luis, 201
Good Times, 186
Goosebumps, 258
Gordon, Jeff, 48
"Gotta See 'Em" campaign, 76–77
Graduation rates for athletes, 40
Grand Floridian Triathlon, 159
Green Bay Packers, 3
Group
  defined, 141
  factors that influence, 248–249
  formal, 242–243
  informal, 243
  managing behavior of, 245–247
  managing team and, 241–265
Group cohesiveness, 246–247
Group conformity, 246–247
Group decision making, 141–146
Group decision support system (GDSS), 296–297
Group dynamic, 244
Group norms, 246–247
Group-oriented making, 136
Group structure, 242–248
Groupthink, 142, 252
Growth strategies, 161
Guzman, Cristian, 76
Gymnastics, 252

H

Hall, Felicia, 62
Hallmark Channel, 114
Halloween Horror Nights, 98
Hamm, Mia, 64
Happy Days, 186
Harding, Tonya, 270
Hard issues, 228
Hardware resources, 290
Harpo Productions, 174
Harry Potter and the Order of the Phoenix, 258
Hayek, Salma, 289
Heisman Trophy, 68
Hendrickson, Doug, 65
Hennepin County District Court, 76
Henry, Nakia, 284
High school athletics, 34–35
Hill, Faith, 148
Hill, Grant, 67
Hispanic-American population, 175, 289
Hispanic market, 172
Hollywood, CA, 277
Homecoming, 89
Home Depot, 264
Houston Aeros, 168
Houston Community College, 223
Houston Fire Department, 284
Houston Oilers, 291
Houston Reliant Energy, 284
Houston Reliants, 223
Houston Rockets, 70, 118
Houston Rodeo and Livestock Show, 91
Houston Super Bowl Host Committee, 238
Houston Texans, 12, 51, 91
Howington, Robin, 284
Hug, Butch, 13
Human resources, 193
  activities, 190
  advertising for applicants, 192
  resume and cover letter, 192
Human resources management
  activities, 190–191
  defined, 7
  for entertainment events, 15
  hiring professional staff members, 10
  for sports events, 10, 35
Hunt Adkins Advertising, 76
Hurricane Andrew, 213

I

IBM, 298
Ice cream, 167
Ice skating, 270
Identity power, 216
I Love Lucy, 186
Implementation, 294–296
  defined, 294
  overcoming, problems, 295–296
  using decision support systems in, 296–298
Implementing
  defined, 5
  function, 121–122
Industrial Revolution, 269
Informal groups, 243
Informal plan, 109
Informal rule, 245
Information
  defined, 289
  gaining competitive edge with, 291–292
Information Age, managers in, 288–289
Information overload, 288
Information resources, 290
Information technology, 286–305
Inputs, 268
Insurance. *See* Liability insurance
Intangible knowledge, 148
Interactive controls, 277
Interactive control system. *See* Control system
Internal analysis, 53
Internal environment, 169
International Olympic Committee (IOC), 36, 163
International Organization for Standardization (ISO), 123
International sports events, 56
Internet, 244
  Atlantis Music Conference (AMC) and, 288
  Broadway and, 287
  for entertainment purposes, 297
  for virtual team concept, 257
Internship program, 202
Interpublic Group, 65
Intranet, 257
Intuitive approach, 135
IOC. *See* International Olympic Committee
iSight, 292
ISO. *See* International Organization for Standardization
Issues, hard and soft, 228

J

Jamboree in the Hills Country Music Festival, 16–17
Jefferson, Thomas, 256
Jeffersons, The, 186
JetBlue, 304–305
Jobs
  sports management, 91–92
  See also Career
Job satisfaction, 218
Job security, 193
Job specification, 191
Joel, Andrew, 65
Jones, Jacque, 76
Jones, Jerry, 70
Judgment decision making. *See* Nonprogrammed decision

K

Kansas City, Missouri, 191
Kansas City Royals, 219
Kate & Allie, 186
Kauffman Marion, Ewing, 219
Kellogg™, 264
Kerrigan, Nancy, 270
Kids' Club, 92
Kingwood Junior College, 51
Kiosk, 171
Knowledge communities, 149–150
Knowledge management, 147–152
Knowledge transmission, 150
Kodak, 95
Kosarzycki, Roxanne, 93
Kwan, Michelle, 160

L

Labor, 88
Labor unions, 193
Larry Micheaux June-Jam-Bo-Ree Basketball Camp, 37
Law enforcement, 178
Leaders
  characteristics of, 215
  how they motivate, 221–226
  See also Management
Leadership
  characteristics of, 65–66
  developing skills for, 217–220
  need for, 214
  skills for, 231
  style of, 222
  types of, 222–224
Lead the Way features
  American Idol, 150
  Debartolo York, Denise, 194
  Hall, Felicia, 62
  Hug, Butch, 13
  IBM and the NFL, 298
  Kauffman, Ewing Marion, 219
  Marcus, Barbara, 258
  Moreno, Arturo, 172
  Oakland Raiders, 111
  Pederson, Steve, 42
  Thompson, Jenny, 278
  Trask, Amy, 93
Liability insurance, 55
Line-and-staff organization, 96
Line authority, 119
Line organization, 95
Local events, managing, 80–85
  importance of planning for, 80–81
  producing and, 81–83
Long-term goals, 53
Lopez, Jennifer, 115, 289
Lopez, Nancy, 274
Los Angeles Lakers, 269
Los Angeles Memorial Coliseum, 93
"Louisiana Purchase," 256
Louisiana State, 68
Lowery, Joseph, 156
LPGA, 156, 274
LPGA ADT Championship, 156

M

Magic Kingdom, 161
Major events, managing, 83–84
  Macy's Thanksgiving Day Parade, 84
  New Year's Eve in Times Square, 83
Major League Baseball (MLB), 144
  attendance decline, 291
  "Bud" Selig and, 115
  college athletes and, 41
  drop in attendance, 169
  insurance regulations, 55
  minorities and, 250
  minority ownership and, 172
  organizational structure, 116
  strategic management, 161
  True Value and, 190
Major League Soccer, 142
Make-A-Wish Foundation, 201
Management
  of amateur sports, 34–38
  of college championships, 11
  control process of, 122–123
  defined, 4
  functions of, 4–5
  functions of, for amateur sports, 35
  of international sporting events, 56
  level of, in college athletics, 32
  of professional sports, 12–13, 91–94
  of sports camps, 27
  three steps of, control, 124
  See also Business information management; Business management principles; Cyber management; Entertainment management; Events; Financial management; Human resources management; Knowledge management; Marketing management; Operations management; Production management; Sports management
Management, sports and entertainment, 78–103
  college events, 86–90
  local events, 80–85
  major events, 83–84
  other events, 95–99
  professional sports, 91–94
  Tournament of Roses Parade, 79
Management basics, 4–14
  business management principles, 6–7
  managing sports and entertainment events, 4–6
  responsibilities, 8
Management functions, 106–131
  of college athletics, 28–30
  implementing and controlling, 121–125
  organizing, 113–120
  planning, 108–112
Management positions, 60–61
Management responsibility, 6, 8, 28, 35
Management strategy, 158–187
  building blocks of, 160–165
  process of, 166–173
Manager(s)
  of comedy club, 17
  characteristics of, 3
  communication between, and employees, 218
  how, influence, 216
  how beliefs influence worker performance, 221–222
  See also Leader
Managerial information system (MIS)
  components of, 290–293
  defined, 289
  implement strategies with, 294
  making decisions with, 290–291
Managerial systems, 256
Managing diversity
  changing demographics, 18
  Commission on Opportunity in Athletics, 40
  in entertainment management, 18
  Florida tourism, 97
  sex discrimination, 40
Managing Diversity features, 18, 40, 57, 97, 124, 148, 164, 198, 223, 257, 276, 289
Manchester United Soccer Club, 243
Marcus, Barbara, 258
Mardi Gras, 15, 97
Marines, 264
Marion Laboratories, 219
Market economy, 88
Marketing and sales, 98
Marketing management, 11, 35
  defined, 7
  of sports event, as recruiting tool for university, 29
Marketing manager, for amateur sports, 36
Marketing plan, 80
Marketing teams, 253
Mary Tyler Moore Show, The, 186
*M*A*S*H,* 186
MasterCard, 95
Masters, Catherine, 107
Matrix organization, 96
McDonald's, 57, 142
McFarlane, Todd, 162
McKey, Derrick, 68
McNair, Bob, 12
Measurements of success, 61
Mechanical organization, 117
Meetings, 97–98
Mendoza, Linda, 289
Merchandise, 30
Merchandising, 48
Merrell Dow Pharmaceuticals, 219
Metrodome, 76
"Miami Sound Machine," 213
Micheaux, Larry, 37
Middle East, 277
Mid-manager, defined, 31
Military and law enforcement, 178
Ming, Yao, 118

Minnesota Amateur Sports Commission, 41
Minnesota Twins, 76–77
Minorities, 250
Minute Maid, 95
MIS. *See* Managerial information system
Miss America pageant, 169
Mission, 53, 167
MLB. See Major League Baseball
Mones, Karen, 284
Money
  to college student athletes, 68–69
  managing, 52–55
  See also Financial management
Monitoring system, 275–276
Monster.com, 87
Monterey Jazz Festival, 124
Montreal Expos, 76, 116
Moreno, Arturo, 172
Motivation, employee, 121
Mrs. America pageant, 169
MRT. *See* Mutual Reward Therapy
MTV, 161, 230, 242
Music production manager, 203
Mutual Reward Therapy (MRT), 224–225

N

Nancy Lopez Golf, 274
NASCAR, 251
  entertainment opportunities and, 162
  female fans of, 175
  over-the-counter drugs and, 225
  sponsors of, 264
NASCAR Racers, 48
Nashville Dream, 107
National Basketball Association (NBA), 41, 171
National Collegiate Athletic Association (NCAA), 210
  Felicia Hall and, 62
  management of college championships and, 11, 66–69
  management of college sports and, 28
  position on paying athletes, 40
National Football League (NFL)
  broadcasting innovations and, 298
  college athletes and, 41
  minorities and, 250
  minority ownership and, 172
  Super Bowl, 238
  True Value and, 190
National Guard, 264
National Hockey League, 41
National Hot Rod Association (NHRA), 117
National Park for the Performing Arts, 217
National Sporting Goods Association, 36
National Women's Business Association, 107
National Women's Football Association (NWFA), 107
Natural resources, 88
Nava, Alicia, 284
Nava, Sheila, 284
Navy, 264
NCAA. *See* National Collegiate Athletic Association
NCAA Basketball, 87
NCAA Tournament, 89
Necessity, 295
Networking
  defined, 198
  delegating and, 196–200
New China Industries Investment Company, 204
New England Patriots, 210
New venture development teams, 251
New Year's Eve in Times Square, 83
New York City, 83–84
New York Yankees, 143–144, 255, 269
NFL. *See* National Football League
NFL Europe, 276
NFL Players' Agents, 69
NHRA. *See* National Hot Rod Association
Nickelodeon, 161
Nike, 241
Nintendo, 161
Nokia Sugar Bowl, 11
Nominal group technique, 144
Nonprogrammed decision, 135–136
Nortel Networks, 57
Nuxoll, Henry, 24
NWFA. *See* National Women's Football Association

O

Oakland Raiders, 111, 269
O'Brien, Nancy, 796
Occupation, 202
Octagon, 65
Ohio State, 5
Olympic Games
  host cities, 5–6
  Michelle Kwan, 160
  state, 41
  Summer (2004), 179
  Venus Williams, 57
Olympic Selection Committee, 6
O'Neal, Shaquille, 64
Opening Act scenarios, 4, 10, 15, 28, 34, 39, 52, 59, 64, 80, 86, 91, 95, 108, 113, 121, 134, 141, 147, 160, 166, 174, 190, 196, 201, 214, 221, 227, 242, 249, 255, 268, 273, 288, 294
Open leader, 223
Operational planning, 53
Operational plans, 162
Operations management, 122, 266–285
  best practices in, 271
  defined, 268
  function, 268–269
  gaining competitive advantage with, 271
  history of, 269
  responsibilities, 268
  women in, 269
Optimizing approach, 135
Orange County Convention and Visitors Bureau, 130
Organic environment, 117
Organization, 193
  defined, 113
  who's in charge, 119
Organizational chart, 59–61
Organizational purpose, 256
Organizational structure, 95–96, 116–119
Organizing, 113–120
  benefits of, 114–115
  defined, 5
  reasons for, 113–114
  staffing and, 188–211
Organizing function, 59–61
Orientation, 193
Outputs, 268
Owner, 70
Oxygen Network, 174

P

Parsons, Dick, 134
Partnerships, business, 98
Paying professional players, 56
Pederson, Steve, 42
People for the Ethical Treatment of Animals (PETA™), 210
People resources, 290
Pepsi 400, 48
Performance review, 201
Personnel. See Employee
PETA™. *See* People for the Ethical Treatment of Animals
Pfizer, 264
PGA, 156
PGA Bank of America Colonial, 143
Philadelphia Eagles, 204
Piggie, Myron, 69
Pitino, Rick, 215
Pixar, 149
Place utility, 87
Planning, 108–112
  defined, 4–5, 107
  importance of, for local events, 80–81
  See also Strategic planning tools
Planning and controlling, 273
Planning process
  purpose of, 108–109
  steps of, 110–111
  Plans, types of, 109
Policy, defined, 168
Political trends, 175
Polk, Daphne, 284
Polk, Tabitha, 284
Population, 175, 289
Portfolio, 203
Position power, 65, 216
Possession utility, 87
Power, 65–66, 216
Price-Hardemon, Angela, 284
Private golf club, 156
Problem-solving, 134–137
Problem-solving teams, 250
Procedure, defined, 168
Product departmentalization, 118
Production, factors of, 88–89
Production management, 7, 30
Productivity, 269
Professional sports, managing, 12–13, 91–94
  catering to young fans, 92
  community involvement, 92–93
  jobs, 91–92
Professional team, organizing, 59–63
Proforma, 98

Programmed decision, 135
Public chat room, 149
Public golf club, 156
Puma, 57

Q

Quality circle, 250
Quality standards, 55
Quantity standards, 54

R

R&D. *See* Research and development
Reál Madrid, 143
Recruiting, 291
Recruiting applicants, 192
Recruiting tool, sports event for college, 29
Red Wings, 210
Reebok, 57
Regionalizing, 40
Reliant Stadium, 12, 91
Research and development (R&D), 148
Resistance, 227
Resources, 53, 290
Resume, 192
Retractable roof, 12–13, 91
Review phase, 171–172
Reward power, 66, 216
Rewards, 295
Riddell, Inc., 3
Risk, of strategic management, 164
Riverboarding, 267
Roberts, Dawn, 93
Robo Cup American Open, 294
Robo Wars, 294
Rock the Universe, 97
Rookie free agents, 69
Rose, Pete, 277
Rose Bowl, 79
Rotational signs, 12
Rowling, J. K., 258
Rozier, Mike, 68
Rule, defined, 168
Runners, 68
Ruth, Babe, 255

S

Safeco Field, 13
Sales, marketing and, 98
Sales and marketing department, 60
Sales promotion, 97
San Diego Chargers, 204
San Francisco Giants, 117
Satisficing approach, 136
Scarcity, 88
Scenario building, 177–178
Scholarships, 40
Scholastic, inc., 258
"Scientific" approach. *See* Optimizing approach
Seattle Mariners, 13
Security, 82, 244
Seike, 163
Seinfeld, 186
Selective, 61
Self-directed work teams, 96
Self-direction, 199
Self-understanding, 217
Selig, Bud, 115–116
Selvaggio, John, 304
Semi-independent teams, 250
Sensor, 274
Sesame Street, 161
Severance package, 230
Sex discrimination, 40
Shafer, Roland, 24
Shannon, Dan, 210
Sherwin Williams, 95, 98
Short-term goals, 53
Shoulder periods, 97
Sitcom, 186–187
Situational leader, 223
Size, of organization, 117
Skills
  what employees need, 199
  See also Leadership
SlamBall, 166
Socialism, 89
Soft issues, 228
Software resources, 290
Song Airlines, 304–305
Sony™, 294
Sorenstam, Annika, 143
Southern Christian Leadership Conference, 156
Southwest, 304
Span of control, 95–96
Spawn, 162
Specialist occupation, 202
Specialization, 114
Sponsor, 175
Sponsorship, 264
Sports, college and amateur, 26–49
  mainstream, losing young people, 35–36
  managing amateur, 34–38
Sports, professional, 50–77
  agents, managers, and ethics, 64–77
  controlling, 54–55
  managing, 52–58
  organizing, team, 59–63
  women's, 57
Sports agent, 204. *See also* Agent
Sports and entertainment management, organizational structure of, 95–96
Sports Business Journal, 93
Sports camp, 27, 37
SportsCenter, 273
Sports events
  financial management of, 52–53
  human resources management, 10–11
  international, management of, 56
  managing, 4–6, 10–11
  organizing resources for, 53
  See also Events
Sports Illustrated for Kids, 36
Sports injuries, 268
Sports management, 10–14, 78–103
  of college championships, 11
  jobs in, 91–92
  organizer of, 204
  of professional sports, 12–13
Sports marketing, 3
St. George, South Carolina, 145
St. Mary's College at Notre Dame, 194
Stability strategies, 161
Stadium, 12–13, 291
  financial management and, 12–13
  information on Internet about, 54
  provide for additional revenue-earning events, 91
Staff authority, 119
Stage crew, 82
Stakeholder, 223
Standard, 54–55, 123, 275–276
Standardization, 117
Standards of performance, 275
State Fair of Texas, 17–18
Steinbrenner, George, 143–144
Stine, R. L., 258
Strategic fit, 179–180
Strategic management, 163–164
  action phase of, 171
  advantages of, 163
  defined, 160
  development phase of, 167–170
  review phase of, 171–172
  risks of, 164
  steps of, 166
Strategic planning, 53, 81
Strategic planning tools, 174–181
  benchmarking, 177
  benefits of strategic fit, 180
  environmental scanning, 175–176
  scenario building, 177–178
  strengths, weaknesses, opportunities, and threats (SWOT) analysis, 176–177
  types of strategic fit, 179–180
  using tools, 178
Strategy
  defined, 160–162
  levels of, 161–162
  of organization, 116
  roots of management, 160–162
  See also Management strategy
Street agents, 68
Streets of San Francisco, 189
Strengths, Weaknesses, Opportunities, and Threats (SWOT) analysis, 176–177
Structure
  departmental, 118
  organizational, 116–117
Student-Athlete Opportunity Fund, 30
Students. *See* College student athletics
Sufficient, 61
Summer Olympic Games (2004), 179
Super Bowl, 13, 238
Supervisor, 8, 31
Supply, 86
Surf Girls, 241
Sustainable, 61–62
Swatch™ Group Ltd., 163
Swimming, 278
Swimming World Championship, 278
SWOT. *See* Strengths, Weaknesses, Opportunities, and Threats analysis
Synchronized, 61–62
Synectics method, 145
Synergy, 61–62, 98

T

Tactical plans, 162
Tamez, Christina-Melissa, 284
Tangible knowledge, 148
Tapscott, Donald, 228
Target market, 4
Taylor, Frederick W., 269
TCM. *See* Turner Classic Movies
Team-based organization, 255

- Team building, 218, 251–254
  - failure, 251–252
  - success, 252–253
- Team concept, 256
- Team organization, 96
- Teams, 143, 249–254, 257
  - autonomous, 251
  - common characteristics, 252–253
  - defined, 249–251
  - forms of, 250–251
  - managing groups and, 241–265
  - marketing, 253
  - members of, 253, 256
  - new venture development, 251
  - problem-solving, 250
  - semi-independent, 250
  - temporary, 250
- Team structure, 255–256
- Teamwork, 199
- Technological trends, 175
- Technology, 117. *See also* Information technology; Managerial information system
- Teenage marketplace, 48–49
- Television ratings, 35
- Temporary teams, 250
- Tennessee Titans, 291
- Texas A&M, 86
- Texas Tech, 5
- Thanksgiving. *See* Macy's Thanksgiving Day Parade
- Theme park, 97
- Thompson, Jenny, 278
- 360-degree-feedback system, 194
- Ticket prices, 5, 42
- Ticket takers, 82
- Tiering, 40
- Time Out features, 6, 13,17, 30, 35, 53, 61, 67, 81, 88, 92, 98, 109, 116, 124, 136, 142, 149, 161, 171, 179, 191, 197, 203, 215, 222, 228, 244, 253, 256, 269, 277, 290
- Times Square. *See* New Year's Eve in Times Square
- Time standards, 55
- Time utility, 87
- Time Warner Inc., 134
- Title IX, 40, 57, 138
- Torantual Excursion Train, 133
- Tostitos Fiesta Bowl, 11
- Total Quality Management (TQM), 32
- Tourism, 97
- Tournament of Roses Parade, 79
- Toyota, 95
- *Toy Story,* 149
- TPS. *See* Transaction processing system
- TQM. *See* Total Quality Management
- Training, 295
- Training and development, 201
- Transaction processing system (TPS), 297
- Trask, Amy, 93
- Travel, war effects on, 130
- Trends
  - business, 197–198
  - economic, 175
- True Value Hardware, 190
- Trump International Golf Club, 156
- T-shirt, 87
- Turner Classic Movies (TCM), 244
- TV Guide™, 251

U

- UCLA. *See* University of California, Los Angeles
- Understanding others, 217
- Unethical behavior, 67
- United, 304
- United Kingdom, 97
- United Sports Labs, Inc., 3
- Unity of command, 95
- Universal Studios, 17
- Universal Studios Orlando Resort, 95–99
- University of Alabama, 68
- University of Arizona, 164
- University of California, Los Angeles (UCLA), 5
- University of Colorado, 204
- University of Indiana, 51
- University of Louisville, 215
- University of Nebraska, 39, 42
- University of Nebraska Athletic Department, 13
- University of Pittsburgh, 42
- University of South Carolina Gamecocks, 210
- University of Southern California (USC), 5, 68, 93
- University of Tennessee, 42
- Upselling, 98
- Upward communication, 114
- U.S. Airways, 95
- U.S. armed forces, 264
- U.S. Figure Skating Association, 270
- U.S. National Championship, 160
- U.S. Olympic Committee, 179
- U.S. Olympics, 41
- U.S. Open, 57
- US Airways, 304
- *USA Today,* 156
- USC. *See* University of Southern California
- USGA, 241
- Ushers, 82
- Utility, 87

V

- Value-chain, 268
- Venue
  - cyber management, 54
  - information on Internet about, 54
  - for professional sports, 56
  - *See also* Stadium
- Vick, Michael, 65
- Video game, 250
- Viewpoint, flexible, 222
- Virtual team, 257

W

- Walt Disney Company, 172
- Walters, Shawn, 68
- War, 130
- Ware, David, 69
- Warner Brothers, 48
- Watt, James, 269
- Weng Xianding, 204
- "Whats-in-it-for-me?" attitude, 232
- Whitney, Eli, 269
- Wie, Michelle, 241
- Williams, Serena, 57
- Williams, Venus, 57, 64
- Wilsons Leather, 57
- Windmill, 24
- Windmill Festival. *See* Comstock Windmill Festival
- Windmill World Trade Fair, 24
- Wind Ranch, 24–25
- Winfrey, Oprah, 174
- Wingo, J. C., 3
- Wingo Sports Group, 3
- Winning Strategies features
  - A Moving Experience, 189
  - Broadway Meets the Internet, 287
  - Dream Football, 107
  - Everything's Coming Up Roses!, 79
  - If Tiger Can Do it, Why Can't I?, 241
  - J.C. Wingo, 3
  - Only the Tough Survive, 159
  - River Rats, 267
  - Success of Sports Camps, 27
  - Hard Road to Success, The, 213
  - Where the West Begins, 133
  - Your Foot in the Door, 51
- Winston Cup, 48, 264
- WNBA, 57, 62
- Wolf Trap, 217
- Wolf Trap Opera Company, 217
- Women, in operations management, 269
- Women's athletic program, 138
- Women's Basketball for NIKE's, 62
- Women's Professional Football League (WPFL), 57, 284
- Women's professional sports, 57
- Women's Soccer Team's World Cup, 57
- Woods, Tiger, 64, 241
- Workforce, reduction in, 230
- Work teams, 122
- World Championship, 160
- World Cup Soccer Championship, 56
- World Grits Festival, 145
- WPFL. *See* Women's Professional Football League
- WPGA, 143
- Wright, Adam, 51
- Wrigley, 57

X

- X Games, 142

Y

- Yahoo! Music, 230
- Yellow Duck Races, 109
- Youth market, 115